Whose Benefit?

Jean Simkins
Vincent Tickner

Whose Benefit?

An examination of the existing system
of cash benefits and related provisions for
intrinsically handicapped adults
and their families

The Economist Intelligence Unit Limited

Published by The Economist Intelligence Unit Ltd
Spencer House, 27 St James's Place
London SW1A 1NT
Telephone 01-493-6711

© The Economist Intelligence Unit Ltd, London 1978

All rights reserved. No part of this publication may be reproduced or used in any form or by any means graphic, electronic or mechanical including photocopying, recording, taping or information storage and retrieval systems without the permission of the publisher.

ISBN 0 900351 70 5

Printed in England by
Page Bros (Norwich) Ltd
Norwich Norfolk

Bound by
Macdermott & Chant Ltd
Enfield Middlesex

Contents

Page 8   List of tables
10   Acknowledgements
11   Foreword
13   Introduction and summary of conclusions

19   **Chapter One   The legislative background**
This chapter outlines the main legislative developments which have produced the existing benefits structure, and the principles enshrined in these.

19   The insurance principle
20   The principle of the relief of destitution
20   The compensatory principle
21   The forty-five years from the Workmen's Compensation Act to the Beveridge Report of 1942
22   The Beveridge Report
22   The post-war years
24   The growth of uncertainty
24   the Supplementary Benefit Act 1966 and the emphasis on 'discretion'
25   differing standards in local authority services
25   the increase in voluntary services
26   variability of treatment of the disabled
26   Attempts to get reform through legislation
27   the Seebohm Report
27   The Chronically Sick and Disabled Persons Act 1970
29   Effects of the 1970 Act
30   Economic and organisational obstacles
31   Pushing the emphasis on to local authorities
32   The increased dependence resulting from the confusion
32   Proliferation of means tests
33   Reports and running repairs since 1970
33   The three elements in welfare
33   Occupational pensions schemes in relation to handicapped people
34   Family Income Supplement
34   Invalidity Pension, its long-term and short-term differentials
35   The significance of the Attendance Allowance
35   The new profession – welfare rights advisory work
36   Side effects of the Rate Rebate scheme

Page 37	Side effects of housing improvement and adaptation provisions
37	The Sharp Report and the future of Invacars and Mobility Allowance
41	Further patchwork – Non-Contributory Invalidity Pension and Invalid Care Allowance
42	Other areas of unmet need recognised in 1974 review
42	disabled children
42	handicapped people in work
43	disabled married women
44	The uncertain status of women in the system
44	The problems as seen by the Supplementary Benefits Commission
45	Conclusions
47	**Chapter Two The resulting tangle**

Chapter Two examines the system of provisions derived from the process outlined in Chapter One, in terms of the tangle of organisations involved, variety of criteria for assessment and of principles – some of them out of date.

48	The organisations – from the administrators' and the clients' viewpoints
49	Composition of an individual's 'package' of provisions
50	the need for repeated applications
50	an unsatisfactory benefit as often as not
51	the difficulties in receiving the benefit
51	Criteria and methods
51	the variety of ways of assessing eligibility
52	the relevance of age
53	the variable factor of taxation
54	the question that is *not* asked – extra outgoings
54	to work or not to work?
55	anomalies in the mobility field
55	to be handicapped or 'sick'?
56	disregards and 'requirements'
58	assessments and their problems
60	overlapping benefits – NCIP and other DHSS benefits
61	overlapping between separate agencies
61	delays and dangers
62	the variable mechanism of appeal
63	Central government benefits
63	Local authority benefits
90	Principles
90	inconsistencies in the treatment of handicap
91	'compensation' for what?
91	changing the rules in the middle of the game
91	the missing principle
91	inappropriate use of the selective principle and resulting 'misappropriation'
92	conflicting principles and the married woman
93	double standards of 'fairness'
93	mobility and work
93	the 'seek and serve' principle
94	freedom to manage one's income – the disappearing principle

Page 95		**Chapter Three The costs of administration**
		This chapter examines the costs of the system to the administrators and the clients.
96		The costs to the administrators: Social Security benefits
96		National Insurance benefits
96		Industrial Injury benefits
97		war pensions
97		Family Income Supplement (FIS)
97		Supplementary Benefits
99		The costs to the administrators: local government services
99		a review of some studies of Social Services administration costs:
100		Essex
100		Leicester
101		Reading
101		Isle of Wight
101		Birmingham
101		Slough
103		Buckinghamshire
104		Hillingdon
111		Rent Rebates and Rent Allowances
114		holidays
116		day care
116		transport
117		meals-on-wheels
119		Home Help Service
121		residential accommodation
121		aids and adaptations
123		The costs to clients of using the system
126		The costs of duplicating assessment procedures
127		The costs of providing unwanted benefits and services
130		Summary
135		**Chapter Four Take-up of benefits and services**
		The first of two chapters devoted to examining the effectiveness of the existing benefits system in reaching the people for whom it is intended, drawing on studies of the proportions of eligible people who claim particular benefits.
135		Factors affecting non-take-up of benefits
137		Handicapped people outside the welfare system
137		local authority registers
143		met and unmet needs
143		who is left out?
144		Take-up of cash benefits
144		Supplementary Benefits
147		Family Income Supplement (FIS)
148		Old Person's Pension
148		Free prescriptions
150		Free dental and optical treatment
150		Rent Rebates and Allowances
152		Rate Rebates

Page 154		Educational benefits
155		Attendance Allowance
160		Mobility Allowance
160	Take-up of local authority services	
160		house adaptations
165		rehousing
166		telephones
168		meals-on-wheels
168		home helps
169		day centres
169		holidays

170 **Chapter Five Non-take-up of benefits: a major problem**
This chapter continues the study of data on take-up rates by analysing reasons for non-take-up, and concludes with some recommendations for improvement of benefit administration.

170	Publicising benefits	
171		preparing publicity
172		publicity distribution
173		publicity campaigns
175		failure of publicity
176	Application forms	
180	Value of benefits to applicants	
180	Difficulties of claim procedure	
181	Pride and fear of stigma	
182	Officialdom and officials' attitudes	
182	Estimating take-up rates	
182		estimating eligible claimants
183		further uncertainties
185	Conclusions and recommendations	

187 **Chapter Six A review of combined assessment procedures**
Reviews of some of the attempts being made to reduce the cost and complexity of multiple assessment through combined assessment.

187	The DHSS Shropshire (Salop) project
187	the M1 form
190	City of Liverpool: multi-purpose benefits form
191	Batley: Rate and Rent Rebates scheme
191	Manchester: Rate and Rent Rebates scheme
192	Merthyr Tydfil: housing and educational benefits scheme
192	Calderdale: centralised benefits assessment unit
194	London Borough of Hammersmith: central assessment unit
195	Coventry: review of combined assessment
195	The Inverclyde project
195	computerised assessment
198	preliminary evaluation of the system
199	Ayrshire Cunninghame District: welfare benefits project
199	Berkshire: review of computerised assessment

Page 200   London Borough of Lambeth: combined assessment form
201   The Finnish computerised pensions system
201   Conclusions and recommendations

204   **Chapter Seven The effect on the client**
This chapter draws on the evidence of case histories to illustrate the effect of the system examined in Chapters One to Six upon its clients among those people with intrinsic handicaps.

205   Supplementary Benefits
206   Inadequate benefits
209   Misinformation
210   The cumulative effects of interacting benefit problems
212   Difficulties caused by long- and short-term rates of benefits
213   Struggling to stay in work
214   Care and attendance
215   the Crossroads scheme
216   Local authority benefits
217   Conclusions

218   **Chapter Eight Implications and recommendations**

223   **Appendix One**
Problems identified in the Disablement Income Group's case files
224   The clients, their problem areas, and major problem benefits
226   National Insurance benefits
227   Attendance Allowance
227   Private Car Allowance
228   DHSS vehicles (Invacars)
229   Supplementary Benefits
231   local authority provisions, including home help, telephones, house adaptations and aids
234   Disabled housewives
235   Conclusions

236   **Appendix Two**
The *Sunday People* form for use with applications for Attendance Allowance

239   **Bibliography**

List of tables

Page 64 **Chapter Two The resulting tangle**
Table 2.1 Central government benefits for people who are handicapped

100 **Chapter Three The costs of administration**
102 Table 3.1 Total unit costs of residential homes, 1969/70
105 Table 3.2 Unit costs of services, Reading, 1972/73
110 Table 3.3 Social Services' salaries costs in a London borough
Table 3.4 Unit costs per worker per year in the Social Services Department of a London borough
113 Table 3.5 Administrative costs of Rent Rebates per tenant in receipt, 1974/75
113 Table 3.6 Administrative costs of Rent Rebates per calculation made, 1974/75
113 Table 3.7 Administrative costs of Rent Allowance per tenant in receipt, 1974/75
114 Table 3.8 Ratio of tenants in receipt of Rent Allowances to number of calculations made, 1974/75
115 Table 3.9 Administrative 'improvements' related to their objectives and effects on cost
117 Table 3.10 Costs per person per mile of different 'alternative transport' facilities, November 1974
118 Table 3.11 Costs for different local authority vehicles
120 Table 3.12 Work patterns of Home Help Organisers and their staff
130 Table 3.13 The estimated administrative costs of benefits and services for adults with disabilities, 1975/76
132 Table 3.14 Expenditure of local authorities in England and Wales on personal social services, 1973/74 to 1975/76
133 Table 3.15 Expenditure of local authorities in England and Wales on personal social services for adults with disabilities, 1973/74 to 1975/76

Chapter Four Take-up of benefits and services
136 Table 4.1 Reasons for people refusing interviews about handicap
138 Table 4.2 Severity of handicap, related to registration with a local authority
140 Table 4.3 Severity of handicap and mobility, related to registration with a local authority
141 Table 4.4 Severity of handicap and use of services, related to registration with a local authority

Page		
142	Table 4.5	Severity of handicap, related to use of services irrespective of registration
157	Table 4.6	Attendance Allowance applications and non-applications for children, related to handicapping disorders
157	Table 4.7	Attendance Allowance awards to handicapped children, related to handicapping disorders
159	Table 4.8	Attendance Allowance awards to handicapped children, related to geographical region
161	Table 4.9	Summary of take-up of cash benefits
165	Table 4.10	Reasons for handicapped people who wanted housing modifications not applying for them, related to registration with a local authority
167	Table 4.11	Reasons for handicapped people not applying to local authority for re-housing, related to age group
167	Table 4.12	Reasons for refusing accommodation offered to handicapped people by local authorities
169	Table 4.13	Reasons for refusing holidays offered to handicapped people by official bodies

177 Chapter Five Non-take-up of benefits: a major problem
Table 5.1 Analysis of acceptability of 66 Rent Allowance forms by 5 criteria

189 Chapter Six A review of combined assessment forms
Table 6.1 Benefits claimed on M1 combined claim form

225 Appendix One
Table A.1.1 Benefits tabulated for study of problem areas in analysis of DIG case files (from 1970 onwards)

Acknowledgements

This book would never have come into its present form without the generous help of many widely differing organisations and individuals: the National Fund for Research into Crippling Diseases, which provided the finance; the Trustees of the Disablement Income Group Charitable Trust, who fostered the idea of carrying out this project, originally put forward by those involved in the running of DIG's Advisory Service; The Economist publishing organisation, which was prepared to adopt the finished report for publication in book form.

From The Economist Intelligence Unit Ltd, the research was carried out by Mrs Jean Simkins (formerly Mrs Millward) and Mr Vincent Tickner, in collaboration with Mr Ken Cooke, working as a full-time researcher with the Disablement Income Group for this purpose.

At the Disablement Income Group, particular acknowledgement is due for the extra work put in by Barbara Macmorland, the social worker responsible for the day-to-day running of the Advisory Service, Dr M Agerholm and Dr Jean Macqueen, both of whom devoted many hours to the production of the book.

The debt to the Mirror Group for permitting the collaboration of its Readers' Service is explained in the Introduction, but we must make clear our thanks to individual members of the team which operates that service, for the effort and time which they personally gave to assist us.

We also acknowledge with gratitude our debt to the more than 200 people up and down the country who contributed to this study their time, their professional expertise and, above all, in many cases the very private details of their own personal problems. They range from people in the most senior positions trying to administer the benefits system as it is, through the middle ranks of local authority Social Services staff, occupational therapists and Welfare Rights Officers trying to make it work, right through to individuals whose case histories and problems have brought them into contact with the Advisory Service of the Disablement Income Group, with the Mirror Group Readers' Service, or with other organisations and individuals to whom they turned when they could no longer find their own way out of the tangle. Their stories are scattered through this report, but we hope not in a form which will lead to the identification or embarrassment of any of those who have so generously assisted us.

Foreword
by Lord Plowden KCB, KBE

As an industrialist I am familiar with the multiplicity of regulations and aids to assist industry: schemes to increase investment generally or selectively, to accelerate investment, to move to development areas or to employ people it would not otherwise be economical to do.

Over the past twenty years, as governments succeeded one another, as schemes failed to achieve the declared objectives or as the objectives changed, so the schemes themselves have been changed with bewildering rapidity.

In spite of the warnings of industrialists expansion was consistently refused or granted with great reluctance in areas of reasonable activity, with the consequence that once thriving areas have become the decaying city centres and that efforts are now made to induce industry to expand there.

Aid was provided in certain areas in a way that caused capital intensive projects to be built with only a small effect on the numbers of unemployed; this was a very extravagant use of the money available.

As a former civil servant I am familiar with the natural desire of ministers to remove anomalies arising from piecemeal legislation by further legislation, often with the result of creating further anomalies.

But nothing in my experience either as a civil servant or an industrialist prepared me for the Kafka-like world in which the disabled and handicapped have to exist as revealed in this fascinating book.

Industrialists enmeshed in the frustrations of schemes to aid them are dealing with legislation nearly all passed since the war.

The handicapped are involved in a world still influenced by the Poor Law of 1601, modified by the many acts and regulations made since then.

On reading this book there were three things that struck me most forcefully:

1. That the handicapped are not homogeneous: indeed they are less alike than able-bodied people. The authors point out, for example, how little there is in common between a wheelchair-bound, articulate person, able to work, and someone mentally handicapped from birth.

2. The extent that the attitude engendered by the Poor Law Acts consolidated in 1601 still prevails – that poverty or need must be proved and adjudged deserving or undeserving. One example given is that local authorities now administer over forty types of means-tested benefits.

3. The complexity of the system which many of the administrators do not understand and which those seeking help cannot possibly understand. The authors give various examples, for instance where some few found themselves getting two or three times the income obtainable by others who had the same disabilities because of their eligibility for differing systems of benefit according to where, how and under what circumstances their disablement arose. Every attempt to rectify the system seems to create further anomalies. So difficult has the system become to administer and so many different authorities are involved that bureaucratic delay is very great. An example is given of a handicapped woman taken to court for non-payment of rent which should have been paid for her by some authority and which she had no reason to suppose had not been paid.

The system has become so difficult to understand that some local authorities have appointed 'Welfare Rights Officers' to aid people to understand and obtain the benefits to which they are entitled.

The system has become so complex that nobody knows how much it is costing. It is in fact a microcosm of our over-governed, over-administered and consequently inefficient system of government.

This is not the fault of the bureaucrats; it is the fault of all of us who fear to upset vested interests or cause people to have to change their jobs.

The authors suggest that a start should be made by raising the level of basic benefit paid as of right as a partial move towards a 'universal' solution and in the meantime an urgent reform of the discretionary element.

This book makes it clear that further tinkering with the worst anomalies, however well intentioned, will only create more anomalies. The first step towards reform should be a root and branch independent inquiry into the whole subject, with a view to complete restructuring of the system. This – a Beveridge for the disabled and handicapped – they strongly recommend. I agree, as I am sure others who read the book will do.

This sober and well-researched account of the problems of the handicapped should be compulsory reading for all politicians, bureaucrats and those in the media concerned.

It is to be hoped it will get wide publicity and lead to the study in depth that it advocates.

Lord Plowden KCB, KBE

Introduction and summary of conclusions

The origins of the study

In 1976 the Disablement Income Group Charitable Trust asked The Economist Intelligence Unit to undertake a study of the United Kingdom welfare benefits system as it affects people with handicaps or disabilities, a study which was made possible by means of a generous grant from the National Fund for Research into Crippling Diseases.

The background to this proposal dates back to DIG's foundation in 1965 by two women with multiple sclerosis, who from their own experience had discovered that the Social Security system offered no help to disabled married women to enable them to meet either the costs of replacing their economic contribution to their families or the extra expenses of their disabilities. They went on to expose other gaps in the system, notably the lack of any recognition of long-term disability as a condition distinct from short-term sickness, and the absence of any 'as-of-right' support for people who lacked the necessary record of insurance contributions. They found too that the hated means-testing of the thirties, believed by many to have disappeared long before, was still active as an intrinsic part of the 'welfare' system.

Established initially to act as a pressure group, DIG very soon found it necessary to set up an Advisory Service to deal with the flood of personal and financial problems that poured in from handicapped people and, increasingly as time went on, from statutory and voluntary agencies acting on their behalf. The files of this Advisory Service came to contain considerable resources of valuable information on the workings of the system of benefits and services as seen from the standpoint of the handicapped client, and the realisation of this prompted the DIG Charitable Trust to ask the EIU to undertake a study of the whole of this system.

The EIU had already carried out one research study on the field of handicap, published as *Care with dignity*; and the part-author of that work, who has personal experience of the problems that handicaps can create for families, was available to direct the present study. The EIU's report, presented to the Trust in January 1977, is made available here in book form, both the Trust and the Unit believing that it offers a much-needed account of the system on which people with disabilities depend and that its material represents a potentially valuable resource to legislators, administrators, doctors and social workers, as well as to handicapped people themselves and their friends, relatives and advisers.

The objectives of the study

The research had three broad aims:
a. to present evidence of the effect upon clients of the workings of the present system of cash benefits (including services, such as the supply of equipment, which directly contribute to the budgets of such clients) created for intrinsically handicapped adults and their families by a complex of legislation that has grown up over many years;

b. to investigate existing material on poverty among the handicapped;

c. to suggest in what ways the existing system of benefits to the handicapped could be changed to obtain a better and more economic coverage of the needs already recognised.

The EIU was asked to study the way in which the many bodies currently involved in the administration of the system function in their various roles, with particular reference to two criteria:

i. shortcomings and anomalies arising out of the overlap and mix of many hands in administering such payments, services, rebates and allowances;
ii. the economics of administering the multiple-outlet system, in terms of personnel, salaries, travelling time and other costs *both* of the potential recipient and of administrators.

Under the first of these criteria, six specific types of problem were highlighted, but it was agreed that the EIU would not exclude others which might come to light merely because they fell outside these groups:

i. miscalculations and errors of benefit which might be described as of a purely arithmetical nature;
ii. misapplication of benefit rules (as when benefits from one paying authority are regarded as a disqualification for a benefit from another even though the intent of the legislation creating them was to provide independently for separate needs);
iii. failure to obtain benefits for which a particular client is eligible because of ignorance of benefit rules (either on the part of client or administrator);
iv. arbitrariness arising from significant variation between one area, or one officer, and another in the application of 'discretionary' rules;
v. the inadequacy, both in real terms and in money terms, of the amount given even when eligibility is agreed;
vi. the inappropriateness of definitions used in determining eligibility for benefits.

Above all, it was intended that the study should be *client* oriented.

The twelve million 'sample'

The Trust intended that this study should be of an analytical nature rather than a statistical exercise, partly because of the limitations of a self-selecting sample of case histories such as that represented by the DIG files. In the course of our researches, however, we were fortunate to receive the whole-hearted collaboration of the Mirror Group of Newspapers, which operates a 'Readers' Service' providing information and advice to the twelve million or so readers of its various publications. We wish to place on record our gratitude to the Mirror Group and in particular to the staff of its Readers' Service for allowing us to compare DIG's sample of experience with the far wider perspective of their readership.

The great significance of our unexpected access to this resource was undoubtedly that it corroborated our findings from the relatively tiny DIG 'sample'. (It was in turn itself confirmed in many respects by the Annual Report of the Supplementary Benefits Commission, published as this study was drawing to a close.)

A note on definitions

In the course of carrying out this study some interest has been expressed in our use of the term 'intrinsically handicapped'. The 1974 government report to Parliament *Social Security provision for chronically sick and disabled people* contained a detailed reference to the lack of consistency in the use of terminology:

'The terms "impairment", "chronic sickness", "disablement", "handicap", etc, are used loosely or with special meanings in particular contexts.'

In the government report, *chronic sickness* means incapacity for work which has lasted more than six months; *disablement* is used as a general description of physical or mental impairment with measurable repercussions; *impairment* and *handicap* are used in the sense given to these terms in *Handicapped and impaired in Great Britain*, Office of Population Censuses and Surveys (OPCS) Social Survey Division, HMSO 1971–72. Thus *impairment* means 'lacking part or all of a limb or having a defective organ or mechanism of the body'; the practical implications of impairment may, however, be negligible. *Handicap* means 'the disadvantages or restriction of activity' caused by impairment serious enough, in a particular context or generally, to limit functional ability.

We have adopted the term 'intrinsic handicap' on the basis of the system of classification proposed by Dr M Agerholm,[1] which has been found in practice (for example, in the Outset study carried out in the City of London) to permit objective recording of the widely different consequences of personal handicapping

---

[1] *Lancet*, Nov. 13, 1976, p.1095; 'The identification and evaluation of long-term handicap', Dr M Agerholm, *Journal of the Medico-Legal Soc.* 43, 1975, p.120; also 'Handicaps and the handicapped: a nomenclature and classification of intrinsic handicaps', *J. Roy. Soc. Health* 1975/3.

disorders, seen apart from social or occupational circumstances which may render them to very varying degrees *disabling*.

The most important aspect of definition, however, for all who deal in schemes of social aid which aim to assist people with handicaps either in cash or in kind, is that 'the handicapped' make up a group which is not in the least homogeneous. People with handicaps, so often discussed as an entity, are in many ways *less* alike than are able-bodied people. There is little in common between the special needs of a wheelchair-bound but articulate person who is able to work and someone mentally handicapped from birth and hence unable to fight his own battles or provide and administer his own finance, or between the armless teenager, part of whose problem is to fend off excessive 'sympathy', and the middle-aged woman with emphysema or epilepsy who meets with hostility or lack of understanding because she has no *visible* handicap. The problems of a young blind person are different from those of the many for whom blindness is part of a complex of sensory handicaps that has come with age, and the problems of the deaf, the agoraphobic and those of exceptionally small stature are each different again.

It will be noted that the term *benefit* has been applied in its wider context, to include, besides the cash benefits of the Social Security system, a wide range of payment exemptions, price concessions, subsidies and provisions 'in kind', all of which are technically available to sick and handicapped people and which interact with the cash benefit system.

Relationship to the literature

We have attempted to digest and absorb as much as possible of the fast-growing literature on the workings of the Social Security provisions for handicapped people, and we hope that we are aware of findings of key importance. Within the time scale of this study, however, we would not claim that an exhaustive study was possible. We have appended a bibliography of some of the studies we found of value, and would like to express our particular thanks to those who allowed us to read other work of a confidential nature or which is not yet published. Where studies are referred to in brief in the text, the bibliography should be consulted for full details.

One document of particular significance published as our study was nearing completion was the Annual Report for 1975 of the Supplementary Benefits Commission. Some of the ways in which it relates to our findings emerge from the final pages of Chapter 1. The report from the SBC states:

'the ideal towards which we would like to see policies directed would be a world in which large social groups such as pensioners, the disabled and students, whose needs are in total reasonably predictable, rarely have to rely on a last-resort, means-tested, labour-intensive service for their incomes.'

From people with handicaps, and their families, there will be heard a heart-felt 'amen' to that.

Summary of Conclusions

Our conclusions and recommendations are set out in full in Chapter 8, and in order to see how they relate to the situation reflected in the DIG and Mirror Group files, and the experience of case workers all over the country, it is necessary to read the intervening chapters. However, to assist busy readers the main points are summarised here (where no specific references are given, the subject is referred to more generally throughout the book):

The present UK system of benefits for handicapped people is a ragbag of provisions based on differing, sometimes conflicting and anachronistic principles, which has not been sorted since 1942 (Chapters 1 and 2).

Benefits do not get to the intended recipients (Chapters 4, 5 and 7).

The system has become so complex that at present no one really knows how much it costs. What *is* clear is that as a country we cannot afford *not* to change it (Chapter 3) because where payment is not made in the form of benefits it is often made in other and ultimately more expensive ways.

The macro-economic arguments pointing to the need for revision are desperately reinforced from the standpoint of individual client households (Chapter 7 and Appendix 1).

A wide-ranging, independent re-structuring is needed – a new 'Beveridge' with the same official status as that of 1942.

Among priorities for tackling in the meantime, perhaps the most urgent is to deal with problems at the fringes of employment, and this must include a more realistic treatment of mobility costs.

The largest *numbers* to be helped could be reached by a real increase in the level of basic benefit (beyond adjustments for inflation). (Together, these last two moves would reduce the numbers dependent on discretionary benefits to a level at which the system might hope to operate as it was intended to do.)

As an ultimate design, a two-part structure is suggested. One benefit should be paid *as of right* for handicapped people to live on – taxable, but tapering off, not cut off abruptly, if employment is possible; the second should be an allowance – not taxable or affected by working – related to the handicap of the individual, which would compensate for the fact that ordinary tax thresholds take no account of the extra costs of disabled living.

Introduction of the second of these elements ought to be the prior aim of the two as it would help most those with the most acute problems.

The most acute and untreated need may well still be among disabled housewives, though some of them are now being helped by the Housewives' Non-Contributory Invalidity Pension.

The possibility should be explored of paying all benefits on a basis which would eliminate the male/female distinction, and would take into account the presence or otherwise of dependants as a matter of fact, not a matter of sex.

Even before any change is effected in the present structure, central government ought to take responsibility for mistakes made and wrong advice given in its name, and to provide recipients automatically with details of the basis upon which their benefits have been calculated (such a legal liability might make a remarkable difference to official interest in effecting real structural improvement).

While the system remains as it is, the possibility ought to be examined of some inversion of the present structure of administration within DHSS offices so that initial contact is with a more senior officer, who will pass to less-experienced staff only clear-cut cases.

The importance, and financial problems, of home care and domestic help as at present provided by local authorities suggest that urgent attention might usefully be given to further extension of the 'Crossroads' care scheme, operated in the Rugby area on a very high level of consumer satisfaction and economic efficiency.

Finally, whatever system is devised, the possibility of abuses should not be allowed to interfere with payment as of right to those genuinely eligible. Organised fraud is insignificant beside the kind of 'cheating' which is created precisely because the system is so extraordinary (Chapter 2 and Chapters 7 and 8 include examples).

Other suggestions are made about matters of detail and it is hoped that the outline of chapters provided in the Contents will enable readers to pursue particular subjects.

Chapter One

The legislative background

Merely to list the legislation which has brought into being the present structure of benefits for people with physical and mental handicaps would be very little help towards understanding either the complexity of the system or its in-built conflicts. Later in this chapter we shall outline the main legislative developments, but first we shall examine the various principles on which these are founded – for there is no single principle underlying the mass of legislation upon which people with disabilities depend today for benefits, even those which are strictly cash.

The basic principles

The insurance principle

The central feature of the British Social Security system is the insurance principle, by which payment is made out of income while earning to provide for benefits to be received as of right in the event of unemployment or sickness. Employers and the state also contribute to the funds from which payment is made.

While the insurance principle may work for the community as a whole – at least so long as those needing to receive benefits remain a relatively small minority – it does not necessarily work for individuals. In order to pay into the scheme, an income is necessary, and in order to have an income one must have employment of some kind. Ability to benefit under this principle therefore depends on two factors – fitness for work first, and then employment – which are to varying degrees denied to people with disabilities. (The most extreme examples are people who have been severely handicapped from infancy.) The British system has never regarded the housewife as being 'employed' and so under this system a married woman caring full time for her family in her own home has been until very recently excluded altogether from benefit except, as a dependant, through her husband's contributions.

Nevertheless, the great majority of people with handicaps are people who have for years contributed to the national scheme of insurance, many of them becoming handicapped only with advancing age. Payments from insured persons in the community as a whole correspond to roughly 5 per cent of total national income tax[1]: a calculation which does not take into account employers' contri-

---

[1] Based on Social Security statistics published by the Department of Health and Social Security, and on National Income statistics published by the Central Statistical Office

butions (the employee's and employer's contributions are equal in size, a factor which necessarily affects the arithmetic involved in determining what wages and salaries employers offer), nor direct state contributions, which come from the taxes also paid by insured persons.

Yet this contributory element does not seem to have altered the outlook which equates drawing benefits with 'scrounging'. With the possible exceptions of the Retirement Pension and the provisions in kind of the National Health Service, this attitude tends to colour people's concept of Social Security in general – and not merely when, as in 1976, massive publicity is given to abuses of the system.

The principle of the relief of destitution

Such an attitude, and the corollary that people who are entitled to benefits are sometimes unwilling to apply for them, is more understandable when it is related to quite another element – one of the oldest of those still built into today's structure of benefits: the relief of destitution under the Poor Law acts, consolidated in 1601. While the principle underlying the Poor Law was public responsibility for the relief of poverty, its effect, as it was administered over the years, was that one had first to prove the most abject poverty and then to be adjudged 'deserving' or 'undeserving' by some impersonal and often uncomprehending body, in order to receive the most parsimonious assistance.

Treatment was meted out on a tripartite basis: 'vagrancy' (which meant leaving one's own parish) was punished (irrespective of how the vagrant came to leave home), the able-bodied poor who could not find work became trapped in the enforced self-help of the workhouse, and almshouses were intended to care for the old and sick. Too often, all three groups found themselves in the same place, and throughout most of the period of the Poor Law there were people who preferred to starve rather than be caught up in the hopelessness of its system. At the same time those in no danger of a pauper's fate resented the taxes raised to pay for it, and there were recurrent protests that too much help was being given to the 'work-shy'.

While the system was set up to deal with *poverty*, not with disablement as such, the effect of a person's handicaps was often to make him unable to support himself or his dependants, and he thus became stigmatised along with able-bodied paupers.

It was from this background, also, that means-testing sprang when, at the end of the eighteenth century, wages below a minimum level became eligible for supplementation from the Poor Rate. This development not only had the effect of undermining the wage structure, but caused additional resentment by bringing the lowest-earning groups of those in work into the same category as those not working.

The compensatory principle

Alongside the Poor Law in the piecemeal growth of Social Security provision was a compensatory principle. This made itself evident first in war pensions: official provision for these goes back to the sixteenth century, but they became much more significant when large numbers of people became disabled as a result of the

1914–1918 war. The community made financial acknowledgement of an obligation to compensate those who in its defence had lost health, strength or faculties for the remainder of their lives, at a time when provision under the insurance principle was only in its infancy.

In the industrial context, compensation began as payment for loss of earnings due to some negligence or shortcoming on the part of an employer, and was widened by the Workmen's Compensation Act of 1897 beyond cases where negligence could be proved. Beginning in industries with obvious high-risk working environments, it was extended more generally from 1906.

The element of compensation for loss of earnings merged with that of loss of faculty in compensatory legislation after the First World War, and loss of faculty chiefly determined entitlement, which was calculated according to a scale of disability rising to 100 per cent. From this arose 'disablement' pensions, payable on top of earnings, for people disabled in war service or in the course of their employment. Neither compensation for loss of earnings nor for loss of faculty, however, included any provision for additional expenses incurred as a direct or indirect result of the disablement suffered.

The pre-Beveridge years

In the forty-five years between the Workmen's Compensation Act and the publication of the Beveridge Report in 1942, financial and social provisions proliferated for a variety of disadvantaged groups on the basis of a mixture of the principles outlined above. Compulsory health insurance for employees (but not for their families) had begun in 1912. Unemployment insurance began for a few industries at that time and was extended in 1920. The first non-contributory pensions, subject to a means test and available at age 70, began with the Pensions Act of 1908, and 1925 saw the introduction of contributory pensions for old age and for widows and orphans. Unemployment insurance had a rough passage because of the wide extent of unemployment, and in 1934 the notorious Family Means Test was introduced into this system. A Royal Commission in 1905–1909 examined the local machinery for the relief of destitution, and the circumstances in which the system operated were in any case being modified by the evolving treatment of unemployment and by the transfer of responsibilities from Boards of Guardians to the local authorities. Separate provisions for certain types of disability began to be added, among the first of which was the Blind Persons Act of 1920. Over this period the combined effect of all these provisions was being affected by changes in the medical system and in provisions for child care, as well as by the growth of friendly societies and of trade union activity in the field of welfare provision.

The Beveridge Report

By 1942 Beveridge could justifiably claim that 'provision for most of the many varieties of need through interruption of earnings and other causes that may arise in modern industrial communities has already been made ... *on a scale not surpassed and hardly rivalled in any other country*'[1] (our emphasis) – a comparison sadly not so favourable in the context of provision for people with disabilities today.

Even Beveridge, however, was not complacent about the system: on the contrary, he noted that *'each problem has been dealt with separately, with little or no reference to allied problems'* and that the provisions as they then existed were *'conducted by a complex of disconnected administrative organs, proceeding on different principles ... at a cost in money and trouble and anomalous treatment of identical problems for which there is no justification'*.[2]

The study that led to the Beveridge Report was carried out for the Committee on Reconstruction Problems. At a period when the war was forcing upon the nation many changes, the writer recognised that he had a rare opportunity 'for using experience in a clear field' and introducing major structural changes into the Social Security provision. He could honestly set himself the task, by analysing the existing structure and making provision to deal with its shortcomings, of making want under any circumstances unnecessary.

So what went wrong? Why, when Alf Morris came to put together the Chronically Sick and Disabled Persons Act nearly thirty years later, did he find no less than eleven ministries involved? And why do disabled people and their families find Beveridge's analysis of the administrative tangle, quoted above, so depressingly recognisable as a description of the situation in the 1970s?

The post-war years

The years immediately following the Beveridge Report were a 'reconstruction' period, during which people with disabilities gained, as part of the whole community, from major reforms such as the creation of the National Health Service (1948), the introduction of Family Allowances (1946), government acceptance of responsibility for maintaining full employment (1944) and the National Insurance and Industrial Injuries Acts (1948). These went a long way towards implementing Beveridge's recommendations.

Social surveys made just before the war, upon whose evidence the process of planning these reforms was based, had reported that most demonstrable want was due to interruption or loss of earning power, and most of the remainder to failure to relate income during earning to family size. Shortcomings in the

---

[1] *Inter-departmental Committee on Social Insurance and Allied Services* (Beveridge Report), Cmd 6404, 1942, part I, paragraph 3
[2] *Ibid*, beginning and end of paragraph 3

existing system of provisions for such circumstances were recognised to exist where benefits available were either below subsistence level or did not last as long as need, and these shortcomings were made worse because supplementary assistance was available only on 'unacceptable terms' – the means tests which had burned themselves into the memories of those who suffered from them in the 1930s.

'Adequacy of benefit' was one of the fundamental principles of the scheme proposed by Beveridge. With adequate benefit levels in the insurance scheme, including children's allowances sufficient for the needs of all dependent children when the responsible parent was in receipt of insurance benefit – plus free school meals and welfare milk and foods for all children – the intended role of National Assistance as introduced by the National Assistance Act of 1948 was a small and diminishing one: purely that of a lifeboat to pick up the 'limited number of cases of need not covered by social insurance' (paragraph 19(x)). It was never intended that the lifeboat should be expected to support a large percentage of the passengers! (There were nearly 7 million claimants in the peak year of 1972, of whom over 6 million were allocated payment of some kind.)

The Beveridge scheme contained an implicit respect for human dignity. It stated that there should not be any means test for an insurance benefit, on the grounds that 'management of one's income is an essential element of a citizen's freedom' (paragraph 21).

One of the scheme's basic tenets, however, was lost in the process of implementation: the idea of introducing benefit at a level adequate for subsistence 'so that individuals may build freely upon it' was rejected. Although Beveridge had insisted that 'a permanent scale of [insurance] benefit below subsistence, assuming supplementation on a means test as a normal feature, cannot be defended' (paragraph 294), such a system was indeed created, and the total number of claimants and dependants eligible for National Assistance or its equivalent rose from 1.5 million in 1948 to over 4 million by 1970. Of the 1970 total, almost 2 million were over pensionable age (many of whom would be people with disabilities), and a further 287,000 of working age were classified as sick or disabled.

In part this development was the result of the original government decision not to phase in the new pension levels as Beveridge had suggested: instead the scheme was implemented in full from the beginning, but the pensions were paid at a much lower rate than he had recommended. Moreover, there was from the outset a failure to appreciate the significance of the problems of people unable to build up contribution records. (The planners could scarcely be blamed for failing to foresee that this, and the problem of single-parent families, would assume even larger proportions as time passed, with changing demographic, medical and social trends.) The proposed provisions for dependent children were also diluted: Family Allowances were set at only two-thirds of the intended rate. It was argued that free school meals and welfare milk and foods were soon to be provided for all children and, although this was not done, the Family Allowances were never uprated to compensate.

During the 1950s and 1960s, no major legislative initiative affected the provisions for people with handicaps created in the post-war years – only changes in the rates of benefit, which were adjusted at different intervals for different benefits in relation to political pressures rather than to any logical long-term policy.

From 1966, earnings-related supplements were added to flat-rate Sickness and Industrial Injury Benefits, from the end of the second week of incapacity for a period of 26 weeks. This was intended to ease the transition from earnings to flat-rate benefits, and was conceived as a first step towards relating Sickness Benefit and Retirement Pensions to previous earnings. The immediate effect, however, was to create a distinction – for many, though again not *all* beneficiaries – between short-term and long-term incapacity.

The number dependent on the 'lifeboat' grew, and contributed further to the distortion of emphasis within the system, away from independence towards a requirement to make supplementary – and indeed supplicatory – applications for discretionary payments in respect of every separate need. Meanwhile, a fresh wave of selective benefits requiring means-testing began, starting with the introduction of Rate Rebates in 1966.

The growth of uncertainty

All through the years – and until November 1975 – there was no payment *as of right* in respect of disabilities except where those disabilities arose from war injuries, injury at work or prescribed industrial disease. Beveridge had recommended a single rate for the Retirement Pension and Unemployment and Sickness Benefit, a rate which represented at the time 27 per cent of average earnings in the case of a single person and 45 per cent for a couple. In the event, however, not only was this basic level not reached, but all the benefit rates afterwards moved differently. Although the standard rates for these three types of benefit followed broadly similar trends up to 1970, the actual amounts received by individuals varied from one benefit to the other in a very complex and seemingly pointless way, often by a few pence per week in either direction. Sometimes the differentials were much wider – as between the payments for dependent children of invalidity or retirement pensioners and the lower rates paid with unemployment benefits. The long- and short-term rates of Sickness Benefit moved apart and graduated Retirement Pensions were introduced. War and industrial injury benefit rates continued to lead the field. A growing number of people received substantial compensation on private insurance for injury in road accidents.

The Supplementary Benefit Act 1966

In 1966 the National Assistance Act 1948 was replaced by the Supplementary Benefit Act. At the time, much was made of the element of 'discretion' built into the new scheme on the grounds that it would give 'flexibility of response to varying situations of human need'.[1]

---

[1] *Supplementary Benefits handbook*, November 1972 edition, page 1

More and more people had become dependent on National Assistance as the years went by, and its level became the accepted official measure of subsistence needs. But already the lifeboat was lying lower in the water. During these years, the real living standards of employed people without handicaps were moving ahead, and the concept of poverty as being definable in terms of subsistence was moving further and further away from the realities of day-to-day living. Poverty has more recently been defined in terms of relative deprivation: 'individuals, families and groups in the population can be said to be in poverty when ... their resources are so seriously below those commanded by the average individual or family that they are, in effect, *excluded from ordinary living patterns, customs and activities*'[1] (our italics).

Moreover, as the number of claimants rose, the emphasis written into the Supplementary Benefit Act 1966 on the fact that 'every person in Great Britain of or over the age of sixteen whose resources are insufficient to meet his requirements shall be entitled, subject to the provisions of this Act, to benefit'[2] underwent a subtle change in practice. As stress was increasingly laid on efforts to control the rising cost of the scheme and the need to guard against its 'abuse', that discretion which had been designed as a means of 'flexibility' became in effect a way of *rationing* benefits. It also meant that it became harder and harder for ordinary people to calculate, or even to understand, the entitlements they should claim.

Local authority services

Similar uncertainty existed in other administrative areas upon which those with disabilities were often dependent. Under the National Assistance Act 1948 there were provisions for local authorities to make available various types of assistance to identifiable groups of people whose needs were not being met, including the elderly and those with disabilities.[3] Such provisions were, however, by no means a 'right' of the people who needed them, the existence of particular services and their availability to any individual depending upon the policy and pocket of the relevant authority. In respect of local authority housing, for example, there was no legislation before 1970 which made it obligatory for authorities to help people with disabilities, who on the ordinary 'points'-scoring system often had little chance of being offered such assistance. Only under Part III of the National Assistance Act 1948 were their needs in terms of bricks and mortar specifically considered – and this, of course, usually meant institutional living.

Voluntary services

During the 1950s and 1960s areas of glaring need increasingly led to the setting up of voluntary bodies to meet specific needs. The Winged Fellowship Trust, for instance, was founded as a result of the discovery that families with severely disabled members were going many years without holidays, and the Spastics Society was established in response to the many problems besetting people with cerebral palsy and their families, and other societies grew up for sufferers from specific disorders. The Disabled Drivers' Association (originally formed under a

---

[1] P Townsend: 'Poverty as relative deprivation: resources and style of living', in D Wedderburn, *Poverty, inequality and class structure*. Cambridge University Press, 1974
[2] Supplementary Benefit Act 1966, section 4 (1)
[3] See particularly Parts III and IV of the National Assistance Act 1948

different title) linked the drivers of three-wheeled vehicles supplied by the government, and other 'mobility groups' mushroomed, pressing for cars and for cash to supplement the National Health Service provisions, and for help for people precluded by their physical and financial disabilities from using public transport or driving their own cars. Voluntary groups helped to bring developments in electronics to the help of the most severely physically handicapped people as Patient Operated Selector Mechanisms (POSSUM) and similar devices became available. It was in this period (1965) that the Disablement Income Group itself was founded by two of those disabled housewives who found themselves without 'rights' under the insurance system, and whose aim was to secure an income *as of right* for all people with disabilities, and by this and other means to improve their economic and social position.

The equation of disability with poverty

People with disabilities are at least as diverse as people without them, and one effect of all these developments was that they became increasingly not merely diverse, but *divided* in the pursuit of what was essentially one common aim: precisely that of joining in those 'ordinary living patterns, customs and activities' from which they were excluded as much by their financial as by their physical or mental state.

A fortunate few found themselves getting two or three times the income obtainable by others who had the same disabilities, because of their eligibility for different systems of benefit according to where, how, and under what circumstances their disablement arose. Assistance with housing, help in the home and the supply of adaptations and equipment could be generous or virtually non-existent for different people with identical needs, depending on which local authority areas they lived in. Again, while those eligible for three-wheelers under the official scheme gained physically and financially as regards mobility, many others were unable to get help, either because the solo vehicles were inappropriate to their needs, or because they were so disabled that they could not drive themselves.

And all the time the equation of disability with poverty continued to develop, and from this followed what has since become a jumble of special exemptions and rebates: for example, exemption from certain taxes, from parking fees under certain conditions, from some bus fares and, for some people, from prescription charges, as well as rebates on rent and rates. The resulting tangle is confusing to those who think they may be eligible, expensive to administer and inimical to human dignity.

Attempted assistance

New moves began in the latter part of the 1960s to get legislative help for those who were disabled. Much of the activity, however, was on the back benches and never reached the statute book.

In July 1968, the Labour MP Jack Ashley, now widely known as a champion of people with disabilities as well as on account of his own handicap of a sudden and total hearing loss, introduced a Bill to set up a Commission which would do for the disabled what Beveridge had done for Social Security in general, namely investigate the problems and tackle the anomalies in their treatment. The Bill fell foul of the end of a Parliamentary session, and was lost.

In November of the same year the Conservative back-bencher James Prior produced a Private Member's Bill which would have helped housewives and others not covered by National Insurance, industrial or war disablement schemes, including those who had been handicapped by illnesses such as polio, muscular dystrophy, multiple sclerosis and arthritis. This Bill also attempted to give ministers power to direct local authorities to reserve a proportion of their housing provision for disabled people and to supply them with necessary special equipment. The Bill, which would have given a pension for the first time to an estimated 200,000 disabled housewives and 140,000 men and women disabled since childhood, was rejected by the House of Commons in February 1969.

Yet another attempt to set up an advisory Commission on the disabled – this time from a Scottish Conservative back-bencher – was lost in March of that year.

At this time Richard Crossman, who was then Secretary of State for Health and Social Security, was preparing the government's massive National Superannuation and Social Insurance Bill, which came to be popularly known as the 'half pay on retirement' Bill. Its provisions included an Attendance Allowance of £4 a week for those so severely handicapped that they needed a great deal of attendance from another person; it was intended that the allowance should be payable to disabled wives and also to the parents of severely handicapped children. It was estimated that 50,000 people would qualify. There was also to be a new earnings-related, long-term Sickness Benefit, payable after 28 weeks of illness. This Bill was lost when the government declared an election in June 1970, but some of its provisions were introduced by the succeeding (Conservative) government.

The Seebohm Report

In the later 1960s, also, an apparently unrelated concern regarding the growing level of delinquency had led to the setting up of a committee on the personal social services whose findings were to be of great significance for everyone closely involved with local authority social services. The committee's findings, better known as the Seebohm Report, were published in 1968 and ultimately led to the combining of the former Welfare and Children's Departments, together with related functions, into the local authority Social Services Departments of the early 1970s, the intention being to secure an effective service for the whole family. The scope of this committee's inquiry, however, only included personal social services at that date administered by local authorities. It was not intended to cover the impact of government Social Security provisions.

The Chronically Sick and Disabled Persons Act 1970

It was another Private Member's Bill which became the most important piece of legislation for the disabled since 1948. Alf Morris began work on his Chronically Sick and Disabled Persons Bill with very little official help, but its wide scope caught the imagination of all, within Parliament and outside, who were concerned with the many aspects of living with disablement. By the time it was published it already involved eleven ministries, and tremendous effort and goodwill from all sides was needed – and given – so that it could avoid the same fate as Crossman's Bill in the pre-election rush. It is an indication of the general commitment to the new Bill that it reached the statute book even though its provisions involved amendment to no less than thirty-nine existing Acts of Parliament, including major statutes such as the War Pensions Act 1921, the Public Health Act 1936, the Education Act 1944, the National Health Service Act 1946, the National Assistance Act 1948, and the Housing Act 1957. It also broke entirely new legislative ground, for example in its various provisions for access to public premises for the severely disabled and in its specific requirements that education authorities should provide special facilities for deaf–blind children and for those with certain less readily recognised handicaps such as autism and dyslexia.

Perhaps the most important new precedent was that created by Section 1, which laid upon every local authority the duty to discover how many persons within its area were in need of the various services for the handicapped. Under previous legislation those authorities which chose to do so had been able to content themselves with meeting need only where it was forced upon their attention. Under the Chronically Sick and Disabled Persons Act, they were to go and seek it out.

Surveys made in conformity with Section 1 led a number of those authorities who faithfully carried it out to some startling revisions of their ideas of the size of their clientele. The Isle of Wight, which was among the first to conduct a special house-to-house survey, discovered 3,000 such people instead of the 600 it had previously assumed. Some very invidious publicity later came the way of local authorities which were less energetic in their efforts to implement Section 1 – not all of it justified.

Section 2 of the Act came to be regarded as a 'charter' for long-term sick and disabled people. Under its provisions it became the duty of local authorities to provide a wide range of services, including practical assistance in the home. Recreational facilities, such as radio and television and domiciliary library services, were to be provided, as were opportunities for intellectual, physical and social recreation and education, and there was to be assistance with transport to enable people with disabilities to take advantage of any such services. Help was to be made available with home adaptations or other facilities to secure the 'greater safety, comfort or convenience' of the client. Help was also to be given to make holidays possible, whether under arrangements made by the authority itself or otherwise (an important provision leaving open a choice between large-scale organised holidays or voluntarily or privately made arrangements). Meals-on-wheels and luncheon clubs were to be provided where there was a need, as was assistance with communications in the form of help to obtain a telephone and any special equipment needed to use it.

Section 3 overlaid the housing responsibilities already implicit in the Housing Act of 1957 with a specific requirement to provide for the special needs of chronically sick or disabled persons.

Sections 4 to 7 created a legal requirement in any building to which the public are admitted to provide for access to and within the structure and its sanitary conveniences for members of the public who are disabled, and for the clear sign-posting of such facilities. Section 8 extended these provisions into educational establishments, so that people who are disabled should no longer be debarred on that account from taking part in education, whether to learn or to teach.

Sections 9 to 16 provided for representation of the interests of chronically sick and disabled persons – where possible by people who themselves had first-hand experience of the problems – on a wide range of central advisory bodies and high-level committees, and in the field of local authority committee work; of potentially even greater importance was the extension of this principle into the employment field.

Section 17 sought to guard against the consigning of chronically sick or disabled persons of working age into geriatric wards while in hospital or Part III accommodation (as provided under the National Assistance Act 1948). The Act required the minister to be informed wherever such a situation did occur, and also to be provided with information regarding the use of chiropody services by people under pensionable age.

Section 20 made legal the use of powered invalid carriages and wheelchairs on footpaths – thereby removing a restriction which had particularly curtailed the movement of some very severely handicapped children and adolescents. The real value of this provision was, however, immediately removed by the circulation of instructions from the Ministry of Health Artificial Limb and Appliance Service to all users of its powered wheelchairs, warning them that they might not use them outdoors. No attempt was made to replace the powered appliances which, the Service claimed, were not designed for outdoor use, though outdoor versions were already available and increasingly used by people in other countries.

Section 21 introduced the 'orange badge' scheme, identifying vehicles being used by either a disabled driver or a disabled passenger, and providing exemption for them from certain of the increasingly restrictive traffic regulations.

Annual reports on research and development work relating to equipment which 'might increase the range of activities and independence or well-being of disabled persons' were provided for under Section 22. Section 23 made changes in the War Pensions Appeals system which were designed to eliminate some of the delays and injustices in that sector which had been brought to the notice of Alf Morris. Finally, Section 24 made new provisions (already mentioned) for the education of deaf–blind, autistic and dyslexic children, and considered the possible creation of an institute of hearing research.

As we have seen, one of the new features of this legislation was that it laid upon the administering authority the requirement to *seek out* those who qualified for its services. What was really much more 'new', however, was the attitude to people with disabilities which underlies the Chronically Sick and Disabled Persons Act, and which to some extent the publicity surrounding its introduction and implementation succeeded in transmitting, if not to the whole community, certainly to a larger number than before. This was expressed in the speech with which Alf Morris presented his Bill for the Second Reading when he spoke of

'a society in which there is genuine respect for the handicapped; where understanding is unostentatious and sincere; where if years cannot be added to the lives of the very sick, at least life can be added to their years; where needs come before means; where the mobility of disabled people is restricted only by the bounds of technical progress and discovery; where the handicapped have a fundamental right to participate in industry and society according to ability; where socially preventable distress is unknown; and where no man has cause to feel ill-at-ease because of his disability.'

The great anomaly

Respect, rights and dignity were intoxicating words to people more accustomed to the anomalies and uncertainties which had grown up around them: their disappointment has been acute in the face of the reality of living since the Chronically Sick and Disabled Persons Act. For while, since 1970, many provisions have been made which accord with the letter of this Act, it is arguable that it has failed *in spirit* because its effect has not been to enhance the dignity or independence of many handicapped people. This fact in itself has created bitter disappointment among some of those who had had the greatest hopes of it.

There were several reasons for this failure. In the first place, by one of the unfortunate accidents of history, the years immediately after the introduction of this 'charter for disabled people' saw an economic downturn not limited to this country alone. Financial obstacles have appeared in the way even of local authorities that really wanted to put into effect the full provisions of Section 2 on the scale shown to be necessary by Section 1. Some local authorities were very slow to move even on Section 1, and delayed action on Section 2 on the grounds that they could not carry that out until they had completed the survey required under Section 1.

Furthermore, no one's task was made any easier by the fact that major reorganisations of local government and of National Health administrative structures were taking place over the same few years.

A number of official circulars were issued (by the Minister of State at the Department of Health and Social Security, and also by associations of local authority bodies) which actively discouraged implementation of the Act in full measure because those who held the purse-strings at various levels were alarmed by the extent of the resources that could become involved. This applied not least to the Treasury, which had already been instrumental in bringing about the withdrawal of some of the ideas originally included in Alf Morris's earlier draft of his Bill.

Less obvious, but at least equally important in its results, was the fact that the effect of the Act, and the long battle to get local authorities to implement it, was to swing emphasis very much toward services and provisions in kind for the disabled, and this at a time when the real value of their cash resources was being eroded very rapidly by inflation. The underlying assumption was that these services introduced things that many people with disabilities would be unable to buy for themselves and, in the state of income provisions we have outlined, this was only too correct.

But by accepting this basis, and by switching the attention of the community to all the special facilities to which people with disabilities were by law 'entitled', the Act did them one disservice more general and possibly greater in its impact for many of them than all the services it did provide: the importance of central government provision, such as was embodied in the major reforms of the post-war years, was reduced, while at the same time there was increasing emphasis on provisions administered by local authorities. One of the advantages of major central government benefits is that entitlements can be universal, clear and comprehensible – as they had been with standard old-age pensions or Family Allowances. By contrast, a great part of the outcry which arose after the 1970 Act came from the variability of the way it was being implemented in different local authority areas.

There is, however, more at issue here than the question of geographical variation. One effect of the additional responsibilities given to Social Services Departments under this Act has been to make it more difficult for them to resist the pressure from the Supplementary Benefits Commission to increase local authority involvement in the lives even of people who did not invite or require it. In theory, the role of the Supplementary Benefits Commission is that of end-stop in the income-maintenance system, while that of Social Services Departments is 'to meet social needs'. In practice, however, the most vulnerable groups in the community, including handicapped and elderly people, found their financial needs re-labelled 'social problems' in order that responsibility for them might be shifted from the benefits machinery to the Social Services Departments. This trend began with payments to prevent children having to be taken into care, under the Children and Young Persons Act 1963, but it has been extended by way of lump-sum payments for fuel debts and rent arrears so that when the Supplementary Benefits Commission took over from the National Assistance Board it was an easy administrative step to refer to local authority departments even claimants who were not previously known to them and whose problems did not involve children. The orientation of the 1970 Act towards local authorities and the post-Seebohm development of social services (see page 27) has made this development even easier, and although officially no such policy exists, its workings have been documented (for example, in *Social Work Today*, 4 March 1976, by Bill Jordan and Peter Moore). Its effect is to create a shadow area of lower-grade public assistance, in which the client may be referred from one department to another in a bewildering and exhausting sequence of buck-passing.

Even this, though the first and most obvious, may not be the worst of the drawbacks of the new arrangement. Local authorities do not have adequate financial resources for the income-maintenance function. They are not bound by a published code regarding their means tests or systems of allocation. (Even a 'system' of the impenetrable complexity of those used by the DHSS has the

31

advantage that it affords grounds for appeal; many local authority systems, on the other hand, are not made known even to their own social workers.) Local authority assistance may well be in kind, not infrequently taking the form of second-hand goods, when the basic problem is lack of cash. Loan, rather than grant, payments are more common than under the Supplementary Benefit system, and the supervision of repayment gives social workers access to areas of a client's life which are unrelated to his original problems. This invasion of privacy leads to resentment and may do great harm to the relationship between Social Services staff and vulnerable people in their areas. It also creates a new dependence among clients, totally mystified as to who is responsible for what.

Another effect of the growing involvement of local authorities has been a mushroom growth of means tests, payment scales and criteria for services and benefits. The one standard means test which was the most Beveridge admitted might be necessary has been lost in a tangle estimated by Michael Meacher[1] to number over *seven thousand*. Moreover, as local authority resources have become more and more strained under the economic conditions of recent years, eligibility criteria have been increasingly used to whittle down the numbers of those to be helped, rather than to establish need.

Last, but not least, so much attention was paid by press and television to the Chronically Sick and Disabled Persons Act (and to the Attendance Allowance and newer Mobility Allowance which stemmed from contemporaneous activity in Parliament) that for every disabled person who found his 'right' to a television set or a telephone to be purely theoretical, there are dozens of able-bodied television-watchers now convinced that anyone who is disabled will be pampered from the cradle to the grave, with free telly all the way! How far from the truth this is, other parts of this book must surely show; nevertheless, many people now genuinely believe that all the provisions of the 1970 Act are a reality for all disabled people. There is no general understanding that disabled people have never been further from that 'control over their own incomes' which Beveridge saw as essential to the freedom of any citizen, nor from the opportunity to use what abilities they have to contribute to the community. Nor is it generally understood that the effect of each new benefit or service announced may not be to add to the income of those who qualify for it, but often merely to change the label on a part of the little they already get, while at the same time adding to the complexity of the choices they must make as to how to obtain the best total deal within their legal 'entitlements'. These effects are discussed elsewhere in this book, insofar as they affect disabled people themselves. They are mentioned here only in relation to their impact on the climate of opinion among the non-disabled part of the community, which in large measure has now lost interest in people with disabilities, considering all their needs to have been met under the Chronically Sick and Disabled Persons Act.

---

[1] In a piece originally published in the *Observer*, reprinted in 1973 in *Better social services* published by the Bedford Square Press of the National Council of Social Services

Also since 1970

Reports and running repairs

Parallel with the events arising from the Chronically Sick and Disabled Persons Act, a number of other developments have contributed to the present structure of benefits for handicapped people. Among these we have already noted the restructuring of local authority Social Services which followed from the Seebohm Report. The relationship between that report and other developments is noted later in this book.

There has been, since 1970, a number of reports and discussion documents at least equal in significance to some of the actual legislation. Indeed, it can be argued that much of the legislation has been piecemeal – as in the case of the growing number of specialised benefits – precisely because the reports, which have served as the basis for policy-making, have not had sufficiently broad terms of reference.

These reports have also tended to approach problems from the administrators' viewpoint, not from that of the clients. Thus, the Seebohm Report concentrated on Social Services administered by local authorities, but was not intended to consider the related provisions of central government, even though the adequacy or otherwise of these has a bearing on the demand for local authority assistance. Similarly, when Baroness Sharp was called in to examine the provisions for mobility in relation to people who are severely disabled, she was required to do so only for the *physically* handicapped and to exclude those whose disablement was associated with old age, despite the fact that the elderly form so large a section of those with physical handicaps. Moreover, the definition of mobility used – which became the basis of the Mobility Allowance – was in terms of ability to walk or to use public transport, and excludes people with socially unacceptable handicaps and also the blind.

It is a tribute to those who were responsible for both the Seebohm and the Sharp Reports that they stretched the limits of their terms of reference and made recommendations which looked beyond them; but it remains a weakness of recent legislation and planning that it has been directed to filling gaps in the existing structure of benefits, rather than to considering whether the structure itself needs replacement. As Professor Titmuss emphasised, there are three major systems of welfare – social, fiscal and occupational – and they do not have to be seen in isolation. Some problems arising at the interface of the social and fiscal systems have been well documented, though chiefly in relation to low-wage earners and low-income groups rather than specifically in relation to people with physical handicaps. One problem area has been created by the successive lowering of tax thresholds in a period when cash benefit levels have maintained a more or less even relationship with average wage rates (see also page 53; other specific areas of friction in the fiscal system are noted on pages 40–41 and 52).

Much less attention seems to have been devoted to the importance of the 'occupational' element in welfare. Yet since the 1950s this has been of growing importance: occupational pension schemes were offered as fringe benefits and then reflected in the various re-draftings of the state scheme of pensions. Many occupational schemes *excluded* handicapped people, at least in the early days, and thus made it more difficult for them at once to get a good job in their working years and to secure an equal income with their peers on retirement. Schemes that did not actually exclude them often admitted them only on unfavourable terms; also, since the whole idea of occupational pension schemes is to provide better benefits for the higher earner, the schemes by their very nature operate against handicapped people, who are usually *lower* earners than they would have been if able-bodied.

For the same reason neither the system of wage-related benefits nor suggested schemes of negative income tax offer much real help to the handicapped, though they cannot escape the effects of any such changes. Policy in relation to cash benefits for the handicapped needs therefore to take a wider-angle view.

Family Income Supplement

There have been good, as well as bad, spin-offs from legislative developments only incidentally involving handicapped people in these years. In order to tackle the problem of low incomes in families – irrespective of whether or not they include members with disabilities – the Family Income Supplement was introduced in 1971, and this has been of incidental help to some handicapped people. It is, of course, yet one more to be added to the list of benefits which depend upon means-testing.

Invalidity Pension

From September 1971, the introduction of Invalidity Pension meant that anyone entitled to long-term Sickness Benefit would be paid full-rate benefit even if his contribution record was deficient, and a special higher rate was paid for dependants of those on the new benefit. Married women contributors, though eligible for Sickness Benefit only at a reduced rate, were also paid standard-rate Invalidity Pension (this category of contributors has now been made obsolete by changes in the contribution arrangements). A new Invalidity Allowance was added, paid at one of three rates according to the age of onset of chronic incapacity, the highest rate going to those affected earliest in life. The principle underlying this arrangement is that those affected while still young have least opportunity to build up financial reserves, but its operation is arbitrary and the results often difficult for people to understand (see also page 52).

The differential between the higher long-term and the lower short-term benefits was widened by successive upratings, but the advantage of the long-term rate is nevertheless insufficient to deal with the cumulative results of living on the initial short-term benefit; for that, many people have to fall back on lump-sum payments from the Supplementary Benefit organisation. The decision to allocate lower payments in the early stages of any break in earnings appears to have its roots in the idea that resources up to the point of interruption have been adequate, and even that there will be savings to fall back on at first. This assumption belongs to the nineteenth century, when thrift was an accepted virtue, and economic conditions did not doom to disappointment those who practised it. In the inflationary 'credit card' era of the 1960s and 1970s people with low incomes from work are usually over-committed even when earning – and this group includes many of those with established handicaps, and particularly with conditions that are progressive. This over-commitment immediately catches up with them when they are forced to give up work. When the motor industry was first hit by unemployment there was an outcry from the unions that their men had heavy hire-purchase and mortgage commitments to meet, and could not be expected to manage on the Unemployment Benefits. Handicapped people have no union, but their problem is a parallel one: barely keeping pace when *in* work, their time of greatest expense may well be when they are first without earnings – yet this is when benefits are lowest.

Attendance Allowance

Perhaps the most specialised and potentially significant development of these years was the introduction, also in 1971, of the Attendance Allowance for those who need substantial care by day and night (the lower rate for those needing such attention *either* by day *or* by night being introduced in 1973). The significance of this benefit, and it remains unique in this respect, is that it is payable as of right, irrespective of means, irrespective of contribution record, and to (or for) any person of age two or upwards purely on evidence of severe disablement, however caused, which requires attendance. Thus it is received by the parents of disabled youngsters, by housewives and by people who have never paid National Insurance contributions; it can be paid on top of other income; and it is paid at the same rate however the incapacity arises, whether as a result of accidental injury or of the diseases of old age developing at the end of a long working (and contributing) life, or from congenital physical or mental handicap. Its main drawback is that, like the post-war benefits, its level is unrealistically low: even the full rate will not buy more than one night's sleep a week for those whose constant attention has to be proved in order to qualify.

Nonetheless, many hopes were pinned to this benefit at the time, as representing a new philosophy in cash provision for disablement. This hope may have been rather misplaced, however: not only has there been no evidence in subsequent legislation of further extension of this principle, but the Attendance Allowance itself is paid as of right *in case of attendance need*, not in respect of disablement alone. It is thus another specialised *incapacity* benefit in the same tradition as the early provisions for the blind. (Similarly, the more recent Non-Contributory Invalidity Pension is paid in respect of absence of any qualifying National Insurance contribution record, not in respect of disablement *per se*.)

The new profession

By this time it had become painfully clear that the structure of rights and benefits for disadvantaged groups within the community was so complex, the various responsibilities of different local authority departments so difficult for the public to understand and the rate of introduction of new regulations so rapid, that no-one other than a full-time professional guide could hope to find a way around the maze; and this problem was by no means limited to people with disabilities. People were simply not getting the benefits designed for them (non-take-up of benefits is discussed in detail in Chapters 4 and 5 of this book). Some community organisations and voluntary bodies were setting up advisory services, and experiments began in various parts of the country in the use of full-time workers within local authority organisations whose whole occupation was to keep abreast of legislative and other changes affecting the system and to advise clients regarding their entitlements.

The first of these Welfare Rights Officers was appointed in Manchester in 1972. They are still few in number, but in effect a new profession has been created – like the high priests of old, to act as intermediary between the layman and the law – in this case the morass of law relating to welfare benefits. Some authorities have begun using computers as an aid to this ever-more-complex exercise (see page 195) and even those whose profession this is are questioning whether the need to involve a computer does not in itself amount to an indication that the system has become unworkable.

Another response to the problems arising from the Seebohm recommendations was the setting up, between 1973 and 1974, of the Personal Social Services Council, which it was intended should form an advisory, research and development body able to take a broad view of personal social services. Its officers hoped to give priority to studying the effect on the personal social services of policies in other spheres, such as housing and education. This body, however, was given a budget in its first full year of less than £200,000, 80 per cent of which was spent on maintaining its offices and paying its staff – and it was hardly to be expected that an organisation on that scale would be able to make any appreciable difference to the torrent of legislation, still less to the amount of resources to be made available for social service uses.

Confusion: Rate Rebates

How much scope there is for looking ahead, at these margins of interaction, is illustrated by the national Rate Rebate scheme, which though not primarily concerned with the affairs of handicapped people, came to affect indirectly the financial circumstances of those of them who depend on Supplementary Benefit. When the scheme was first introduced it was intended that qualifying income levels should bear a close relationship to the levels of 'requirements' in the Supplementary Benefit system, so that there would seldom be any advantage to be gained by a Supplementary Benefit recipient from claiming a rebate instead. However, in April 1973 the government proposed substantial increases in qualifying incomes, in order to cushion the impact of rent increases due under the Housing Finance Act of the previous year. The result was a situation in which large numbers of Supplementary Benefit recipients could be better off by switching to housing benefits (Rent and Rate Rebates and Allowances), and this number was further increased when a revised Rate Rebate scheme came into operation in April 1974.

The situation thus produced led to so much confusion that it called for a massive joint exercise between local authority Housing and Rating Departments and local offices of the Department of Health and Social Security to identify those Supplementary Benefit recipients who might gain by transferring to housing benefits. Nearly 90,000 eventually opted to make the transfer, but it took until 1976 to complete the operation and set up a mechanism for the consideration of new Supplementary Benefit claimants, in order to advise them if it seems they would be better off with housing benefits (see also page 61). It is significant that this was yet another factor tending to shift recipients of central government cash benefits into the ambit of local authorities.

Confusion: housing

Housing is recognised to be a crucial area for handicapped people, yet here again patchwork legislation has produced confusion, particularly on the questions of rehousing and housing adaptations. The responsibility of local housing authorities for adaptations, originating in the National Assistance Act 1948, was made more explicit under the Chronically Sick and Disabled Persons Act 1970, with the result that District Councils (as housing authorities under the 1957 Housing Act) have the statutory responsibility. Under Sections 56 and 61 of the 1974 Housing Act, Improvement Grants became an area of interacting responsibility between Housing and Social Services Departments. This is a complication even where, as in London, they are two departments of the same local authority, but the complexity is even greater where the authority responsible for housing is a different one from that providing social services, as in the counties. Shared financial arrangements are worked out, but as economic restrictions cause all authorities to examine spending more critically, both must be tempted to shift responsibility. Expenditure for people living in local authority housing is the responsibility of the housing authority, and their outlay in this connection has received a 66 per cent subsidy from central government. For handicapped people in private sector housing any necessary work must be done by the Social Services Department: in this case a means test may be applied. Social Services outlay comes wholly from local finances and, though these include rate support grants, there is clearly an advantage to local authorities in trying to shift the cost on to the subsidised sector by rehousing rather than doing major adaptations.

There are in any case problems in using Improvement Grants to finance adaptations. A required adaptation – be it an extra room for renal dialysis or a lift in the corner of a room – is not necessarily an 'improvement' from the standpoint of any subsequent occupant. If work is to be done under the Improvement Grant provisions it would normally be aimed at bringing the general condition of the house and its facilities up to standard on a ten-point scale, which may involve the occupant and the authority in far more work than they require or can pay for. Moreover there is a (relatively low) rateable value barrier, beyond which the making of an Improvement Grant cannot be considered, and this regulation cannot be waived to allow individual cases through, though certain other provisions can be waived by housing authorities in respect of work undertaken for handicapped people; the age qualification of the property is one example (normally it must be pre-October 1961). The basic problem lies in the use of unsuitable legislation, never designed for this purpose. The authorities are evidently well aware of the difficulties: in February 1976 a discussion document was issued by the relevant ministries for use in trawling for ideas about possible changes around the local authorities and voluntary bodies involved.

The mobility tangle

Another very significant report, which has already been mentioned, was commissioned in 1972 and presented in 1974. This was Baroness Sharp's report, *The mobility of physically disabled people*. This inquiry was ordered at a time when there was increasing disquiet about the lack of help available to people too badly disabled to drive, and when the Department of Health and Social Security's Vehicle Service was already under pressure to issue cars instead of three-wheelers. A number of minor changes had been introduced as an interim arrangement. Thus, although the terms of reference were 'to consider the means by which the limitations on mobility imposed by severe physical disablement can be mitigated', medical and surgical aspects were left aside, some attention was given to housing and means of mobility within the home, but the issues surrounding the Vehicle Service dominated the inquiry. The question of the relationship between income and mobility was not specifically considered except insofar as it was recognised in discussion concerning priorities, and means-testing of those who might benefit.

A long-standing campaign had been fought against the DHSS three-wheelers on grounds not only of their shortcomings from the safety standpoint, but also for the anti-social aspects, arising because they could not carry passengers – forcing severely disabled people to travel unaccompanied, dividing families and posing problems for disabled mothers. The three-wheeler was originally conceived between the wars as an alternative to a bathchair rather than to public transport: a personal vehicle enabling its user to overcome inability to walk. The subsequent development of the Vehicle Service in many ways typifies the piecemeal growth, under a variety of expediencies, of the whole system of provisions for the handicapped. War pensioners were the first to drag the vehicle system into the contemporary world: for them, since 1948, small cars have been a permitted alternative to the three-wheelers, and these could be driven by a nominated driver such as the pensioner's spouse or parent, if the pensioner was unable to drive. From 1964 the option of a car for their own use was extended to strictly limited groups of civilian clients of the Vehicle Service, such as households where two related members would both qualify for three-wheelers, and some parents responsible for the sole care of young children. In 1972 haemophiliacs were included. Vehicle Service beneficiaries received not only a vehicle, but also free maintenance and insurance and exemption from Vehicle Excise Duty, adding up to a useful contribution to their personal budgets. With the exception of the war pensioners, however, they had to be able to drive the vehicle themselves. If they could not drive, perhaps because they were too severely disabled, they received no help at all.

Alongside these provisions there had grown up a number of cash alternatives for those who were able, and preferred, to run ordinary cars of their own rather than use a three-wheeler or a car supplied by the Vehicle Service. Some of the war pensioners who qualified for cars in 1948 were allowed the alternative of driving their own cars and receiving a maintenance allowance equal to that given in connection with government cars. When cars were allowed in 1964 to the first limited groups of NHS applicants, they too had this option. The rate of maintenance allowance for private cars moved ahead of that for government vehicles after 1953, but was never geared to actual maintenance costs. From 1973 it was also possible to get a contribution (then £90 maximum) towards the cost of converting a car from foot to hand controls, as an alternative to the supply of a three-wheeler. In 1972, anyone qualifying for a three-wheeler could take the alternative of an annual tax-free allowance of £100 for his own car, provided that it was registered and insured in his name and that he held a valid driving licence. This Private Car Allowance carried with it exemption from Vehicle Excise Duty. This last concession, worth £25 at the time of its introduction, was later extended to those among the disabled non-drivers who:

a. satisfied the medical criteria used for the Vehicle Service (specified amputation, inability to walk, or reduced ability to walk coupled with the type of social/employment 'need' accepted under the scheme);

b. needed to be driven;

c. were in receipt of the Attendance Allowance at either the higher or lower rate; and

d. owned a vehicle registered in their own name which was 'conspicuously and permanently adapted' for their use.

This, however, was merely another patching job, since it still left unaided those many disabled passengers who needed no permanent or conspicuous adaptation and those who did not have a constant-attendant-cum-driver in their household; the fourth criterion was, in fact, later dropped.

Baroness Sharp, reporting in 1974, recommended that cars should actually replace the three-wheelers, with the continuing alternative option of an annual allowance. Disabled non-drivers should, she suggested, be eligible on the same terms as disabled drivers, but the terms of that eligibility were to be tougher: 'severe physical disablement should not, of itself, entitle any NHS applicant to a car'. She proposed, in addition, that there must be demonstrable *need* for a car in order to maintain the individual and the family, or to contribute to family support. When this need ceased, cars would be withdrawn, though arrangements for *purchase* of the car at written-down cost were suggested.

Alternative methods of replacing the existing Vehicle Service with capital grants adequate to enable disabled people to buy their own cars were also mentioned, as was the fact that such grants could more easily be subject to a means test.

It was argued that, vehicle for vehicle, the proposed switch to cars would not cost more than the three-wheelers were by then doing. More realistically, however, it was seen that a greatly increased proportion of eligible people, previously deterred by the unsocial or performance aspects of the three-wheelers, would take up such an option.

Under pressure from the safety lobby as well as from those anxious to end the deprivation of the disabled non-driver, and wary of the likely cost of so popular a provision as the car, the government did not adopt Baroness Sharp's recommendations. Instead, in stages from January 1976, they introduced a Mobility Allowance – a cash payment to those who were 'unable or virtually unable to walk because of severe physical disabilities' and were likely to remain so for at least a year, but who were capable of making use of the allowance. By so doing they created at least as many anomalies and difficulties as they solved:

a. The Mobility Allowance ceases at retirement. This apparently constitutes a legacy of the idea – surely out of keeping with the spirit of the Chronically Sick and Disabled Persons Act – that vehicles for the disabled are only a means of getting to work. The rule, however, has the advantage (from the resource standpoint) of automatically excluding the very large number of retired disabled people. It seems curiously inconsistent that the 'travel-to-work' qualification available under the old Category 3 has at the same time been eliminated.

b. Moreover, tied to the state system of retirement pensions, the Mobility Allowance rules ignore all 'equal opportunity' legislation and penalise women, who lose their Mobility Allowance five years earlier than men, despite the fact that they live longer and are more likely to run their own households in those years.

c. Learning nothing from what happened with post-Beveridge benefits, the Mobility Allowance was introduced at a rate totally inadequate for its theoretical purpose: £5 a week in 1975, or £7 a week in 1977, might make possible a couple of social outings by taxi for someone whose income was otherwise adequate but it will certainly not finance any sort of daily movement for someone housebound by their existing income. Theoretically the Manpower Services Commission can be asked for help by handicapped people who still cannot afford to get to work, but such help is subject to a complicated means test and is available only to a very few people (313 in 1975/76); and its recipients, moreover, are paid no money to spend on travel for any other purpose.

Perhaps the greatest loss is to handicapped teenagers, who could formerly look forward to a real increase in independence when they became eligible for a three-wheeler on their sixteenth birthday. The Mobility Allowance will not even begin to provide them with the facility to go, *by themselves*, to see a friend, look at the shops or visit a library when they want to do so.

d. The Mobility Allowance was at first presented as an *alternative* to the vehicle option (see leaflet NI 211, published in September 1975). But the axe which had clearly hung over the three-wheelers since before the Sharp inquiry began did not take long to fall, and there has never been any commitment to the development of a new race of specialised vehicles. In 1976 it was announced that the production of three-wheelers would be phased out over five years. In the meantime, however, three-wheelers issued under Categories 1 and 2 are not promptly withdrawn on retirement, as is the Mobility Allowance. Similarly, war pensioners retain their cars beyond pensionable age. At a time when the whole issue of retirement ages is under examination, anomalies of this sort are particularly noticeable.

e. The Mobility Allowance has been made taxable, in order, it was stated, to 'give most benefit to those in greatest need'. In the context, taxation does seem to be a rather blunt instrument for so delicate a use. The practice assumes a purely financial assessment of 'need'; it can only produce further anomalies and it makes the pretence that the Mobility Allowance is 'not means-tested' mere playing with words. To dignify this expedient with the name of 'income redistribution' is in any case specious, since handicapped people as a whole already belong to a sub-group in greater financial need than their non-handicapped peers. War Disablement Pensions, Industrial Injury Benefits and contributory as well as non-contributory Invalidity Pensions are all non-taxable and payment of any of these benefits depends on where, when and how a person becomes disabled. The tax-free base income from benefits thus varies greatly between disabled people and it bears no relation to the degree of disablement or the financial needs of the individual. Indeed a disabled person who is working may, after paying income tax and expenses, receive *less* net income than a similarly disabled person with similar family responsibilities who is paid one of the tax-free Social Security benefits. To add a *taxable* Mobility Allowance on top of this 'lucky dip' structure of income maintenance cannot possibly have anything other than random effects even among those who qualify – and how does such income redistribution help those, even worse placed, who fail to meet the technical requirements of eligibility?

f. But perhaps the most potentially hazardous precedent created by developments surrounding mobility is the conversion, without any option, of a provision (in this case a personal vehicle) introduced by law as a part of the *service* of one government agency (in this case the Artificial Limb and Appliance Centres of the Health Service) into *cash* from quite another agency under the Minister for Social Security. The criteria used for the two provisions are not the same, nor are the cut-off points.

Further patchwork

In July 1974, while the mobility issue was still under discussion, a review of existing Social Security provisions for chronically sick and disabled people was carried out.[1] (This was provided for in Section 36 of the Social Security Act 1973.) The exercise showed up some more of the gaps in the structure, and plugs for some of these gaps have subsequently been introduced. Thus the needs of those unable to build up contribution records were recognised in the introduction of the Non-Contributory Invalidity Pension to compensate for the shortcomings of the insurance principle. There was recognition too of the needs of those who have lost their rights to benefit because they have stayed at home to care for a relative who was disabled, and the Invalid Care Allowance was created to provide at least some of them with an income other than from means-tested Supplementary Benefit (though it is not payable to *wives* who give up work to care for husbands or relatives, nor is it available to non-relatives, so that a caring relationship which may have lasted many years – between friends, say, or between fostered children and their foster-parents – still leaves no alternative at the end but Supplementary Benefit.)

The extra costs arising from disablement were acknowledged, though no general help was offered. Certain specific areas of additional cost such as mobility and

---

[1] *Social Security provision for chronically sick and disabled people*, a report to Parliament by the then Secretary of State, Mrs Barbara Castle, 31 July 1974

attendance have become the subject of additional benefits, but other expenses, as far as Supplementary Benefit claimants were concerned, were assumed to be already met within the existing system. Thus the higher long-term scale rates technically 'include a margin for special expenses' and 'disregards' are considered to incorporate them; extra allowances for accepted diets, extra heating or essential domestic help were included in the catalogue of such help. Attention was also called to the availability of lump-sum Exceptional Needs Payments for 'necessary expenditure which cannot be met from weekly benefit'. (The adequacy of an arrangement which officially pronounces an expense 'necessary' but then often pays for only *part* of it was not questioned.)

. . . Sometime . . . ?

Three other areas of unmet need were recognised in that review:

a. disabled children;

b. handicapped people *in work*, disqualified under the existing system from cash support by earnings which are yet too low in themselves to provide support; and

c. disabled married women who have not worked outside the home, for whom no benefit existed.

Disabled children

The first group had begun to receive some help only in the previous year. The ten-year battle on behalf of those children with congenital handicaps traceable to thalidomide ended in 1974 in the award of substantial damages – only to raise an immense furore as the tax authorities descended to put in their claim. In 1973, while the issue in the courts was still undecided, the government had set up a £3 million fund, to be known as the Family Fund, managed by the Joseph Rowntree Memorial Trust. This has since been further augmented and its help, originally intended only for children with very severe congenital handicaps, is now available to any severely handicapped child. Out of the personal tragedies of this one group of children there arose at least some help for a group of handicapped people always previously at a great disadvantage – those disabled at the beginning of their lives; but it was claimed that government was largely groping in the dark as regards the unmet need of handicapped children and their families, and research on the subject was said to be an essential next stage, though many organisations insisted that sufficient information was already available.

Workers with disabilities

Three problem areas were recognised for handicapped people in work: the additional *expenses* which are for many of them an inescapable part of the very act of going into a working situation, the *low returns* which many receive, and the fact that existing benefit arrangements act as a disincentive to employment because they recognise *no intermediate stage between 'total' incapacity for work* (and the receipt of Invalidity Benefit) *and full-time work* (and earnings). The idea of some cash benefit payable at the same time as earnings was noted. (In the form in which such a scheme is reported to operate in Germany, it can act as an *incentive* to return to work.) It was also admitted that the £4.50 limit then imposed on 'permitted earnings' – the maximum one may earn before disqualification from Invalidity Benefit – was not acting as an easement but as a restriction.

Even less progress has been made with the problem of the *low earnings* of handicapped people in work. There are several reasons for this problem. Many experience life-long interrupted work patterns; moreover, those handicapped early in life often begin work with lower educational attainments, as a result of their corresponding problems during their youth. Furthermore, older handicapped people tend to be consigned to less well-paid and lower-status jobs, a tendency which the quota scheme for the employment of handicapped people has done little to correct.

The report mentioned the possibility of creating a separate standard benefit to be paid to severely disabled people who are working despite their disablement, but more discussion and consultation were said to be needed. The situation remains unchanged except that during 1975 an end was put to the *wage stop*, which limited benefit paid to people while they were not working to the level of their previous earnings. This had operated with particular severity in the case of handicapped people, whose earnings while in work were already low.

In the field of rehabilitation close co-ordination between the various central and local government services was seen as necessary to 'ensure an efficient, intelligible and accessible programme for the use of cash and non-cash resources'. The subsequent course of events surrounding the Vehicle Service – already discussed – does not suggest that that aim has yet been met.

Disabled married women

The disabled housewife has in some respects had the worst deal of all. The 1974 review accepted the tentative OPCS estimate of 40,000 such women below pension age with husbands at work, and accepted the seriousness of the impact of her incapacity upon the household budget and the economic value of a housewife's work. It pointed out that her exclusion from benefit was technically because both National Insurance and Supplementary Benefit were designed to provide a substitute for maintenance from earnings. Never having established a record of earnings outside her home, the housewife was therefore unable to qualify for such a substitute when she became disabled. It was also admitted in passing that the lack of contribution record was partly the result of the option for married women not to contribute – an option created by the state system for the conditions of an earlier period – and partly even of the basic pattern of employment for married women. Changes made under the Social Security Act 1973 to the qualifying conditions for Invalidity Pension would, it was claimed, enable more of those who had had paid jobs outside the home to qualify after 1975, since the married woman's option in respect of pension contributions was to be removed under the government scheme for future pensions. This, however, was a long-term promise of self-help without any relevance to existing disabled housewives.

Subsequently a 'Housewives' Non-Contributory Invalidity Pension' actually reached the statute book, only to be postponed as part of the cuts affecting the whole field of public expenditure in 1976. There are also difficulties of definition arising from the decision to make this benefit payable only to women who are incapacitated *both* for paid employment and for their 'normal household duties'. This benefit was introduced from November 1977.

This benefit will involve new overlaps with other benefits. The whole system of benefits, taxation and retirement pensions is at present at variance with itself as regards the status of women. At many points in the system the basis is still the idea that a married woman will 'normally' be at home; non-payment of the Invalid Care Allowance to married women, for instance, is justified by the claim that 'they would probably be at home anyway'. This is despite evidence that women are now the breadwinners in 20 per cent or more of UK households[1].

Yet the basis of the pension schemes is that it will be 'normal' for women to have a full contribution record. A widow's income geared to the contribution record of her late husband does not bear much relation to the needs of the living, especially if the husband was handicapped and therefore a low earner.

The administrator's view

As this chapter has shown, the idiosyncracies of the system all too frequently cause handicapped people to become dependent upon that lifeboat intended for a tiny minority, Supplementary Benefit. It is, therefore, worth noting here the comments of the Chairman of the Supplementary Benefits Commission, Professor David Donnison, in the first separate Annual Report produced by the Commission, published in September 1976. He pointed to five strategic problems of the service, which will have to be tackled before long if it is not to become completely unworkable.

The first is the growing reliance on *discretionary* powers, with all that this means in terms of increased workload and uncertainty among clients. The second is the *complexity* of the system, which means that its officers have to work from instructions so long, so complex and so frequently amended that even they have difficulty in understanding them. The third area troubling the Commission is what are described as *'frontier problems'* among the various agencies involved – for example with Social Services Departments, the Employment Services Agency, housing authorities, education authorities and many others. The fourth question concerns the mechanism for dealing with *appeals* and the last is the question of the *cost in staff*, now that the Supplementary Benefits Commission has become so labour-intensive a service under the weight of numbers, calculations and ancillary services that have been thrust upon it.

Professor Donnison's warnings were published when our work was virtually completed, but it is interesting that they provide official backing for many of the conclusions embodied in this book.

---

[1] See report of the first six months of the Equal Opportunities Commission, by Lady Howe, June 1976

Conclusions

In one sense there are no 'conclusions' to be drawn from the material in this chapter, which is merely the on-going story of government action. It is, however, possible to sum up the course of events to date. The salient points seem to us to be:

a. Beveridge inherited a complex of piecemeal legislation built on a mixture of the principles of *insurance*, *compensation* and the *relief of destitution*, the latter bringing with it means tests and all the indignities historically associated with the Poor Law.

b. Working at one of those rare points in history when major change was possible, he set out what became the basis of a new post-war structure of sickness, unemployment and retirement provision for the community as a whole; but those provisions which particularly affect handicapped people were to some extent watered down in the course of implementation.

c. The result was a much greater dependence upon means-tested National Assistance (later Supplementary Benefit) than he had envisaged.

d. Through the 1950s and 1960s there was growing emphasis on the use of 'discretionary' payments and local authority involvement in provisions for handicapped people. By 1970 there was once more a large complex of overlapping provisions and ministerial responsibilities. All that has happened since has served only to increase these complexities.

e. The Chronically Sick and Disabled Persons Act 1970, coupled with the reorganisation of local Social Services Departments, placed still more responsibility with local authorities, laying down the principle that they should *seek out* those chronically sick and disabled people who needed the services they were empowered to provide. Its supporters also set out to provide a new dignity and independence for this section of the community.

f. A consequence of recent legislation has been a blurring of the essential separateness of the national cash benefit system for income maintenance and the provision of social services by local authorities.

g. Subsequent developments have included many piecemeal efforts in line with the letter of the 1970 Act, but the effect has been to create a system so complex and so full of anomalies that even the administrators have found it increasingly hard to keep pace. Cost and manpower usage have soared, and a new *dependence* (upon someone to guide them through the maze), rather than independence, has been the result for handicapped people.

What is needed now (and probably at intervals in the future will again be needed) is a 'new Beveridge' – a radical re-examination of the whole structure which must be given much broader terms of reference than the Royal Commission of Enquiry into the National Health Service, or the inquiry into the working of the Supplementary Benefits system, if it is to avoid the trap of adding to the patching effect. If the conclusions of such a review were allowed to form the basis of a new system, towards which the present one might be headed in a series of logical moves, even if not in the comparatively short space of time that was possible in the post-war reconstruction, one might hope for the avoidance of the mistakes of the 1940s and early 1970s, in watering down the essential elements of Beveridge and the Chronically Sick and Disabled Persons Act.

Chapter Two

The resulting tangle

In the previous chapter, we set out the background of legislation and the underlying principles of the emerging provisions for handicapped people. We tried there to bring out the pattern in a way which would be meaningful, not from the standpoint of senior administrators who must look at the demarcations between benefits, but from that of the would-be recipients and those in direct contact with them, who must be able to reach some understanding of the system in order to secure its benefits.

If there is any such reader who was *not* confused by the picture presented in Chapter 1, we can only admit defeat and try to give a more accurate impression in this chapter, the aim of which is to present a series of snapshots of the resulting position at the time of writing.

In setting out to portray the present 'system' to anyone not involved full-time in its operation, we feel we are attempting to describe the indescribable: a tangle of such complexity and at times unbelievable illogicality that the most hopeless traffic jam looks, by comparison, orderly and simple of solution. In fairness it must be said that any Social Security scheme would have to be complex, since it has to deal with the endless variety of human circumstances and human need. The DHSS description of the existing provisions as a 'network' does, however, prompt one to remember that Roman gladiators used a net *as a weapon*. For this tangle is more complicated than any traffic jam, because its confusion extends in so many dimensions. The tangle operates:

a. in terms of *organisation*, in that so many authorities are involved;

b. in terms of *methods* in that different criteria are used to assess the eligibility of people who have the same intrinsic handicaps if these arise from different causes, at different dates or in different parts of the country, and their treatment with regard to taxation and other matters may also differ; and

c. in terms of *principles*, in that different and even conflicting principles underlie the various arrangements now in use. Some of these are related to social and demographic circumstances that are part of history and make little allowance for conditions in the 1970s.

The organisations in the tangle

We began this study with a list of over a dozen benefits, generally described as obtainable through 'the Department of Health and Social Security or the local authority Social Services Department' – as though that comprised only two agencies. The list has grown steadily to comprise over fifty different benefits in cash (see Table 2.1, page 64) and many more in kind, such as telephones, holidays, aids and adaptations. We do not claim that this list is exhaustive.

The number of organisations involved depends on the point of view. From the administrator's standpoint, two main agencies are involved: the DHSS and the local authority of the area in which the handicapped person lives, with the additional involvement of the income tax authorities and the Department of Employment.

Viewed from the standpoint of the would-be user, however, the system explodes into a bewildering array of different offices and agents. A DHSS benefit may be centrally assessed by a specialised unit (as is the Mobility Allowance) and day-to-day payment then made through the local DHSS office (this happens with the Attendance Allowance), or it may involve *only* the local office (as with Invalidity Benefit), or *only* a specialist department (as has been the case with the Artificial Limb and Appliance Centres, where assessment for vehicles and powered wheelchairs has also been carried out). Alternatively the Supplementary Benefits machinery, with its own separate structure of Appeals Tribunals, may be concerned. All these agencies operate from different places. Application forms are required for many benefits; these are obtainable in theory, but often not in practice, from post offices. Medical statements (corresponding to the old medical certificates) repeatedly have to be obtained, thus involving general practitioners or hospital doctors.

The situation becomes still more complex when local authority benefits are added. One local authority Social Services office may deal with applications for home helps, day centre places and transport to them, and meals-on-wheels, but other local authority departments deal with Rate Rebates (Treasurer's Department), re-housing or home adaptations if local authority property is involved (Housing Department) and allowances for clothing or free school meals for school-age members of low-income households (Education Department). Moreover, for some items such as disposables and special clothing for incontinent people, the application route may be through a doctor-attached nurse in a primary health care team.

Procedure is not even the same from one borough to another. Depending on whether a London borough, metropolitan area or county authority is involved, the administrative structure is different, even before variations in local policy regarding procedures are taken into consideration. As an example, among a sample of only 100 local authorities, 66 different types of form for Rent Allowance applications were in use in 1974 (see page 176).

Even then, the seekers have not finished. Motor Taxation Departments are involved if the handicapped person's vehicle qualifies for exemption from Vehicle Excise Duty (and it is possible to make anything up to four trips to wrong local offices of one sort or another to discover how to go about obtaining exemption). Handicapped people not currently in work may be required to 'sign on' at Department of Employment offices, and to visit a different office again if they later need financial help from the Manpower Services Commission for getting to work.

The benefits package and applying for it

The system is so arranged that almost every handicapped person's Social Security provision consists of a package made up roughly as follows:

a. A basic cash benefit – under National Insurance (if the handicapped person has a satisfactory contribution record) its amount will vary depending upon whether the person is over or under retirement age, whether or not he or she has recently been employed, or whether or not he or she qualifies for long- or short-term invalidity benefits. If handicapped as a result of service or industrial injury or prescribed industrial disease the benefit will be larger. If neither of the above applies, the person may receive Non-Contributory Invalidity Pension. Failing any other benefit, Supplementary Benefit may provide the only basic income. (The married woman is excluded from both National Insurance and Supplementary Benefit income maintenance systems except where, since November 1977, she may qualify for the Housewives' Non-Contributory Invalidity Pension).

b. Regular 'topping-up' payments from Supplementary Benefit if the client is still considered, on official criteria, to have requirements which exceed his or her income (and this may even apply for handicapped people in work who have a family and qualify for payments from Family Income Supplement if income from employment is low, but again the married woman is excluded).

c. Special additions related to the handicapped person's incapacities. Examples include Attendance Allowance, and local authority benefits such as meals-on-wheels or a home help, or day centre care for those who find self-care impossible. Other instances are additions to Supplementary Benefit scale rates, travel and television licence 'concessions' for the blind, Mobility Allowance payments for some of those unable to walk and dietary allowances for some of those with special dietary problems – such as diabetics – if they are receiving Supplementary Benefit.

d. Additions in respect of environmental problems derived from the person's handicap, such as housing, heating, aids and adaptations, according to his or her circumstances.

e. Other items, such as help with holidays, telephones or other services designed to contribute to the 'greater safety, comfort or convenience'[1] of a handicapped person but which, had the person an adequate income, he or she would normally buy out of that income.

---

[1] CSDP Act 1970, section 2

The permutations of this jigsaw are as variable as the circumstances and inclinations of 3.5 million variously handicapped people and the first thing that must be said about it is that it rarely works out as generously as either the legislators intended or the able-bodied believe, a matter discussed in more detail below. The second is that each person may be eligible for several distinct benefits if his or her 'package' is to do the job it was intended to do, and will thus be involved with several of the different organisations indicated at the beginning of this chapter. Each of these will require documentary evidence upon which to establish whether or not he or she is eligible, the widely varying selection including pay-slips, rent books, bills, and so forth, as well as birth, marriage and medical certificates. Dates for local authority assessment vary, so that, for example, a disabled person with children might need to apply for Education Department benefits three times a year before a new term begins, for Rate Rebates at six-monthly intervals (which do not coincide with the school terms), and for other assistance such as holidays or aids at yet other times. On each occasion he or she must go again through the time-, energy- and even cash-consuming task of presenting evidence as to family income, rent and so on. Moreover, one office may require the information to be expressed on a weekly basis, and others may need it in monthly or even annual terms. (Note that this is *in addition* to any dealings with the National Insurance or the Supplementary Benefits or Employment offices.) Unless the applicant already has a telephone, and the officers in question visit, every application will need to be either in writing (which may be difficult) or in person at various different locations, with all the problems of access, cost and time that such travelling around implies for people with handicaps. In addition, since most offices are closed at times when working able-bodied partners would otherwise be able to call, the need for these partners to take time off work presents a further difficulty. The combined assessment procedures examined in Chapter 6 are being tried in various parts of the country in an effort to achieve at least a partial reduction of this waste of resources. Welfare Rights Officers, too, are part of the attempt to clear a way through the tangle.

The recent tightening of budgets in all departments has, however, if anything made the growth more resistant than ever to any attempt at pruning. Every agency is anxious to avoid paying from its over-burdened budget for anything that can be justifiably determined to be some other agency's responsibility – so the passing of applicants from one office to another, as well as the delays, are made even worse.

In theory, the Supplementary Benefits mechanism is the end-stop for financial assistance, but we have already shown that, since the 1970 Chronically Sick and Disabled Persons Act and the local authority reorganisation after Seebohm, there has been an increased tendency to pass applicants to local authority services on the grounds of the 'social' rather than financial aspects of their problems (see page 31). There, resources for many authorities are already strained, and likely to become more so, and even the 'second-class public assistance' described in Chapter 1 may be secured only after a long and tiresome sequence of application and re-application or may in the end be refused. Handicapped people are finding that the eligibility criteria for such services as telephones are being applied with great rigidity in order to rule out any but the most unavoidable of cases, rather than being used objectively to assess 'need'.

Even when eligibility has been established and the benefit is being paid, the problems are not over. Some publicity has been given to the number of closures of sub-post offices recently. For handicapped people in receipt of regular, long-term cash benefits, the distance to their nearest post office is very significant. This is because the normal method of payment is either by a pension book containing a quarter's payment slips, to be cashed over a post office counter week by week, or by Giro cheque, which most recipients will also want to convert into cash rather than have it paid into a bank. Inflation has so increased the face value of thirteen weeks' benefit that there is a growing problem of attacks by organised gangs on pensioners for these books. This may well be one area of the existing system which changing circumstances will make it necessary to re-examine. It has always been a fertile area for annoyance when new books or Giro cheques fail to arrive, signatures are not accepted, or mistakes have been made at issuing offices, leading to wasted journeys for the handicapped. Moreover, not only are post offices less numerous than they once were; they nowadays seldom offer places where a handicapped person can *sit down* before a writing surface while struggling to produce an acceptable signature. Thus there may be a need for changes. These could perhaps include a pass, with a photograph of the beneficiary or person normally collecting the benefit, rather than the book of pay slips.

Criteria and methods

What do they want to know?

To illustrate the tangle of criteria needed to make the present system work, let us consider a person with one or both legs amputated[1]. If he is seeking a payment under War Pensions or Industrial Injury schemes, he must first establish where and how the damage was caused, and then the size of the payment made to the amputee would depend on a schedule, in 10 per cent steps, in effect needing a reply to the question: *'how much of the limb/limbs have you lost?'*

---

[1] See the introduction to this report concerning intrinsic handicap. The implications in terms of *disablement* in our hypothetical case would depend on the age of the person, his physical condition in other respects, and whether the reason for the loss of limb was external and once-for-all (as in the case of war or industrial injury or accident) or due to some continuing condition (for example, of the circulatory system). It might be possible for him, using an artificial limb, to resume work, and even maybe to use public transport. On the other hand he might be obliged thereafter to use a wheelchair. Thus the extent of disablement will vary even between those whose actual amputation is of the same extent. In addition there are, of course, variable social and occupational factors: a classic example is that of a concert violinist, who may be professionally disabled by damage to a single finger which would be hardly more than a minor irritant to many other people. The problems which any system has to cope with are exemplified by the well-known story of Douglas Bader, who qualified for a 100 per cent disability pension at the same time that he was officially admitted to be 100 per cent fit to fly an aircraft into battle.

For the Mobility Allowance the question would be *'are you unable or virtually unable to walk, and likely to remain so?'* – the applicant who can walk a relatively short distance with the help of artificial limbs may not get the allowance even if he has no feet.

If an Attendance Allowance were being sought, the question is *'how much help do you have to have?'*

For the contributory benefits the approach is 'never mind the leg, *how about your payments record?'*

For Supplementary Benefits, or to find out how much a home help would cost (if one is available), the question is *'how poor are you?'* and for some local authority benefits, *'how isolated are you from relatives whom we might expect to help you?'*

For some local authority benefits the key question may well be *'where do you live?'* For a few people who lived in the wrong spot at the time of local government boundary re-organisation, entitlement vanished overnight without the applicant moving from his bed.

And of course if the amputee is a 'housewife', the authorities are not interested in her leg, only in the answer to: *'what kind of contribution record or income does your husband have?'* And for the single woman: *'are you cohabiting with a man to whom you are not married?'*[1].

What type of housing?

From the housing benefits or adaptations angle, the possibilities may differ greatly according to whether the applicant lives in local authority or private sector housing. The reasons for the difference are, in part, discussed on pages 37 and 48.

Age

The age at which the individual becomes handicapped is also a factor to be considered. This is particularly true for Invalidity Allowance, where an extra birthday can cost the applicant £1 a week or more. When incapacity begins before age 35 the rate (at November 1976) is £3.20; if its onset is between 35 and 44 inclusive, £2.00; from 45 to before 60 for a man or 55 for a woman, £1.00 (see page 34).

Age is also highly significant at the arbitrary margin of the official retirement age – 60 for women and 65 for men – where the contributory benefit suddenly becomes taxable.

For widows, however, there may be more advantageous changes: a widow is not allowed to receive Invalidity Allowance in addition to her Widow's Pension, but when that Widow's Pension becomes a Retirement Pension she may also be paid Invalidity Allowance (overlapping benefits are discussed on pages 60–61).

---

[1] The new phrase is 'living with a man who is not your husband'. Since November 1977, however, the questions to the 'housewife' have changed: see page 43.

Taxation

Historically, it was intended – by Beveridge, for instance – that all benefits should be at a sufficiently high level to count as the 'income' of the recipient (who would have been encouraged to add to them by his own efforts) and should be taxable. Because this proved too difficult from the administration standpoint, over the years a curiously inconsistent pattern of taxation has developed. War or Industrial Injury payments are not taxable. Mobility Allowance is taxed, but Attendance Allowance is not. Among contributory benefits, sickness and invalidity benefits are tax free (as is Non-Contributory Invalidity Pension); but tax must be paid on a Retirement Pension.

In recent years, however, a new and broader problem has arisen with respect to taxation at the junction of the fiscal and social systems of welfare, in the overlapping of tax and benefit thresholds. This has been much discussed, though chiefly in relation to low-wage earners and low-income groups rather than specifically in relation to people with handicaps. It may seem to many to be obvious that the point at which a person is earning enough to pay tax should be *higher* than the point at which that person is deemed to require income support from the Social Security system. Inflation of wage rates, particularly in some sectors, has steadily increased the value of 'average gross earnings' and successive Chancellors of the Exchequer have brought down the percentage of average gross earnings at which income tax becomes payable (the 'tax threshold'). Whereas in 1950–51 a single man did not pay tax unless he was earning at least 40 per cent of average gross earnings, by 1976 he was liable for tax even if earning only 21 per cent of the average. A married man with two children in 1950–51 did not pay tax unless earning *more* than average gross earnings; in 1976 he became liable to pay tax at earnings of only 44 per cent of the average.

This fall in the income tax threshold raises problems in relation to Supplementary Benefits. While the threshold has dived, the percentage of average earnings which benefit rates represent has changed very little over the years: it was around 17 per cent in 1950 for a single householder, and around 39 per cent for a married man with two young children. From a brief peak in 1967 when the corresponding figures were 20 per cent and nearly 45 per cent, the relationship has moved back again, and in the past three years the figures have been around 17 per cent and 37–38 per cent respectively.

Now that virtually everyone in work is paying tax (even including some people receiving Family Income Supplement, payable only to 'low-income' families), the percentage of net average earnings at which net income equals Supplementary Benefit levels has risen, so that by 1976 it was 30 per cent of the average for a single householder and 53 per cent for a married man with two children. (These figures take account of Family Allowance where relevant, and refer to ordinary rates of Supplementary Benefit, including rent additions.) Thus other things (such as housing costs) being equal, a single householder whose earnings fall between 21 and 30 per cent of the average will be *worse off* if earning, and thus paying tax and National Insurance contributions, than on Supplementary Benefit – even before any extra costs of disablement are considered. For a married man with two children the situation is still more difficult: taking up employment will impoverish him if his earnings are between 44 and 53 per cent of the average. This is clearly of particular relevance to handicapped people, whose earnings are frequently below average.

... and what not?

It will be noted in all we have said regarding criteria that none of the authorities is interested in the *extra outgoings* occasioned by handicap unless such outgoings fall into one of a few tidy categories such as mobility expenses (and then only if the applicant is under retirement age) or attendance costs (the criteria in this case would be unlikely to allow in our hypothetical amputee, unless there were other factors). In certain circumstances, the Supplementary Benefit offices will help also with additional costs for clothing or bedlinen, or for heating. Mavis Hyman's study[1], however, has shown that the extra costs of disablement (including outgoings and opportunity costs) incurred by her sample of wheelchair users *out of their own resources* – in addition to benefits from central or local government – averaged 24 per cent of income and for this general increase there is no provision.

To work or not to work?

Going to work is a major source of extra expenditure, yet the tax paradox examined above is only one of the confusing aspects of the situation surrounding the handicapped person of working age who actually tries to 'participate in industry', to use Alf Morris's phrase (see page 30). His increased costs may well be highest when his circumstances are first changed by his handicap – and this is confirmed by Mavis Hyman, who found that a number of people referred to particular financial difficulties in the early stages of their disablement – but the benefits system appears oblivious of this consideration. His personal payment received from Unemployment or Sickness Benefit (twenty-eight weeks) will at first be £12.90,[1] plus earnings-related supplement for twenty-six of those weeks (not the first two), plus £8.00 if he has a dependent wife and £4.05 for a first or only child. Only after twenty-eight weeks will he graduate to the higher rate of Invalidity Benefit: £15.30 personal benefit, his dependent wife now counting for £9.20, his first or only child for £7.45, plus a further £3.20, £2.00 or £1.00 Invalidity Allowance according to his age. This money is not taxable.

Suppose, however, that he finds a full-time job. It will quite probably be less well paid than the one he held prior to disablement; he will nevertheless now lose *all* the above payments and become liable to pay tax, but will receive nothing to help with his additional expenses except just possibly help with the cost of travel to work. And supposing further that his health or the local employment situation forces him to give up that job, he drops back to the *lower* rate of benefit if he had managed to stay at work for thirteen weeks or more[2], despite the fact that his intrinsic handicap has remained unchanged throughout. If the disabling condition is one of the recurrent, relapsing conditions, such as multiple sclerosis or, in some cases, epilepsy, the person who tries to work during his 'good' periods is even more heavily penalised. His interrupted work pattern will tend to dis-

---

[1] Mavis Hyman, *The extra costs of disabled living*
[2] This is because periods of interruption of earnings are only linked if separated by less than 168 days (excluding Sundays); if the intervening spell of work is longer, waiting days, short-term rates etc. begin again as if this were a *new* cause of interruption of earnings no more connected than a bout of 'flu and a sprained ankle

qualify him from contributory benefits, and his intermittent periods *in* work will disqualify him from the higher long-term Supplementary Benefit rate, because the two-year qualifying period is counted from the end of the last period of his employment.

In many ways the real financial disaster areas for handicapped people lie at the point of change from working to not working and even more from not working to working. Many such people need to use more effort than the fit to find work, to get ready for work, to get work and to do their work; these people are understandably bitter about a system which is supposed to be based on a work ethic yet recognises no virtue in intermittent or part-time work, and which moreover penalises them if they try to raise their own incomes (by immediately taking away *the whole* of an invalidity pensioner's benefit if he earns more than a derisory 'therapeutic earnings' sum – though others, such as war or industrial disablement pensioners, are not penalised in this way). This is especially galling when the publicity for organised Social Security racketeers and 'scroungers' is rubbing off on to genuinely handicapped people.

The anomalies of the Vehicle Service in respect of working have been somewhat overshadowed by the prospect of the even greater anomalies of the Mobility Allowance (see page 40), but they are still sufficiently recent to affect some handicapped people. One example was that of a handicapped person still a few years short of retirement age but no longer quite equal, on health grounds, to full-time working. Even where an employer was prepared to allow what, for the fit, is now known as 'phased retirement' – the working of a gradually reducing number of hours or days per week – the Vehicle Service was not. As soon as full-time working ceased, so did entitlement to a vehicle under Category 3, and the handicapped person's only choice lay between early retirement entailing loss of possible improved pension rights – lowering income both in the short-term and in the longer-term future – and continuing full-time work with the possibility of a complete breakdown of health (even then probably before full retirement age). Not until 23 July 1976 did the government announce that it would no longer withdraw a three-wheeler (or Private Car Allowance) from a person who had been awarded it for the purpose of travel to work if he or she ceased working. It is ironical that this concession was not made until seven months after acceptance of fresh applications for vehicles had ceased because of the switch to Mobility Allowance. So those who had vehicles withdrawn under the old ruling cannot make new applications for vehicles which under the concession they could in fact have retained, but must rely on the Mobility Allowance, if they qualify, or cash from the Manpower Service Commission (which of course is means-tested, and is solely for travel to work and has not the spin-off into more general mobility of the surrendered vehicle). As we said in Chapter 1, the whole area of mobility is at the present time full of anomalies, and we shall return to this subject later in this chapter.

The disincentives of the system with regard to working are, however, by no means limited to getting there. There are particular difficulties for people with any of those conditions in which they are handicapped but not sick. A person moderately handicapped by cerebral palsy (a 'spastic'), for instance, may be in good health but have great difficulty in walking or getting up and down steps and, both for this reason and because of the social attitudes of fellow passengers, finds using public transport a great trial. Nevertheless he may be presented with a situation in which, if seeking work, he is required to make frequent and regular trips, which are either expensive (by taxi) or possibly hazardous, in order to sign on for work and keep in touch with the officer responsible for seeking out job opportunities for the disabled. Such a person is not infrequently advised to go on to *sickness* benefits, thereby avoiding the necessity to visit the Employment Office regularly. But if he does so he is technically no longer 'available for work' and will moreover tend to be overlooked for job opportunities. Perhaps more seriously, he is falsifying his own health record for possible future employers, while the doctor's written declaration that he is 'sick' is an expedient nonsense which some doctors may, with every justification, object to signing. That this should be a recognised way round the situation is no fault of the people involved: DHSS officers, Employment Officers, the handicapped person and the doctor are all obliged to put themselves in the wrong because the system does not acknowledge in those of working age anything between 'sickness' (plus the appropriate benefits) and 'fitness' (when benefits depend upon 'availability' for work).

Where the people concerned had no entitlement other than Supplementary Benefit (or where their entitlement had to be 'topped up' from this source) one reason why they have sometimes been advised to claim sickness benefits is because the requirement to sign on for work halved the amount of net income from part-time earnings which could be 'disregarded' before benefit was reduced (from £4 to £2 at November 1975 rates. For a single parent a higher disregard has since been introduced). The basis of this regulation seems quite inappropriate to people who are permanently handicapped; the distinction may be relevant in truly temporary periods of unemployment (between jobs, for instance) or as part of an effort to persuade the 'work shy' to find work, but in either of those cases it is doubtful whether the amount is large enough to have much effect. As a permanent feature of the calculations of a handicapped person on a very low income, however, it has been a much more important factor.

Disregards and requirements

The whole question of what can be 'disregarded' by various agencies in calculating the resources of handicapped people is a cause of confusion, with the Supplementary Benefit mechanism and local authority means-tested benefits the largest areas of uncertainty.

For both kinds of benefit, the basic method of assessment is the same: a two-stage process which first determines the applicant's 'requirements' according to official practice (based on family size, outgoings in respect of housing, and so on), and then calculates the 'resources' which he has coming in to meet these. If other eligibility criteria are satisfied, the *amount* of benefit (or, conversely, the extent to which the applicant may be required to contribute towards the cost of a benefit such as a home help) will depend on the extent to which his resources fall short of his recognised requirements. In calculating resources, the income of a household is taken as a unit. Income from National Insurance benefits of the income-maintenance type (such as Unemployment, Retirement, contributory or non-contributory Invalidity Pensions or Invalid Care Allowance) is fully taken into account. For Supplementary Benefit claimants, an owner-occupier's house is disregarded and the treatment of other capital or savings is codified: the first £1,200 is disregarded, and after that the *actual* income is ignored, a standard scale of income is assumed, and benefit is reduced by 25p per week for every complete £50 of capital. The use of assumed rather than actual income can lead to problems in dealing with capital, but the variable level of *earnings* which can be disregarded is a much more frequent cause of confusion.

The two levels of earnings disregards within the Supplementary Benefit system have already been noted. War and industrial disablement benefits are payable in full whether the claimant is in work or not but only £2 of war and industrial disablement pensions can be 'disregarded' for Supplementary Benefit calculations (in the permitted disregards for 'other' income). As recently as 1975 the battle was still on to end the unrealistically low limits on 'therapeutic earnings' permitted to those on Invalidity Benefit before benefit was affected and these were even smaller for long-term invalidity pensioners than for those on Sickness Benefit (£4.50 compared with £7 at 1975 rates). The sum of £20 was completely disregarded under the earnings rule for certain dependants (for instance, the 'dependent' wife of an invalidity pensioner) and also for retirement pensioners and certain dependants under the retirement pension arrangements. This sum was increased to £35 in the November 1976 revision of benefits. It is worth noting that earnings disregards under Supplementary Benefit rules, when introduced in 1966, at £2 were 9.9 per cent of average weekly earnings but although by 1975 the rate was higher (£4), the comparable figure had fallen to only 6.6 per cent.

Last, and perhaps more important still, 'requirements' tend to be calculated on official ideas of the minimum needed. However, handicapped people do not depend upon one or other of the benefits for a limited period of interruption of a reasonable chance to earn, but possibly for the rest of their days, and they are justified in requiring us as a community to be more honest in our public attitudes. The calculation of their requirements even for basic subsistence items often assumes an ability *which they do not have* to make the cheapest substitutions – such as moving about to keep warm, for instance, or eating the cheapest foods which they cannot 'shop around' for. Moreover, they may not be able to digest such foods, or be permitted them for medical reasons: allowance is made for certain recognised conditions such as diabetes, but not for the general inability to fill up with cheap foods for fear of becoming overweight, an important consideration for wheelchair users. The result is often utterly inadequate payments: examples in 1976 included 85p per week for *both diet and laundry* for someone on a fat-free diet and incontinent of urine, and 80p per week for heating when one bag of coal costs the respondent £2.66. For some, the impossibility of meeting electricity bills leads to the use of paraffin heaters by people who ought never to use them – such as those with multiple sclerosis, for whom disturbance of balance consequently means an ever-present risk of injury or death by fire. Yet in describing our provisions for people who are handicapped no government spokesman has ever proclaimed that 'we support them – just – but of course they *are* expected to live for the rest of their days on the cheapest foods and to economise on fuel by becoming voluntarily bed-ridden for one day a week[1] and buy all their clothes from jumble sales'. Nevertheless, for many this is nearer to reality than the 'dignity and independence' Alf Morris sought to secure for them by the 1970 Act.

Assessment

Eligibility for benefits has to be assessed purely on objective fact in very few instances (such instances include contribution record for National Insurance purposes and the death of a spouse for widows' benefits). The great majority of benefits, not merely the means-tested ones, require in addition that the awarding agency be satisfied on many points which have to be assessed for each individual case.

Medical

Assessment of medical aspects is usually the task of a general practitioner or specialist, who may or may not be cognisant of the home conditions of the person being assessed. In some cases medical officers or panels forming part of the administration may be required to assess, or confirm assessment of, a person coming to them 'out of the blue'. There is disturbing evidence, not only from the DIG sample but from the much larger sample of Mirror Group Readers' Service clients, that not enough attention is paid to existing records or enough imagination directed towards day-to-day living conditions in making such assessments. The design of forms is also felt – not least by the medical profession – to be a hindrance. So many severely handicapped readers were refused Attendance Allowance on the basis of the official forms that the Readers' Service was prompted to issue a supplementary form (Appendix 3) for its readers to send in when they returned the official one, or when applying for a review, and this has had a high success rate. Its main advantages over official forms are, firstly, that it is in language people can understand and, secondly, that it asks questions which build up a picture of the limitations on the applicant for everyday living rather than solely of their need for 'care' in professional nursing terms.

Practical

Medical assessment apart, one reason for the sometimes unthinking meanness noted above in respect of 'requirements' is that the method of assessment places very heavy demands upon the judgement of the junior ranks of staff within the Social Security and Social Services departments. Technically, of course, the decision-makers are officers of some experience and there is a right of appeal, but in practice the decision must be based on evidence provided on forms (for further comment on the shortcomings of these see also Chapter 6) or case notes written up by the person whom the applicant actually sees and talks to. It is not easy even for people with some experience of living with handicap, and of human pride, to ask the right questions and to read correctly between the lines of half-answers to understand the real 'need' of people who come to them, out of the context of their daily life and work. Yet because of the large numbers now having to be assessed for benefits (see Chapter 1) this must be done every day by officers interviewing at local office counters and by young Social Service case workers

---

[1] This period is based on the many comments of DIG members who go to bed two hours earlier or get up two hours later each day simply in order to keep warm without using heating; assuming a normal waking day of twelve hours they have only to do this six days a week to be, in effect, giving up a waking day

with relatively little experience either of life or of disability, with the added pressure of excessive numbers to deal with so that they are always conscious that extra time spent probing one case may mean extra delay for someone else. They are also acutely aware that total resources are strictly limited, and that the next applicant's need might be even greater. It is hard enough to be fair if the applicant is articulate, helpful (both in attitude and in supplying the necessary documentation) and knows what is available. When faced with someone who does not know, cannot explain the necessary details or resents the need to do so, it is harder still. For an officer on a counter with a restive queue, it is easier to be discouraging to an applicant whose case is complex than to go into lengthy explanation, and if every doubt was referred to a more senior officer the system would grind to a halt. The possibility of having to deal with claims for other benefits than the one for which the applicant first presented is often avoided on the 'if they don't ask, don't tell them' basis.

All very human, very understandable, but *a handicapped person's livelihood ought not to depend on such a loaded gamble.*

Consider a specific example. A couple, both badly handicapped, were refused a telephone, not on the grounds of 'no funds available' but because they 'had access to a neighbour's telephone', this in fact belonged to the occupant of the only other flat on their level, who was old, afraid to open the door, and so confused that she herself was taken into medical care within weeks of the refusal. The result was that if a doctor was needed the couple had to wait *up to a week* for someone to call; and when a haemorrhage occurred in the night they had to try to attract the attention of sleeping neighbours thirty-two stairs up by shouting. One is impelled to ask how such an assessment could arise? Was it on the basis of a form the applicants filled in, which asked some such question as 'do you have a neighbour with a telephone?' – to which they could only in truth reply with an affirmative, but misleading, answer? Or was it on the basis of a discussion in an office where perhaps they were asked the same question and, not realising why the information was required, again answered truthfully but misleadingly? More disturbing still, was it on the basis of a visit – and if so, did the visiting worker actually talk to the neighbour? (We don't know the answer because, when interviewed, the couple could not recall exactly how assessment had taken place; this case is discussed in more detail on page 232).

Financial

Quite apart from experience, the complexity of the tangle outlined in this study calls for intellectual (and particularly mathematical) ability from the staff concerned far in excess of what is required or paid for when the job is offered, and more time to keep abreast of new legislative developments and regulations than any of the lower-ranking officers are, or are ever likely to be, given. In its 1975 annual report, the Supplementary Benefits Commission has placed on record its own protest at the 'volume of instructions ... so long, so complex and so frequently amended that officials themselves often find them very difficult to understand' (page 13). At the local authority level, senior staff have complained to us that they 'need to take an accountant with [them] to carry out the complex calculations called for'. One of the aspects of the tangle which makes

59

the calculations so difficult for everyone is that of overlapping benefits.

Overlapping benefits

The general rule is that 'only one payment can be made from public funds for the same purpose for the same period'. The difficulty here is to understand what the administrators mean by 'purpose'. Thus, the purposes of Unemployment Benefit, Invalid Care Allowance, and Widow's Pension would seem to most lay people to be quite different: but the official purpose of each is *income maintenance*, and they therefore overlap. That is to say, no two income maintenance benefits may be paid in respect of the same person at the same time: whichever of the two is payable at the higher rate will normally be paid.

At first glance that seems to take care of the problem. The reason why it does *not* is because, as we have seen, the piecemeal growth of the system has had the effect that each benefit now carries different implications for the recipient's total income, in terms of whether, or how much, extra money may be added by part-time earning, whether other benefits in cash or kind are 'attached' on a passport basis, whether Rent or Rate Rebates can be obtained or not, whether or not the benefit itself is means-tested, whether or not it carries with it 'credits' to safeguard pension rights – and so on and so forth.

A glimpse of the implication of calculations like these is provided by the introduction of Non-Contributory Invalidity Pension. The level of this benefit was set below Supplementary Benefit rates, and it is taken fully into account when Supplementary Benefits are calculated. Its effect on many of those eligible is thus to reduce the amount of Supplementary Benefit to which they are entitled, and make the same total sum come from two sources instead of one, at greater administrative cost. (The government's own estimate was that only about 7 per cent of disabled people receiving Supplementary Benefit would be relieved of the need to claim it by NCIP, and only 15,000 who were not previously on Supplementary Benefit would be eligible[1].) Some recipients of *contributory* benefits whose contribution record is such as to have left them with only a low rate of benefit can have their income 'topped up' by NCIP (in this case the contributory benefit takes precedence). But there is no compulsion on Supplementary Benefit recipients to claim NCIP, and some will choose not to do so for convenience if they are among those severely handicapped people to whom Supplementary Benefit is being paid *without* a requirement for regular medical certification, since NCIP does require continued certification, even though at lengthening intervals. In staying on Supplementary Benefit, however, they may find that they forgo the Class I (employed earners) pension contribution credits built into the NCIP provisions and possibly also Rent and Rate Rebates which may be payable with NCIP if income is low and rates high. On the other hand, there is a country-wide view among case workers that it is more difficult to get lump-sum payments for exceptional needs if one is not in receipt of regular Supplementary Benefit (even though in theory this is possible if income is very near the borderline). So how can the potential NCIP applicant know whether or not it would be to his advantage to apply? Since senior DHSS officials themselves admit to being unable to

---

[1] House of Commons Hansard vol. 892, 12 May 1975, col. 22

follow the implications in many cases, and since the shifting pattern of relative values for benefits such as Rate Rebates and heating allowances can overturn any given calculation within weeks, the only true answer is that *he can't*.

Both Supplementary Benefit and the NCIP are administered by the Department of Health and Social Security, but overlapping also occurs between totally separate agencies. We have already (page 36) noted the overlap between Supplementary Benefit and the Rent and Rate Rebates and Allowances, which has resulted in the scrutiny of thousands of records by DHSS officers and the transfer of some 85,000 beneficiaries from Supplementary Benefit to local authority benefits, where their income is thereby increased. There is some indication how far out of control the system has gone when the Chairman of the Supplementary Benefits Commission himself can write (in his 1975 report): '*There are probably similar numbers of people on the books of the local authorities who would be better off on Supplementary Benefit, but finding them would be an even more daunting task*' (paragraph 2.25). Perhaps most significant of all, that was the end of the paragraph ... nobody is going to *try*.

For a few of those thousands of people, a Welfare Rights Officer, local social worker or well-informed friend may give the right advice. The rest will continue to struggle on, not even getting all their little entitlement; and how many times this story is repeated is indicated in the discussion of the problems of non-take-up of benefits later in this book.

Held up at the frontier

Another effect of involving so many agencies in the provision of support and essential services for people with handicaps is that there are so many internal hurdles to surmount. It is clear from Chapter 6 that a great deal of attention and time has already been devoted to this problem, with only limited success. The growing part played by local government has increased the number of departments involved and the wasted journeys and delays experienced by claimants have likewise increased. *Delay* in obtaining local authority assistance was a major factor among the comments of DIG members (see Appendix 1), particularly in relation to aids. The same complaint is made, however, in a more dangerous context, in relation to the frontier between agencies administering so-called 'direct payment'. This is not, as the uninitiated might suppose, payment direct to the beneficiary: on the contrary, this payment is something the beneficiary never handles at all. The system applies where an authority takes over responsibility for making payments such as telephone charges for handicapped people, and it is also used where an individual or family has a record of non-payment (for instance, of rent, rates or fuel bills). The local authority or DHSS office concerned will then make the payment direct to the relevant body rather than making a larger payment to the individual from which to pay his or her own bills.

This is described as 'making it easier for them to pay' – which may be true as regards the telephone account, but often nothing except an increase in regular financial resources would really make it 'easier' for them to pay such charges as rents, and the true effect is only to make it *less* easy for them to do something else, such as to buy an adequate diet.

What is more disquieting, however, is that the direct payment system creates a state of dependency which is alarmingly vulnerable to bureaucratic mistakes and delay. We were told by case workers from one area that 'on more than one occasion telephones have actually been cut off for non-payment' because the procedure for paying the rental charge is 'so overloaded with bureaucracy'; while in London in 1976 a handicapped woman was taken to court for non-payment of rent which she had no reason to suppose was owing, as she was still being paid the amount to which she had been reduced at the time of the direct payment decision. Owing to some administrative breakdown, however, payment had not been made – yet it was not the administrators who were held responsible when the summons was issued.

Yet another aspect of the 'frontier' problem is that where the operations of different departments do not overlap, they may actually leave gaps. One northern authority is concerned that no agency now seems to accept responsibility for providing powered wheelchairs for people over retirement age. They have had applications from people who otherwise are housebound but could get out with a powered chair. Health authorities have said they cannot supply them. Since there is theoretical provision under the Chronically Sick and Disabled Persons Act, the applicants have turned to the local authority. The sum involved is around £250 for each chair, and in the present state of resources the authority cannot countenance this provision being quietly slipped on to its plate as yet one more 'aid' from its Social Services budget.

Appeals

Even when a decision has been made, applicants are often confused about their rights in respect of appeals – a further effect of the multiplicity of authorities and methods in use. Appendix 1, referring to cases on the DIG files, mentions that ignorance and misunderstanding of the appeals system were often found to be significant, and that many cases which did go to appeal were successful. Reference has also been made (page 58) to the Mirror Group Readers' Service's analogous experience in connection with reviews of Attendance Allowance decisions after fuller information was given. Other organisations have established the need for claimants to be represented by, or accompanied by, experienced Welfare Rights or similar workers if they are to have the best chance of making their case on appeal. Many claimants, however, do not appreciate that a tribunal such as the Supplementary Benefit Appeals Tribunal is a separate structure and that their evidence needs to be presented afresh, nor that it is possible to appeal against a decision on a discretionary award on the grounds that the sum awarded is too low to meet the need.

Although a recent study commissioned by the DHSS[1] suggests that the time-lag on appeals may be only some three weeks, many people seem to feel it is not worth appealing. Although the right and method of appeal is explained in most of the official leaflets dealing with benefits and in the letters informing claimants of decisions against which they may wish to appeal, it is still difficult to convey to

---

[1] *Research study on Supplementary Benefit Appeal Tribunals.* Kathleen Bell, DHSS. HMSO, 1975

possible appellants that the effort may be worthwhile. Once more, however, as elsewhere in the system, the heaviest burden of effort, and possibly of expense, falls on those least fitted to carry it – and the returns may be remarkably small even if the appeal is successful.

Central government benefits

Table 2.1 on pages 64–87 sets out some of the basic features of the central government benefits most likely to affect handicapped people. We are very grateful to senior DHSS staff for the work they put into making sure of the accuracy of this for us. In the process, however, they reinforced our awareness of the yawning gap between the language of the administrators and that of those whose only preparation for dealing with the benefits tangle is their need. What, for example, would the entries in the fourth column for the main benefits convey to the average man in the street? We originally had in mind a listing of the persons who perform the vital function of providing entry to eligibility. For most people (other than applicants for war or industrial injury benefits) the people whose impressions and decisions *matter* will be the doctor who provides any necessary medical statement, the visiting officer or officer on duty at the counter of their local DHSS office. It is not, of course, the case in legal terms that these people determine eligibility – but in practical terms? The person who is technically responsible for the official decision will often not be directly accessible to the claimant.

The difficulty concerning the 'purpose' of a benefit has been referred to earlier in this chapter: we did not succeed in finding a satisfactory form of words to provide a separate column stating the *function* of each benefit, and this is for the most part included, by inference, in the eligibility conditions. For explanation of the term *maintenance benefit* see page 60.

Local authority benefits

We have already pointed out the wide variation in the organisation, methods and policies employed by different local authorities in trying to meet their growing responsibilities for providing help for handicapped people. These variations made it impossible to produce a tabulation of local authority benefits comparable with Table 2.1. Too often, basic criteria for eligibility are not clearly defined even for those trying to work with a particular authority. Usually no statutory right of appeal exists, and any effort to appeal tends to travel in a circular fashion back to the place where the original decision was authorised – to the Director of Social Services, for instance. Generally, provision for dependants is not made except incidentally: that is, if housing adaptations are under consideration, or if the strain on an able-bodied partner is one of the considerations surrounding an application for help with holidays. In the post-Seebohm construction of Social Services Departments, however, it is easier to consider any family as a whole than it was when Children's Departments and Welfare Departments worked separately; this is one area in which the number of internal divisions has in general been reduced.

The activity among local authorities experimenting with combined assessment is covered in Chapter 6, but it has not so far done much to relieve the load either on applicants or on case workers in Social Services Departments arising from the need for repeated and various application to different departments for grants,

Table 2.1 Central government benefits for people who are handicapped

Benefit and date introduced	Basic eligibility conditions	How to claim	Eligibility determined by
Basic civilian benefits (below retirement age)			
1. Sickness Benefit (1911–1912) (see also 50)	Incapacity for work supported by medical evidence; contribution conditions to be satisfied; age between 16 and 70 (65 for a woman); see below for procedure after 28 weeks	On medical certificate ('Doctor's Statement' as from October 1976)	Insurance officer
2. Invalidity Benefit (September 1971); consists of two parts, *pension* and *allowance*	*Pension*: previously entitled to Sickness Benefit for 28 weeks; aged between 16 and 70 (65 for a woman) *Allowance*: paid in addition to pension if under age 60 (55 for a woman) when incapacity began	On medical certificate ('Doctor's Statement' as from October 1976)	Insurance officer
3. Non-Contributory Invalidity Pension (November 1975)	Incapable of work for over 28 weeks; aged between 16 and pension age; satisfies conditions as to residence and presence; extended to married women who are also incapable of housework in 1977	On claim form included in leaflet NI 210 supported by evidence of incapacity for work similarly on Leaflet NI 214	Insurance officer
4. Attendance Allowance (6 December 1971; an alternative lower-rate allowance was introduced in 1973)	For adults and children aged 2 or over who *i.* are so severely disabled either physically or mentally that they have needed a lot of looking after for 6 months or more; and who *ii.* satisfy the condition as to residence or presence The Allowance is payable at a *higher rate* for those who require attendance by day *and* at night; *lower rate* for those who need attendance either by day *or* at night	On claim form (DS2) at the back of leaflet NI 205	*i. Medical conditions*: The Attendance Allowance Board or its delegated medical practitioners *ii. Other conditions* Insurance officer
5. Invalid Care Allowance (July 1976)	Prevented from working by need to care for severely disabled relative. (Other conditions relating to age, residence, and the fact that this benefit is not available to married women, are similar to those for NCIP)	On claim form included in leaflet NI 212	(As for NCIP)

Appeal to	Provisions for dependants	Method of payment	Whether taxable	Overlap
Local appeal tribunal; National Insurance Commissioner	Increases of benefit payable for one dependent adult and dependent children	Girocheque weekly or fortnightly	No	Cannot be paid at same time as any other maintenance benefit of equal or higher amount
Local appeal tribunal; National Insurance Commissioner	Increases of benefit payable for one dependent adult and dependent children	Girocheque weekly or fortnightly or order book payable weekly at post office	No	Cannot be paid at same time as any other maintenance benefit of equal or higher amount
Local appeal tribunal; National Insurance Commissioner	Increases of benefit payable for one dependent adult and dependent children	Girocheque or order book payable weekly at post office	No	Cannot be paid at same time as any other maintenance benefit of equal or higher amount
No right of appeal against the decision of the Board or its delegates on question of fact or medical judgement, but decisions may be reviewed by the Board or their delegates Appeal may be made to the National Insurance Commissioner	None	Order book payable weekly at post office Where possible payments to adults are combined with payments of Retirement Pension, Widow's Pension, Invalidity Pension or Supplementary Benefit	No	Normally paid in full in addition to all other Social Security benefits. However, if a Constant Attendance Allowance is being paid under the Industrial Injuries Scheme, or with a war pension, the Attendance Allowance will be affected. Supplementary Benefit is not affected unless it includes a special payment to meet attendance needs
(As for NCIP)	(As for NCIP)	By order book payable weekly at post office	Yes	(As for NCIP)

Benefit and date introduced	Basic eligibility conditions	How to claim	Eligibility determined by
Mobility benefits			
6. Exemption from Vehicle Excise Duty for disabled non-drivers (April 1971)	Unable or virtually unable to walk; needing a full-time constant attendant for which an Attendance Allowance is payable; has a vehicle registered in own name which is suitable for use by the disabled person	Written application to DHSS Artificial Limb and Appliance Centres	Medical examination, administrative decision
7. Invalid three-wheeler vehicles	Unable or virtually unable to walk because of physical disablement and likely to remain so for at least 12 months. Able to control such a vehicle; aged 16 to pensionable age	For those currently eligible for Mobility Allowance on claim form included with leaflet NI 211. For those not yet eligible for Mobility Allowance but who are under pensionable age, by writing to the address given on page 5 of leaflet NI 211	If not eligible to claim Mobility Allowance, by administrative decision
8. Mobility Allowance (phased introduction over 3 years from 1 January 1976)	Unable or virtually unable to walk because of physical disablement, and able from time to time to make use of enhanced facilities for locomotion; likely to remain so for at least 12 months. Eventually available to those aged 5 to pensionable age but being introduced over 3 years by age groups in the broad order 15–50, 5–14, 51–pensionable age. Residence and presence tests	On claim form in leaflet NI 211	Insurance officer
Industrial benefits			
9. Injury Benefit (5.7.48 for industrial accidents and certain prescribed industrial diseases; later dates for other prescribed industrial diseases)	Incapable of work because of personal injury suffered by industrial accident or prescribed industrial disease; satisfies conditions as to insurability and presence. Payable for maximum of 26 weeks from date of accident or development of prescribed disease	On medical certificate supporting incapacity – replaced by doctor's statement from 4.10.76)	Insurance officer; Medical Board or Pneumoconiosis Medical Board

66

Appeal to	Provisions for dependents	Method of payment	Whether taxable	Overlap
None	None	Not applicable; certificate of exemption is issued which entitles holder to exemption	No	Cannot be granted if Mobility Allowance is in payment or if any benefits supplied under the old NHS Invalid Vehicle Scheme
If not eligible to claim Mobility Allowance, none	None	Not applicable	No	Mobility Allowance, allowances and vehicles under former NHS Vehicle Schemes
i. *Medical questions*: Medical Board; Medical Appeal Tribunal; National Insurance Commissioner (point of law only); ii. *Non-medical questions*: Local Appeal Tribunal; National Insurance Commissioner	None	Order book payable weekly at post office	Yes	Cannot be paid at same time as payments or provision of vehicles under former NHS Vehicle Service or a three-wheeler invalid vehicle. May affect any special payment under the Supplementary Benefit Act specifically made to meet a person's mobility needs
Local tribunal; National Insurance Commissioner; Medical Board or Pneumoconiosis Medical Board Medical Appeal Tribunal (in certain circumstances); National Insurance Commissioner on point of law (if leave to appeal granted) Limited provisions for review	Increases of benefit payable for one adult dependant and for children	Girocheque payable weekly	No	Cannot be paid at same time as any other maintenance benefit of equal or higher amount. Limitation on amount payable by way of Injury Benefit and Disablement Pension(s) (for accident and prescribed disease or more than one accident)

67

Benefit and date introduced	Basic eligibility conditions	How to claim	Eligibility determined by
10. Disablement Benefit (5.7.48 for industrial accidents and certain prescribed industrial diseases; later dates for other prescribed industrial diseases)	Suffers, as result of industrial accident or prescribed industrial disease, from loss of physical or mental faculty in respect of which disablement is assessed at not less than 1 per cent. Satisfied insurability condition. Not available until after end of Injury Benefit period, if any	On claim form BI 100A, BI 100B, or BI 100(Pn)	Insurance officer; Medical Board or Pneumoconiosis Medical Board
11. Unemployability Supplement (normally payable only as increase of Disablement Pension)	Permanently incapable of work because of results of industrial accident or prescribed industrial disease. Condition may be satisfied if unable to earn more than a specified limited amount	On claim form BI 101	Insurance officer
12. Allowance for partial disablement under the Pneumoconiosis, Byssinosis and Miscellaneous Diseases Benefit Scheme for certain diseases contracted as a result of specified employment which was wholly before 5.7.48 (Current scheme introduced on 1.3.66)[1]	Suffering some disablement which is likely to be permanent as a result of one of the scheduled diseases contracted as a result of specified employment prior to 5.7.48	On claim form PN 201 available from and submitted to the Pneumoconiosis, Byssinosis and Miscellaneous Diseases Benefit Board, Norcross, Blackpool, Lancs, FY5 3TA. Leaflet available at local Social Security Office	The Pneumoconiosis, Byssinosis and Miscellaneous Diseases Board

[1] A person entitled to an allowance under this scheme may also be entitled to Unemployability Supplement, Constant Attendance Allowance, or Exceptionally Severe Disablement Allowance on the satisfaction of similar conditions to those prescribed for these benefits under the Industrial Injuries Scheme

Appeal to	Provisions for dependants	Method of payment	Whether taxable	Overlap
Local tribunal; National Insurance Commissioner; Medical Board or Pneumoconiosis Medical Board Medical Appeal Tribunal (in certain circumstances); National Insurance Commissioner on point of law (subject to leave to appeal being granted) Limited provision for review	Not payable with basic Disablement Benefit	Disablement Pension: by order book payable weekly at post office; disablement gratuity: normally lump sum	No	Limitation on amount payable by way of Injury Benefit and Disablement Pension(s) (for accident and prescribed disease or more than one accident) Limited to 100 per cent Disablement Benefit if separate assessments of disablement total more than 100 per cent
Local tribunal; National Insurance Commissioner Limited provision for review	Increases of benefit payable for one adult dependant and for children	Order book payable weekly at post office	No	Cannot be paid at same time as Special Hardship Allowance or any other maintenance benefit of equal or higher amount
No appeal. The Board's decision is final, but may be reviewed if it can be shown to be erroneous in the light of new facts or because it was based on a mistake as to the facts, or there has been a relevant change of circumstances since it was given	Increase of an allowance in respect of total disablement can be paid for a male claimant's wife and/or child(ren). A claimant receiving Unemployability Supplement with the allowance may be entitled to an increase in respect of a wife or other adult dependant and/or child(ren)	By order book payable weekly at post office	No	Generally, where there is title to two or more allowances under either the Benefit Scheme or the Workmen's Compensation (Supplementation) Scheme the aggregate weekly payment of all allowances will be limited to the rate of allowance for total disablement

Benefit and date introduced	Basic eligibility conditions	How to claim	Eligibility determined by
13. Major or Lesser Incapacity Allowance under the Workmen's Compensation (Supplementation) Scheme for the effects of industrial accidents or diseases incurred as a result of employment prior to 5.7.48. (For accidents or disease resulting from employment prior to 1.12.24 there is also a basic allowance) (Current scheme introduced on 1.3.66)[1]	*i.* Entitlement to weekly payments of Workmen's Compensation for the accident or disease at some time since 5.7.56 in the case of Major Incapacity Allowance, and 1.3.66 in respect of an existing loss of earnings for Lesser Incapacity Allowance *ii.* For Major Incapacity Allowance; totally incapable of work as a result of disease and likely to remain so for at least 13 weeks *iii.* For Lesser Incapacity Allowance; partially or totally incapacitated as a result of the accident or disease *iv.* For the basic allowance the conditions are partial or total incapacity for work as a result of an accident or disease incurred in employment prior to 1.1.24 and a right or underlying right to weekly payments of Workmen's Compensation on or after 21.3.51	On a claim form WS 70 or WS 80 available from and submitted to the Workmen's Compensation (Supplementation) Board, Norcross, Blackpool, Lancs, FY5 3TA Leaflet available at local Social Security Office	The Workmen's Compensation (Supplementation) Board
14. Constant Attendance Allowance (Industrial Injuries)	In receipt of 100 per cent industrial disablement pension; needs constant attendance	Claim form BI 104	Secretary of State
15. Special Hardship Allowance	Unable to work in regular occupation (pre-accident) or work of an equivalent standard as a result of an industrial accident or a prescribed disease	Claim forms BI 103 or BI 103A	Insurance officer
16. Industrial Death Benefit	Payable in respect of a widow, widower, child, parent and certain relatives of a person whose death results from an industrial accident or a prescribed industrial disease, and to a woman having care of a child of the deceased	Claim forms BW 1 (widow) or BI 200 (others)	Insurance officer

[1] A person entitled to an allowance under this scheme may also be entitled to Unemployability Supplement, Constant Attendance Allowance, or Exceptionally Severe Disablement Allowance on the satisfaction of similar conditions to those prescribed for these benefits under the Industrial Injuries Scheme

Appeal to	Provisions for dependants	Method of payment	Whether taxable	Overlap
No appeal. The Board's decision is final; but it may be reviewed if it is shown that it was based on a mistake or there has been some relevant change of circumstance since it was given	Where a claimant is receiving an Unemployability Supplement with the allowance an increase may be paid in respect of a wife or other adult dependant and/or child(ren)	By order book payable weekly at post office	No	Generally, where there is title to two or more allowances under either the Supplementation Scheme or the Pneumoconiosis Byssinosis and Miscellaneous Disease Benefit Scheme the aggregate weekly payment of all allowances will be limited to the rate of the 100 per cent Disablement Pension payable under the Industrial Injuries Scheme
Secretary of State reviews on request	Not applicable	Order book	No	Takes precedence over ordinary (non-war pension, non-industrial) Attendance Allowance
Local tribunal; National Insurance Commissioner	Not applicable	Order book	No	Aggregate weekly rate of Disablement Benefit cannot exceed 100 per cent rate of Disablement Benefit
Local tribunal; National Insurance Commissioner	Not applicable	Order book	Yes	National Insurance Widow's Benefit not payable at the same time as Widow's Industrial Death Benefit; increases of other benefits in respect of dependent children not payable at same time as Child's Industrial Death Benefit

Benefit and date introduced	Basic eligibility conditions	How to claim	Eligibility determined by
Services benefits 17. War Disablement Pension (1917 in current form)	Must be suffering from disablement due to the continuing effects of service in armed forces after 3 September 1939	By writing to DHSS Blackpool Central Office, Norcross, Blackpool, Lancs, FY5 3TA or by calling at any local office of the department	Entitlement officer
18. Mercantile Marine Scheme: disablement pension	Must be suffering from disablement due to war injury or war risk injury	By writing to DHSS Blackpool, Central Office, Norcross, Blackpool, Lancs, FY5 3TA or by calling at any local office of the department	Entitlement officer
19. Civilian Scheme: disablement pension	Must be suffering from disablement due to war injury or war service injury	By writing to DHSS Blackpool Central Office, Norcross, Blackpool, Lancs, FY5 3TA or by calling at any local office of the department	Entitlement officer
20. Unemployability Supplement	So seriously disabled as to be unemployable. Pensioned disablement must be main cause of unemployability	By application to DHSS Blackpool Central Office, Norcross, Blackpool, Lancs, FY5 3TA, the nearest War Pensions Office, or any local office of the department	Entitlement officer
21. Constant Attendance Allowance (1917)	Pensioned disablement 80 per cent or more and such that regular attention of a personal nature is needed	By application to DHSS Blackpool Central Office, Norcross, Blackpool, Lancs, FY5 3TA, the nearest War Pensions Office, or any local office of the department	Entitlement officer
22. Allowance for Lowered Standard of Occupation	Payable where there is an earnings loss because pensionable disablement permanently prevents pensioner from following his regular occupation or work of an equivalent standard.. Allowance and pension together cannot exceed the 100 per cent pension rate	By application to DHSS Blackpool Central Office, Norcross, Blackpool, Lancs, FY5 3TA, the nearest War Pensions Office, or any local office of the department	Entitlement officer

Appeal to	Provisions for dependants	Method of payment	Whether taxable	Overlap
Pensions Appeal Tribunal	Increases payable for wife and children	Payment voucher monthly or order book payable weekly at post office	No	Does not overlap with any other benefit
Pensions Appeal Tribunal	Increases payable for wife and children	Order book payable weekly at post office	No	Does not overlap with any other benefit
Pensions Appeal Tribunal	Increases payable for wife and children	Order book payable weekly at post office	No	Does not overlap with any other benefit
No statutory right of appeal but can put case to his/her local War Pensions Committee	Increases payable for wife and children	Allowance included in basic Disablement Pension order book	No	Overlaps with Sickness Benefit, Invalidity Benefit, Non-Contributory Pension, Unemployment Benefit, Widow's Pension, Retirement pension, Unemployability Supplement and Injury Benefit under the Industrial Injuries Scheme
No statutory right of appeal but can put case to his/her local War Pensions Committee		Allowance included in basic Disablement Pension order book	No	Overlaps with National Insurance Attendance and Industrial Injuries Constant Attendance Allowances
No statutory right of appeal but can put case to his/her local War Pensions Committee		Allowance included in basic Disablement Pension order book	No	

Benefit and date introduced	Basic eligibility conditions	How to claim	Eligibility determined by
23. Severe Disablement Occupational Allowance (introduced 1961)	Must be receiving Constant Attendance Allowance at one of the two rates above the normal maximum and despite handicap be following employment	Eligibility is automatically examined when Constant Attendance Allowance is awarded at qualifying rates	Entitlement officer
24. Exceptionally Severe Disablement Allowance (introduced 1966)	Pensioned disablement of exceptional severity and Constant Attendance Allowance payable at one of the two rates above the normal maximum	Eligibility is automatically examined when Constant Attendance Allowance is awarded at qualifying rates	Entitlement officer
25. Clothing Allowance	Where the pensioned disablement or the use of an appliance for the pensioned disablement causes exceptional wear and tear of clothing	By application to DHSS Blackpool Central Office, Norcross, Blackpool, Lancs, FY5 3TA, the nearest War Pensions Office, or any local office of the department	Entitlement officer
26. Comforts Allowance	Payable in addition to Constant Attendance Allowance and/or Unemployability Supplement	Eligibility is automatically examined when Constant Attendance Allowance or Unemployability Supplement is awarded	Entitlement officer
27. Age Allowance (introduced 1957)	Must be 65 or over with a pensioned disablement assessed at 40 per cent or more	Automatically awarded when pensioner eligible	Entitlement officer
28. Education Allowance	Payable where an allowance is in payment for a child of 5 or over, the circumstances of the family are such as to require it and the Secretary of State is satisfied that the proposed education is suitable for the child	By application to DHSS Blackpool Central Office, Norcross, Blackpool, Lancs, FY5 3TA, the nearest War Pensions Office, or any local office of the department	Entitlement officer
29. Treatment Allowance	Where a pensioner is receiving treatment for his pensioned disablement of a kind which prevents him from working for more than 7 days	By application to DHSS Blackpool Central Office, Norcross, Blackpool, Lancs, FY5 3TA, the nearest War Pensions Office, or any local office of the department	Entitlement officer
30. Increase in the amount of personal Treatment Allowances (1943)	Where a pensioner is eligible for Treatment Allowance, but is not eligible for such National Insurance benefits as Sickness Benefit, Invalidity Pension, Retirement Pension, etc.	Enquiries made by DHSS Blackpool Central Office when Treatment Allowance is awarded	Entitlement officer

Appeal to	Provisions for dependants	Method of payment	Whether taxable	Overlap
No statutory right of appeal but can put case to his/her local War Pensions Committee	—	Allowance included in basic Disablement Pension order book	No	Not payable with Invalidity Benefit, Non-Contributory Invalidity Pension and Retirement Pension
No statutory right of appeal but can put case to his/her local War Pensions Committee	—	Allowance included in basic Disablement Pension order book	No	—
No statutory right of appeal but can put case to his/her local War Pensions Committee	—	By Giro order	No	—
No statutory right of appeal but can put case to his/her local War Pensions Committee	—	Allowance included in basic Disablement Pension order book	No	—
No statutory right of appeal but can put case to his/her local War Pensions Committee	—	Allowance included in basic Disablement Pension order book	No	—
No statutory right of appeal but can put case to his/her local War Pensions Committee		By Giro order	No.	—
No statutory right of appeal but can put case to his/her local War Pensions Committee	Increases for wife and children if pensioner's assessment is less than 100 per cent	Basic pension topped up to 100 per cent rate by Giro order	No	—
No statutory right of appeal but can put case to his/her local War Pensions Committee	Increases for wife and children	Weekly in advance by Giro order during duration of award	No	—

75

Benefit and date introduced	Basic eligibility conditions	How to claim	Eligibility determined by
31. Part-time Treatment Allowance	Where a pensioner is receiving treatment for his pensioned disablement of a kind which prevents him from working for 7 days or less. Allowance based on loss of earnings subject to maximum rate and the limits of ordinary Treatment Allowances	By writing to DHSS Blackpool Central Office, Norcross, Blackpool, Lancs, FY5 3TA, the nearest War Pensions Office, or any local office of the department	Entitlement officer
32. Invalidity Allowance (introduced 1971)	Where Unemployability Supplement is in payment and the unemployability began 5 years before retirement age (provided this was not before 1971)	Automatically considered when Unemployability Supplement awarded	Entitlement officer
Retirement benefits[1] 33. Retirement Pension (on own contributions) (First contributory retirement pension scheme 1925)	i. Minimum age 65 (men) and 60 (women) ii. Retirement up to age 70 (men) and 65 (women) iii. Contributions *paid* in any tax year on earnings of at least 50 times the lower earnings limit for contributions (£13 in 1976/77) *and* contributions paid or credited to the same level in about 9/10ths of the tax years in the working life[2]	Normally on form BR 1	Insurance officer
34. Retirement Pension (wife on husband's contributions)	i. Minimum age 60 ii. Retirement up to age 65, and husband's retirement iii. Conditions for pension on own contributions satisfied by husband	Normally on form BR 1A	Insurance officer

[1] An age addition is payable with the pensions of all people aged 80 or over
[2] An increase of both basic and graduated pension can be earned by deferring retirement beyond minimum age

Appeal to	Provisions for dependants	Method of payment	Whether taxable	Overlap
No statutory right of appeal but can put case to his/her local War Pensions Committee	—	Paid by Giro order	No	—
No statutory right of appeal but can put case to his/her local War Pensions Committee	—	Paid by Giro order	No	—
Local tribunal and National Insurance Commissioner	Adult dependant and children	*Either* weekly by order book, *or* four-weekly in arrears by crossed order, *or* quarterly in arrears by crossed order	No	The main benefits with which there is overlap are Sickness, Invalidity, Unemployment, Widow's and Non-Contributory Invalidity Pensions but this list is not exhaustive. If there is entitlement to more than one basic pension only the higher of the two will be paid
Local tribunal and National Insurance Commissioner	None	*Either* weekly by order book, *or* four-weekly in arrears by crossed order, *or* quarterly in arrears by crossed order	Yes	The main benefits with which there is overlap are Sickness, Invalidity, Unemployment, Widow's and Non-Contributory Invalidity Pensions, but this list is not exhaustive. If there is entitlement to more than one basic pension only the higher of the two will be paid

Benefit and date introduced	Basic eligibility conditions	How to claim	Eligibility determined by
35. Retirement Pension (women widowed before age 60 and not remarried at age 60) (August 1957; April 1971 for *iii. A*)	*i.* Minimum age 60 *ii.* Retirement up to age 65 *and* *iii. A.* Pension at the same rate as the Widow's Pension she was receiving before age 60 *or B.* Contribution conditions as for pension on own contributions but late husband's contributions can be used to satisfy the first contribution condition *and* can be used instead of the widow's own record for periods up to the end of the tax year in which he died	Normally on BR 1	Insurance officer
36. Retirement Pension (women widowed over age 60)	Contribution conditions based on husband's record satisfied as if he had retired on date of death	Form BW 1 or form BD 8 if she is already receiving a pension on her husband's contributions	Insurance officer
37. Retirement Pension (women divorced over 60) (August 1957)	Contribution conditions based on husband's record satisfied as if he had died on date of decree absolute	BR 1 or by letter if she is already receiving a pension on her husband's contributions	Insurance officer
38. Retirement Pension (women divorced under age 60, and not remarried before age 60) (August 1957)	*i.* Minimum age 60 *ii.* Retirement up to age 65 *iii.* Contribution conditions as for a pension on her own contributions except that she can use her former husband's record instead of her own, for the second contribution condition, up to the end of the tax year in which the marriage ended	Normally form BR 1	Insurance officer

Appeal to	Provisions for dependants	Method of payment	Whether taxable	Overlap
Local tribunal and National Insurance Commissioner	Children, but she could receive Widowed Mother's Allowance instead of Retirement Pension	*Either* weekly by order book, *or* four-weekly in arrears by crossed order, *or* quarterly in arrears by crossed order	Yes	The main benefits with which there is overlap are Sickness, Invalidity, Unemployment, Widow's and Non-Contributory Invalidity Pensions but this list is not exhaustive. If there is entitlement to more than one basic pension only the higher of the two will be paid
Local tribunal and National Insurance Commissioner	Children, but she could receive Widowed Mother's Allowance instead of Retirement Pension	*Either* weekly by order book, *or* four-weekly in arrears by crossed order, *or* quarterly in arrears by crossed order	Yes	The main benefits with which there is overlap are Sickness, Invalidity, Unemployment, Widow's and Non-Contributory Invalidity Pensions but this list is not exhaustive. If there is entitlement to more than one basic pension, only the higher of the two will be paid
Local tribunal and National Insurance Commissioner	Children	*Either* weekly by order book, *or* four-weekly in arrears by crossed order, *or* quarterly in arrears by crossed order	Yes	The main benefits with which there is overlap are Sickness, Invalidity, Unemployment, Widow's and Non-Contributory Invalidity Pensions, but this list is not exhaustive. If there is entitlement to more than one basic pension, only the higher of the two will be paid
Local tribunal and National Insurance Commissioner	Children	*Either* weekly by order book, *or* four-weekly in arrears by crossed order, *or* quarterly in arrears by crossed order	Yes	The main benefits with which there is overlap are Sickness, Invalidity, Unemployment, Widow's and Non-Contributory Invalidity Pensions, but this list is not exhaustive. If there is entitlement to more than one basic pension, only the higher of the two will be paid

F

Benefit and date introduced	Basic eligibility conditions	How to claim	Eligibility determined by
39. Graduated Pension (April 1961)	i. Age and retirement as for Retirement Pension ii. 2½p for each unit of graduated contribution paid up to 5 April 1975 when the payment of graduated contributions ended. A unit is £9 (woman) and £7.50 (man)[1]	Normally on same BR 1/ BR 1A as for Retirement Pension. Graduated pension, on its own, can be claimed on BR 1	Insurance officer
40. Non-Contributory Retirement Pension for people over 80 (November 1970)	Over pension age at 5 July 1948 *and* normally living in England, Scotland or Wales at time of claim, *and* have lived in the UK for at least 10 years in the 20-year period ending on the day before 80th birthday	Claim form in explanatory leaflet NI 184	Insurance officer
Widow's benefits 41. Widow's Allowance	Under 60 at widowhood *or* late husband not entitled to Retirement Pension; single contribution conditions satisfied on late husband's insurance	On claim form BW 1	Insurance officer
42. Widow's Earnings-related Addition (October 1966 – known as Widow's Supplementary Allowance prior to April 1975)	Widow entitled to Widow's Allowance; late husband had reckonable earnings of specified amount	On claim form BW 1	Insurance officer
43. Widowed Mother's Allowance	Qualifying child under 19 and residing with widow; contribution conditions satisfied on late husband's insurance	On claim form BW 1 – follows Widow's Allowance	Insurance officer
44. Widow's Pension	Aged 50 or over either at widowhood or when Widowed Mother's Allowance ceases; contribution conditions satisfied on late husband's insurance	On claim form BW 1 – follows Widow's Allowance or Widowed Mother's Allowance	Insurance officer
45. Age-related Widow's Pension (April 1971)	Aged between 40 and 50 either at widowhood or when Widowed Mother's Allowance ceases, contribution conditions satisfied on late husband's insurance	On claim form BW 1 – follows Widow's Allowance or Widowed Mother's Allowance	Insurance officer

[1] An increase can be earned by deferring retirement beyond minimum age

Appeal to	Provisions for dependants	Method of payment	Whether taxable	Overlap
Local tribunal and National Insurance Commissioner	A woman divorced over age 60, or a widow, can receive half her husband's entitlement on her own retirement	Normally with Retirement Pension. Where there is no entitlement to Retirement Pension Graduated Pension is paid *either* weekly or four-weekly by order book, *or* four-weekly or quarterly by crossed order	Yes	As for Retirement Pension
Local tribunal and National Insurance Commissioner	Adult dependant, children, former wives and widows	As for Retirement Pension	Yes	As for Retirement Pension
Local Appeal Tribunal; National Insurance Commissioner	Increases of benefit payable for dependent children	Girocheque *or* order book payable weekly at post office	Yes	Cannot be paid at same time as any other maintenance benefit of equal or higher amount
Local Appeal Tribunal; National Insurance Commissioner	None	Girocheque *or* order book payable weekly at post office	Yes	None
Local Appeal Tribunal; National Insurance Commissioner	Increase of benefit payable for dependent children	Order book payable weekly at post office *or* crossed order four-weekly or quarterly in arrears	Yes	Cannot be paid at same time as any other maintenance benefit of equal or higher value
Local Appeal Tribunal; National Insurance Commissioner	None	Order book payable weekly at post office *or* crossed order four-weekly or quarterly in arrears	Yes	Cannot be paid at same time as any other maintenance benefit of equal or or higher value
Local Appeal Tribunal; National Insurance Commissioner	None	Order book payable weekly at post office *or* crossed order four-weekly or quarterly in arrears	Yes	Cannot be paid at same time as any other maintenance benefit of equal or higher value

Benefit and date introduced	Basic eligibility conditions	How to claim	Eligibility determined by
46. Non-Contributory Widowed Mother's Allowance (November 1970)	Qualifying child under 19 residing with widow; husband over 65 at July 1948, conditions as to residence and presence satisfied	On claim form BW 1	Insurance officer
47. Non-Contributory Widow's Pension (November 1970)	Aged 50 or over either at widowhood or when Widowed Mother's Allowance ceases; husband over 65 at July 1948, conditions as to residence and presence satisfied	On claim form BW 1	Insurance officer
48. Non-Contributory Age-related Widow's Pension (April 1971)	Aged between 40 and 50 either at widowhood or when Widowed Mother's Allowance ceases; husband over 65 at July 1948, conditions as to residence and presence satisfied	On claim form BW 1	Insurance officer
49. Death Grant	Contribution conditions satisfied on insurance of deceased or deceased's spouse. If deceased is a child conditions may be satisfied on parent's insurance. If deceased incapable of work since age 19 conditions may be satisfied on insurance of a near relative	On claim form BD 1	Insurance officer
Earnings-related Supplements to other benefits 50. Earnings-related Supplement to Unemployment Benefit, Sickness Benefit, Injury Benefit and Maternity Allowance, Widow's Earnings-related Addition is payable with Widow's Allowance (October 1966)	Entitlement to the appropriate flat-rate benefit. For PIEs[1] beginning before 2 January 1977 it was necessary to have reckonable earnings of more than £500 in the relevant income tax year. Reckonable earnings were earnings amenable to income tax under Schedule E and from which tax was deductible under PAYE system. From 2 January 1977 it became necessary to have an earnings factor (derived from Class I contributions paid) of more than 50 × the lower earnings limit for contributions in the income tax year	No specific claim is necessary. It is paid automatically where appropriate	As for the benefit which it supplements

[1] Periods of Interruption of Employment

Appeal to	Provisions for dependants	Method of payment	Whether taxable	Overlap
Local Appeal Tribunal; National Insurance Commissioner	Increases of benefit payable for dependent children	Order book payable weekly at post office *or* crossed order four-weekly or quarterly in arrears	Yes	Cannot be paid at same time as any other maintenance benefit of equal or higher value
Local Appeal Tribunal; National Insurance Commissioner	None	Order book payable weekly at post office *or* crossed order four-weekly or quarterly in arrears	Yes	Cannot be paid at same time as any other maintenance benefit of equal or higher value
Local Appeal Tribunal; National Insurance Commissioner	None	Order book payable weekly at post office *or* crossed order four-weekly or quarterly in arrears	Yes	Cannot be paid at same time as any other maintenance benefit of equal or higher value
Local Appeal Tribunal; National Insurance Commissioner	None	Girocheque	No	None
As for the benefit which it supplements	Not applicable	As for the benefit it supplements	No	Each supplement is treated as part of the benefit it supplements. Amount of supplement not to be reduced under overlapping benefit rules. Amount of Widow's Earnings-related Addition to be deducted from any other benefit for the same period calculated by reference to contributions of deceased. Widow's Earnings-related Addition may be payable as well as ERS of other benefits

Benefit and date introduced	Basic eligibility conditions	How to claim	Eligibility determined by
Supplementary Benefit			
51. Supplementary Benefit (replaced National Assistance 1966)[1]	Aged 16 or over; not in full-time work; not a woman living with husband or with man as husband and wife. If claimant's 'resources' are less than his 'requirements' the benefit payable is the difference between the two	On claim form included in leaflet SB 1, or if registered for employment on form B 1 available from Unemployment Benefit Office	Supplementary Benefits Commission
Miscellaneous benefits			
52. Family Income Supplement (August 1971)	Families with dependent children, where the head of family is in remunerative full-time work (30 hours a week), and where the gross weekly income falls below a prescribed amount determined by the number of children in the family	On claim form included in leaflet form FIS 1, supported by evidence of wages and other income	Supplementary Benefits Commission
53. Help with charges for spectacles (1951)	Under 16 or still at school; receiving FIS or Supplementary Benefit; receiving free prescriptions or free welfare milk because of low income; others with low income	By declaration to optician; and for those with low incomes not receiving a 'passport benefit' by claim on form F1	Claimants on low income grounds by Social Security office; others by Family Practitioner Committee (in practice, the optician)

[1]*a.* The blind: the 'requirements' of blind claimants are set at a higher level than those of other claimants.
b. Discretionary additions: the Supplementary Benefits Commission may, at their discretion, increase the level of weekly benefit paid in order to meet exceptional circumstances; these may include extra heating needs, special dietary needs, special laundry costs, special clothing needs as a result of disability etc. *c.* Discretionary lump-sum payments: 'one-off' Exceptional Needs Payments may also be made at the Commission's discretion for such items as bedding, essential furniture and clothing

Appeal to	Provisions for dependants	Method of payment	Whether taxable	Overlap
Supplementary Benefit Appeal Tribunal	Higher level of requirements if married; increases for dependent children	Girocheque or order book (sometimes combined with Retirement Pension or Unemployment Benefit) In emergency cash	No	As this is a means-tested benefit, overlap is avoided simply by including other benefits as 'resources'. Family Allowance, Child Benefit, Family Income Supplement and main National Insurance pension and benefits (including NCIP and ICA) are taken fully into account. Beneficiaries entitled to AA receive an attendance requirement of the same cash amount and it is thus effectively disregarded. Mobility Allowance is disregarded. Up to £4 is disregarded from War and Industrial Disablement Pensions
Local Appeal Tribunal	Maximum payment increases by 50p for each additional child	Order book payable weekly at post office	No	Taken fully into account if recipient subsequently claims Supplementary Benefit. Ignored when calculating entitlement to National Insurance benefits
No statutory right	Children under 16 or at school exempt; dependants covered if claim based on low income or receipt of other benefit	Glasses provided free or at reduced charge	No	None

Benefit and date introduced	Basic eligibility conditions	How to claim	Eligibility determined by
54. Help with dental treatment (1951)	Under 16 or still at school; between 16 and 21 still at school (except for dentures); expectant mothers; women who have had a child within the past year; receiving FIS or Supplementary Benefit; receiving free prescriptions or free welfare milk because of low income; others with low income	By declaration to dentist; and for those with low incomes not receiving a 'passport benefit' by claim on form FID	Claims on low income grounds by Social Security office; others by Family Practitioner Committee (in practice, the dentist)
55. Free prescriptions (present arrangements April 1968)	Under 16; over pension age; expectant mothers; women with child under 1; person with specified medical condition; war pensioner (for accepted service disablement); low income; receiving FIS or Supplementary Benefit	Expectant mothers claim on form FW 8; women with child under 1 on form FP 91; low-income claimants on form PC 11; war pensioners, recipients of FIS and Supplementary Benefit apply to Social Security office for exemption certificate; people claiming on age grounds sign declaration on back of prescription. Persons suffering from a specified medical condition claim on form FP 91	Claims on low income grounds by Social Security office; others by Family Practitioner Committee (in practice, claims based on specified medical condition or accepted war disablement certified by doctor; age declaration accepted by dispenser)

Note that for many benefits in this table, benefit may be lost if claims are delayed

Appeal to	Provisions for dependants	Method of payment	Whether taxable	Overlap
No statutory right	Children under 16 or at school exempt; dependants covered if claim based on low income or receipt of other benefit	Treatment provided free or at reduced charge	No	None
No statutory right	Children under 16 automatically exempt; dependants covered if claim based on low income on receipt of FIS or Supplementary Benefit	Certificate of exemption or single prescription issued free as necessary	No	None

rebates, allowances, or assistance of the many types theoretically available. The broad headings under which people with various types of handicap *may* be able to get help (actual availability will vary geographically) are as follows:

Local authority housing (this may or may not be purpose-built)

Grants for necessary adaptation work on property where they live (see page 37 regarding the administrative problems surrounding the application of Improvement Grants in this way)

Adaptations to council property in which they live

Rent Rebate/Allowance

Rate Rebate

Assistance with holidays: either by outright provision, for instance, of group holidays, or by grants towards costs of other arrangements

Provision of or help with installation or rental cost of *telephones*: an area of very variable provision and one in which the squeeze on local authority budgets has been particularly restrictive

Help with the cost of *television*, also occasionally the provision of *radio*; much the same comments apply as to the supply of telephones

Disposables: this is one of the many administrative 'grey areas' between Area Health Authorities (via hospitals or Community Nursing Services) and local authorities' Social Services Departments; in 'good' areas where the two work together well, this overlap does not greatly affect the client, but elsewhere it may give rise to difficulties

Laundry services for those with incontinence problems: these, too, are variable in availability, and cost cutting has tended to reduce the number of calls per week, leading to an accumulation of soiled laundry that can create problems of its own

Day care: limited numbers of day centre places for people with various types of handicap are provided, but in this more than most benefits *location* can be the factor which determines availability

Transport for disabled people: this is a very varied area of provision including concessionary bus passes, free parking permits, transport in tail-lift vehicles to day centres, the operation of a whole fleet of specialised vehicles by some authorities. It is an area in which demand has been increased by the central government switch from personal vehicles to Mobility Allowance, and is particularly under pressure for older people needing transport to luncheon and other clubs (see below); voluntary organisations often help

Walking (or other personal) aids: generally supplied through Social Services Departments, with assessment usually by an occupational therapist; there may be some overlapping agency problems in that hospitals, Community Nursing Services and voluntary bodies may also be involved

Meals-on-wheels: a very variable service as to the frequency of meals that can be provided; while most authorities have been improving the service since 1970, growing financial problems have been experienced in the past two years; there is still considerable involvement of the WRVS who in most places originally operated the service

Luncheon clubs for those who are able, and prefer, to go to local authority centres for meals; these are of great importance to many disabled people because of the saving on fuel costs at home

Home helps: provision of specified kinds of domestic help to people in need – the elderly and the younger disabled are their main clients; usually application is via the Social Services Department to a Home Help Organiser, and some authorities require means-tested contributions from clients; the number of hours which can be provided varies greatly. The potential value of this service is probably reflected in the relatively high incidence of problems concerning this service among DIG cases. The Rugby area operates a special care scheme – the '*Crossroads care scheme*' mentioned on page 215 – composed of domestic help and home nursing elements and much more flexible to clients' requirements than more usual home help services

Residential care: application is usually via the Social Services Department, but the provision itself is widely variable, ranging from warden-controlled flatlet schemes and open hostels which mentally or physically handicapped people can use as a sheltered but semi-independent home of their own, through all kinds of local authority Part III accommodation, 'young chronic sick' units, private or voluntary organisations' residential homes and nursing homes, to the long-stay wards of hospitals

There are many other local authority services – varying from one place to another – which may involve handicapped people and their families, such as Education Department benefits like free school meals or school uniform grants; but these are designed for low-income households, rather than specifically for people whose problems arise from handicaps.

There are also facilities such as POSSUM (Patient Operated Selector Mechanism) whose provision is on a national basis but access to which tends to be via local authority Social Services, because they act as the agency informing the potential applicant of the existence of the service.

This *information function* in itself is one of the most significant and the most variable of local authority 'benefits'. Where it is good it can be *very* good – as in Newcastle upon Tyne, where there is a central reference point manned by people who are themselves handicapped, together with a showroom with expert staff where aids to handicapped living can be seen and tried, supplying a good range of services and alert to the likely trend of needs through its own research. Such a department will chase central government bodies, for instance, for up-to-date copies of leaflets on benefits. Unfortunately not all local authorities' provisions for the handicapped even attempt such a standard.

Principles in a tangle

It was pointed out in Chapter 1 that there is no single principle underlying the Social Security benefit system as it affects handicapped people. In view of the historical pattern of development outlined in that chapter it would be surprising if there were. There is nothing wrong with using more than one principle to meet an evolving situation; the trouble arises from out-of-date or conflicting principles.

One source of problems is the fact that the present structure does not (with the inevitable few exceptions) deal with disablement or handicap *as such*. The condition of the handicapped person in our society is treated as an incidental aspect of either poverty, or of interruption of earnings, or of old age.

Poverty

Even on these bases, the regulations are full of inconsistencies arising from conflicting or sometimes anachronistic 'principles'. Thus, it is conceded, in effect, that the *poverty* of chronically sick or disabled people is 'not their fault' – a distinction flowing directly from the days of the Poor Law – so they are nominally 'entitled' to income maintenance in one form or another. Yet in the application of means tests and the patronising structure of 'concessions' and rebates and 'free' this and that, society shows every inclination still to use *shame* as a way of limiting the demands of disabled people upon its resources. The means-testing which Beveridge sought to remove from the system has increased in significance, because it is now the basis of allocation for many local authority benefits as well as for Supplementary Benefits. Yet by mixing incompatible criteria, anomalies are created so that, for example, even wealthy diabetics can get free prescriptions under the NHS, but the same 'concession' may be denied to poor patients whose diseases or handicaps are less administratively easy to deal with. Rent and Rate Rebates also mix two principles, both being designed on a means-tested basis but larger sums being awarded if people are registered as disabled with the local authority.

Interruption of earnings

Handicap, in a person of below retirement age, is treated as just one of a collection of undifferentiated contingencies that may lead to interruption of earnings. As a result, handicapped people are often treated in the same way as if they were voluntarily unemployed, yet the regulations are so designed as to make it well-nigh impossible for many of them to work to the limited extent that they might without losing all their benefit (see page 54). But without an adequate background of continuous employment they are not covered under the contributory principle.

Age

For the large number of older people who become handicapped, even the treatment of disability as an incidental aspect of old age is not consistent, because old age, as a qualification for income maintenance, has given place in recent years to *retirement*, and there is even less direct association between disablement and retirement at an arbitrary date than between disablement and old age. Thus, for instance, a fit retirement pensioner may be entitled to benefits and concessions denied to a person handicapped by premature ageing who has not yet reached the official retirement age.

Compensation – for what?

Only within the carefully circumscribed area of war and industrial injury schemes is disablement dealt with *as such*, and even these schemes vacillate between the principle of compensation for loss of earnings (as in the Allowance for Lowered Standard of Occupation) and that of compensation for loss of faculty (in the disablement scales themselves), having long ago abandoned the basis of loss of earning power because it proved impossible to administer.

Changing principles

The switch away from the 'loss of earning power' principle illustrates a vital difference between those who devise benefits and those who depend on them: the administrators can, and do, change the rules when the going gets rough. The handicapped cannot. Indeed one of their greatest problems in recent years has been the tendency of the administrators to change the rules in the middle of the game, as with the decisions whether or not to make taxable new benefits as they are devised (contrast Attendance Allowance and Mobility Allowance). The most obvious current examples arise in respect of personal vehicle provision, but the extent to which recent rule-changing will affect the numerically much larger area of retirement pensions in the future is only now emerging, and is a matter which ought to be under very close scrutiny.

The missing principle

In the legislation which applies the various principles upon which central government benefits are based, nothing gives any explicit recognition to the one way in which handicapped people are *not* similar to the rest of the community: those non-optional areas of extra expenditure which arise directly from their disabilities. Because of this difference, the principles outlined above are often inappropriate as bases for determining the benefits due to handicapped people.

The selective principle

Herein lies the shortcoming of the newer benefits which have been introduced since 1970 on the selective principle of helping identifiable groups of handicapped people who have a particular need, such as a need for attendance or for help with mobility. If the principle underlying such payments is that a special and abnormal need has been (very rigorously) identified, a need for which the claimant's existing resources cannot make sufficient provision, then it must be logical to *add* this allowance to existing resources. It is illogical to offset it in some way (as was done when the Mobility Allowance was made taxable) or to pay a part of the cost when the client has no way of supplying the remainder. The basic problem is that the identified needs are particular areas in a wider background of additional expense arising from the handicap; yet these areas are picked out and the rest left untreated. As a result the benefits awarded are often technically misappropriated to pay for other extra expenses whose existence is not officially recognised. Examples from DIG's case histories include allowances given for petrol for Invacars but used to pay for extra electricity or to meet telephone bills, Exceptional Needs Payments given for 'a coat and shoes' used to pay fuel bills, and the use of Attendance Allowance to pay for extra heating.

Long-term generosity?

In recent years it has been a matter of principle to provide more generously for longer-term incapacity relative to that for short-term sickness (or dependence upon Supplementary Benefit). Yet because the operation of this is still tied to the principle of incapacity *to earn* – not to intrinsic handicap – the permanently disabled who can work only intermittently find themselves relegated to 'short-term' rates.

Principles and the married woman

In relation to married women, conflicting principles lead to some very curious situations. The resources and requirements of family groups are calculated on a basis which pays no regard to legislation on equal opportunities for men and women. A family unit for benefit purposes is regarded as being a *man*, a *dependent adult* (usually his wife) and such *children* as there may be. A wife is a kind of variable benefit voucher – discounted (that is, her earnings offset against benefit) in some situations, such as sickness or unemployment, if she earns more than £8, but allowed to earn up to £35 before benefit is affected in some others, as when on Retirement Pension. If she should need to claim under the insurance principle on the basis of her own record the 'normal' (i.e. male) contribution requirements apply – even though the reason why she may not now have such a record may be the 'married women's option' which was created by government in the period concerned, to suit conditions of society which have now changed. (Should not the legislation on equal opportunity have incorporated a moratorium on such effects of the principles which preceded that legislation?)

If, on the other hand, a wife has given up work to care for a sick or handicapped husband, she will find that the Invalid Care Allowance is not available for her – despite the fact that it was introduced 'for those of working age who would be breadwinners in paid employment but for the need to stay at home and act as unpaid attendants to people who are severely disabled and need care'. To most people in today's society, in which women are breadwinners in 20 per cent of households, this sounds like a perfect description of a wife who has a handicapped husband. The catch, however, lies in that word *breadwinner* – for the existing principles upon which benefits are constructed do not admit to that category a married woman who lives with her husband: Family Income Supplement, for instance, cannot be paid to a couple unless the *man* is in full-time work with a suitably low income. The married woman must be content to live on her variable estate as a dependant on her husband's benefits, and if these are not adequate, on Supplementary Benefit.

If the housewife herself is disabled, she must pursue the will-o'-the-wisp 'Housewives' Non-Contributory Invalidity Pension'. Even though this was on the statute book it continued to be without substance until November 1977, and will remain so except for those who can satisfy the administrators that they are incapable of 'normal household duties' as well as of doing work for which an outside employer would pay. (For men unable to work, NCIP is payable if contribution records are deficient, without any such additional conditions.)

The principle of 'fairness'   The most extraordinary double standards are used in defence of 'natural justice' or 'fairness' under the existing system. Thus, it is not considered right to pay non-contributors as much as contributors despite the fact that there is no pretence that contributory benefits are paid for out of the money paid in as National Insurance contributions: they require substantial supplementation (£600 million in 1974) from government funds, themselves raised by taxation on the community at large. Yet benefits such as NCIP are fixed at only 60 per cent of the level of equivalent benefits within the contributory sector. Since the level even of these contributory benefits is frequently inadequate for the needs of handicapped people, the 60 per cent principle merely guarantees that most of those who are eligible for NCIP would still have incomes below Supplementary Benefit levels.

Yet it is considered quite 'fair' to give all sorts of special benefits, particularly in the mobility field, to two small groups of handicapped people (those coming within the scope of war or industrial injury schemes) on the basis of where and when they were disabled, rather than on the fact of their disablement.

The whole question of whether it is 'fair' to take away mobility benefits from a woman five years earlier than from a similarly handicapped man is being ducked at the present time because it is associated with the question of retirement age under the national scheme of retirement pensions.

Mobility and work   So long as mobility benefits end with retirement, however, the need for any means of getting about in the community is being denied except as *a means of getting to work*. It is utterly inconsistent that the old 'Category 3' qualification for assistance with personal mobility (which was precisely this one, of need for assistance to get to work) has at the same time been abandoned, and the government has even stated that those who *have* Invacars or allowances under the old scheme will *not* now lose them if they cease working. So *do* we believe handicapped people should only be able to go out if it means they will work? If so, what is the point of all the access provisions under the 1970 CSDP Act? And if working *is* considered a virtue, to be 'rewarded' or facilitated with help towards mobility, why is the system in other respects allowed to remain so constructed that it penalises handicapped people who struggle to work, as we have indicated earlier (page 54)?

The 'seek and serve' principle   Under the Chronically Sick and Disabled Persons Act 1970, and in various other ways, legislation has extended the principle of the responsibility of local government for providing care and certain benefits for handicapped people. Deep-rooted in the system, however, is the principle that the Supplementary Benefit mechanism is the end-stop for *cash* benefits. Moreover, the new responsibilities of local authorities have never been adequately reflected in the movement of funds out to the local departments which incur the costs of the new benefits, and the present economic situation has led to the imposition of limits which make a dead letter of this particular principle for many handicapped individuals. Having found their disabled citizens, local authorities are unable to provide the services they need.

An essential element of freedom

Perhaps nothing strikes more deeply at the dignity or desire for independence of people with handicaps than the betrayal of Beveridge's principle that the 'management of one's income is an essential element of a citizen's freedom'. Handicapped people find themselves unable to calculate or understand how much money they will receive. They find that new benefits do not add to their resources. When the inadequacy of these resources leads them into debt they may find that 'direct payment' (see page 61) further circumscribes their ability to manage their incomes. And if they cross the boundary into 'pensionable age' they will find their income arbitrarily *reduced*, by taxation (payable on Retirement Pension but not on Invalidity Pension) or by the cessation of even that small contribution towards the cost of mobility outside the home presented by the Mobility Allowance.

Chapter Three

The costs of administration

Part of the brief for this study was to analyse

'the economics of administering the multiple-outlet system in terms of personnel, salaries, travelling time, etc, both of the potential recipient and of administrators, and including unnecessary duplication of the processes of assessment, and the cost of alternatives which do not even represent what the client wants, such as unemployment benefits rather than a means of getting to work, residential care rather than adequate finance or domiciliary support to live at home, where the latter alternatives are unavailable to the client because of the technicalities of eligibility, etc.'

This comprises four areas: the costs of administering the system to the administrators, the costs of administering the system to the potential recipients, the costs to both of duplicating assessment procedures, and the costs of providing benefits and services that are considered acceptable by the providing agency but which are unwanted by the client.

The analysis of these four areas has been considerably limited by several factors:

a. The information on costs available from both central and local authorities does not lend itself to analysis of this kind.

b. The work considered necessary for the extraction of such information was regarded by central and local authorities as prohibitive in the time and with the staff available.

c. Recipients of benefits and services were largely unable to assess from memory the extent of time, effort and cost involved in obtaining the benefits and services.

d. Costings of the assessment processes for different benefits and services are rare, and often difficult to obtain accurately.

Accordingly, where the analysis has been possible from readily available data, it has been provided, and where the data is not available an analysis of the constraints of obtaining it and an appraisal of the usefulness of doing so have been presented.

The costs to the administrators: Social Security benefits

In 1975, it was estimated that the expenditure of central government in the administration of Social Security and miscellaneous services for the year ending 31 March 1977 would be £424 million (at 1975 prices), compared with £381 million for 1974/75, £289 million for 1973/74 and £120 million for 1966/67.

In 1976/77 these administrative costs would be in the ratio of 1:22.6 with the cost of benefits themselves, compared with ratios of 1:17.8 in 1974/75, 1:18.8 in 1973/74 and 1:21.1 in 1966/67.

In 1975, 91,500 people were employed in the civil service in social services. This constituted an approximate average administrative cost per person in Social Services Departments of the civil service of £4,164.

At the end of 1975, about 82,200 DHSS civil servants were working on Social Security operations, the great majority in the regional organisation which administers, through the local office structure, both contributory and non-contributory benefits. This organisation consisted of a Regional Directorate (500 staff), 12 regional offices (3,000 staff) and 928 local Social Security offices (60,200 staff). About 30,000 local staff worked on Supplementary Benefits and about the same number on other benefits.

The estimated total annual cost of the regional and local offices was around £275 million, a figure based upon the numbers of staff in post at the end of 1975 at current pay and prices and including staff pay, accommodation, services, postage and telephone charges; of this amount staff pay accounted for about £190 million. An appraisal of the costs of individual Social Security benefits is set out below.

National Insurance benefits

The expenditure of National Insurance funds on administration and miscellaneous services (which has since 1969/70 included payments to the Post Office) for the year 1973/74 was £165.6 million. Of the benefits covered by these funds, four are under review: Retirement Pension, Old Person's Pension, Invalidity Benefit and Sickness Benefit.

In 1973/74 **these administrative costs for National Insurance benefits were in the ratio of 1:23.9 with the costs of the benefits themselves**, compared with 1:27.8 in 1966/67.

Industrial Injury benefits

The expenditure of Industrial Injuries funds on administration and miscellaneous services for the year 1973/74 was £16.24 million. Almost 90 per cent of the funds distributed under this scheme are for Industrial Injury Benefit and Industrial Disablement Pensions.

In 1973/74 **these administrative costs for Industrial Injuries payments were in the ratio of 1:8.7 with the costs of the benefits themselves**, compared with 1:9.4 in 1966/67.

War pensions

At 31 March 1975, 440,610 war pensions were being paid out, of which 328,160 were War Disablement Pensions. In 1974/75 the cost of the local and central administration of these pensions, including costs incurred by departments other than the DHSS, amounted to £7.73 million. Relating this to the numbers of recipients it is estimated that the administrative costs of administering War Disablement Pensions in 1974/75 was approximately £5.75 million.

In 1974/75, £132.50 million was paid out in War Disablement Pensions.

Thus in 1974/75, **the administrative costs for War Disablement Pensions can be estimated to have been in the ratio 1:23 with the costs of the benefit itself**, compared with 1:22.2 in 1967/68.

Family Income Supplement (FIS)

The estimated expenditure on FIS for 1975/76 was £13 million, of which approximately £1 million was spent on administration including staffing but excluding advertising costs (which amounted to £100,000 in 1975). Accordingly **the costs of administering FIS were in the ratio 1:12 with the costs of the benefit paid**.

At the end of 1975 there were 59,638 awards being paid. During the year 1975 there had been 124,733 claims dealt with, of which 59,638 were awarded (26,967 being renewals), 63,733 were rejected and 1,362 were withdrawn. Accordingly, the approximate average cost of administering each claim dealt with was £8. The average payment for the whole year was £209. Only about 7 per cent of the recipients of FIS are disabled. Therefore, the cost of administering FIS to disabled recipients for 1975/76 is probably about £70,000.

Supplementary Benefits

There were about 30,000 staff working in local Social Security offices on Supplementary Benefits at the end of 1975. The estimated annual cost of work done in the regional and local offices on Supplementary Benefits amounted to about £140 million of which staff pay accounted for about £95 million. At the end of 1975 it was estimated that the annual cost of payments for Supplementary Benefit claims was about £1,420 million gross, and that the total costs of administering these payments including postage and encashment charges, at pay and prices then current, were about £190 million. Thus **the ratio of the costs of administration to the costs of benefits paid is approximately 1:7.5**.

It has been estimated that roughly two-thirds of the work done by Supplementary Benefits staff is on *Supplementary Allowances* which demand a much greater administrative input than Supplementary Pension cases. Additional administrative expense has been incurred by the emphasis on discretion within the system, which makes decisions harder and calls for experienced officials and a lot of visiting. The Annual Report of the Supplementary Benefits Commission for 1975 maintains that 'discretion is very expensive in staff to administer properly' (page 12), but gives no further breakdown in cost terms of how this has affected the system in 1975.

Another important administrative cost in 1975 was that of *uprating*. Scale rates were increased twice in 1975 to keep up with inflation, and this 'imposed a severe strain on the service and on the staff responsible for carrying through the uprating' (*SBC Annual Report* 1975, page 31). No figures for the administrative costs of upratings are available, although 'extra staff are always needed and overtime has to be worked to calculate the new rates' (*ibid*, page 111).

At the end of 1975, 2.79 million people were claiming Supplementary Benefit (of which 1.68 million were paid Supplementary Pensions and 1.11 million Supplementary Allowances). During the period 4 December 1974 to 2 December 1975, 5.13 million claims were received, of which 157,000 were awarded Supplementary Pensions, 2.68 million were awarded weekly Supplementary Allowances, 1.41 million received single-payment benefits and 886,000 were unsuccessful or not pursued. About 256,000 claims were by retirement pensioners, and of these about 175,500 were successful. The proportion of retirement pensioners receiving Supplementary Pensions has been falling slowly to 22 per cent in 1975 (1.56 million people). It is not known what proportion are people with disabilities.

In addition to retirement pensioners, 242,000 'sick and disabled' people were receiving Supplementary Allowances in December 1975. Of these, 54,000 were receiving Invalidity Benefit, 40,000 Non-Contributory Invalidity Benefit and 15,000 Sickness Benefit. The number of 'sick and disabled' receiving Supplementary Allowance alone was 165,000 at the end of 1975. This group has been increasing at about 1 per cent a year. About 23,600 of this group were also receiving Attendance Allowance. 57,750 of the 'sick and disabled' receiving only Supplementary Allowance were under 30 years old. Although 117,600 of the 'sick and disabled' are most probably 'disabled' it is not known what proportion of the other 124,400 are 'disabled'. Without knowledge of the exact numbers of 'disabled' receiving different Supplementary Benefits or a clear idea of the costs of administration of each type of Supplementary Benefit, it is difficult to estimate the proportion of administrative costs that is apportionable to people with disabilities, but it is probably in the range of £15 million to £35 million.

In 1973, the cost per day of a DHSS official was estimated at £20–£25[1], assuming that the official was paid around £1,700 per annum and that the total cost of hiring is three times this figure (the normal commercial ratio used). The difference between the two amounts is accounted for by overhead costs including holidays, pensions, offices, a share of typing, supervisory and accounting costs, a share in the cost of the department that recruits staff, and travelling expenses.

In 1973, in assessing the costs of administering heating allowances, it was estimated that a DHSS official could make six effective visits per day, and that accordingly the cost per visit was around £4. With an estimated score rate of one in three, the cost per grant was likely to reach £12; by comparison, paying a weekly 25p allowance costs £13 per annum. The Supplementary Benefits Commission has, since then, attempted to improve the efficiency of visits, recognising

---

[1] *Care with dignity*, page 69

that 'visiting claimants is a labour-intensive operation and therefore costly, yet it may not always be the most effective way of finding out about their needs and circumstances' (*SBC Annual Report* 1975, page 108). Postal reviews and postal inquiries have been more widely used since then, and the Inspectorate of the Supplementary Benefits Commission has been investigating the efficiency of these changes since the spring of 1974. Nevertheless, between 1973 and 1975, the number of Exceptional Needs Payments increased from 808,000 to 945,000, and the number of Exceptional Circumstances Additions from 753,000 to 1.09 million. This increase in the number of discretionary payments entails both extra administrative burdens and further difficulties of assessment. The lack of mobility of many people with disabilities probably necessitates more visits on the part of DHSS officials than they might otherwise make under the new system, thus keeping up the costs of administration.

The costs to the administrators: local government services

In 1973/74, local authorities in England and Wales spent £522.43 million from revenue and special funds on personal social services, and £74.31 million on capital works for personal social services. Local authorities in Scotland spent £56.30 million out of revenue on social work in 1973/74, and £6.24 million on capital works for social work.

In addition in 1973/74, local authorities in England and Wales spent £1,028.45 million from revenue and special funds on housing to which the Housing Revenue Account relates, and £282.71 million on other housing. On capital works they spent £1,106.66 million on housing to which the Housing Revenue Account relates, and £773.79 million on other housing. In Scotland in 1973/74, £226.99 million was spent on housing out of revenue, and £184.95 million on capital works.

The analysis of local authority accounts in an effort to establish the costs of administering particular benefits and services is not easy as local authority accounts are mainly kept for other objectives. Some authorities, in assessing the efficiency of different services, have made such analyses, but often with considerable difficulties. Legg and Brion in their study found, as we did, that 'very often information had to be obtained from departments or sections other than the one in which we were based and from staff who were under considerable pressure to finish work of an urgent nature for the local authority' (page 153).

Local authorities can often provide aggregate costs on two different bases, depending on the nature of the service or benefit, and their accounting practices. Where they have established individual cost rates for clients in each category, they can provide aggregates by multiplying individual cost rates by numbers of clients in each category. These are called 'rate-computed costs'. Some authorities can provide 'declared costs' as a response to specific questions. Declared costs are usually more accurate, but in Susan Stone's study on holidays for the physically handicapped (Section 251) it was felt that 'for those authorities for which both declared and rate-computed costs are available there is a sufficiently acceptable level of correspondence to justify the substitutions when arriving at national aggregate costs'.

The Essex study

The study undertaken by R Wager in Essex in 1969 for the Institute of Municipal Treasurers and Accountants (IMTA) on a cost-benefit analysis of care for the elderly was primarily concerned with comparing the comparative costs of institutional and community care. The analysis of cost data based on 1969/70 prices excluded expenditure on central administration, but included administrative expenditure that was directly attributable to individual services, such as the cost of home help organisers. The unit costs of residential homes were estimated (see Table 3.1). These costs were calculated net of charges for staff board and lodging and certain minor sources of income.

Of the running costs, 69 per cent were attributable to staff, the remainder deriving from provisions, laundry, fuel etc. The cost of home helps was put at 42.1p per hour and of meals-on-wheels at 16.2p per meal (the range was from 12.5p to 23p per meal).

Table 3.1 Total unit costs of residential homes, 1969/70

	Size of home			
	20 places	40 places	50 places	60 places
Average no. of places occupied	19.16	38.32	47.91	57.49
Capital cost per resident per week	£	£	£	£
at 10%	—	6.54	5.83	5.17
at 5%	—	3.49	3.12	2.78
Running costs per resident per week	10.93	9.75	9.16	8.57
Total costs per resident per week				
at 10%	—	16.29	14.99	13.74
at 5%	—	13.24	12.28	11.35

Source: Wager (1972), page 45

The Leicester study

In 1971, PA International Management Consultants conducted a study for the City of Leicester to evaluate social services expenditure. At 1970/71 prices, and excluding central administration costs, the following cost estimates were obtained: £8.96 per resident per week (after resident contributions) for local authority residential accommodation for the elderly, 45p per hour for the home help service, 15.71p per meal for mobile meals, 50p per person per week for laundry service, £5.09 per resident per week for day care (excluding transport) and 11.52p per meal for day club meals. Most of their data related specifically to the elderly or to children under five, and thus are not readily applicable to chronically sick and disabled people outside these age groups; nor did the analysis extend to administrative costs.

The Reading study A survey undertaken in Reading in 1973 under the Chronically Sick and Disabled Persons Act tried to establish the costs of supplying and administering different services for the chronically sick and disabled as part of an assessment of need for planning purposes. The survey first tried to establish the average amount of each service received per person receiving it, and differences between different client groups. Unfortunately the only service for which disabled people were clearly differentiated was that for aids and adaptations. The unit costs of services were obtained by dividing the estimated running costs of each service in 1972/73 by the estimated usage, and those applicable to the benefits and services under review are set out in Table 3.2. However, the differences of estimated usage by different client groups, particularly people with disabilities, could not be broken down, nor was it attempted to isolate the administration costs of every service.

The Isle of Wight study The Isle of Wight Social Services Department worked out its unit costs in 1973/74. Gross unit costs for homes for the mentally disordered ranged between £11.55 and £26.46 per person per week, and those for homes for the physically handicapped between £26.92 and £39.90 per person per week. The gross meals service unit cost was 29p per meal, and the gross domestic help unit cost was 66p per hour. The average cost of adaptations for the chronically sick and disabled was £312, and that of aids £5.70. These figures do not, however, include the administration charges, which include costs of management, administrative, central office and area clerical staff, provision of office accommodation and a proportion of county common services. These overheads were considered to represent 15 per cent of all services provided.

The Birmingham study The Birmingham Social Services Department has also made extensive efforts to cost service provision for the chronically sick and disabled at 1973/74 prices, including a differentiation between one-off and continuing costs. However, because it used a cluster analysis approach to arrive at a comprehensive list of the mix of services considered appropriate to each group for its final analysis, unit costs for individual services were not a prime element in the published presentation. Services for which costing was possible were: aids to mobility, widening of doors, bath aids, shower, bath attendants, stair handrails, ramps, raised seats, clothing gadgets, special cutlery, telephone, alarm system, home help, meals service, short-term residential care, holiday grant, social work assessment, social work support and occupational therapy. No attempt was made to estimate the costs of services involving transport or capital costs, such as attendance at day centres or residential accommodation. Services for people with mental handicaps were unfortunately excluded from the original cost estimates.

The Slough study The 1976 Slough Mencap Study looked at the costs of maintaining a home for mentally handicapped adults in Slough, Berkshire. The researchers pointed out some of the difficulties of isolating administrative costs when they said that:

'The cost of administering residential services in Social Services Departments should be recognised in the costs of a hostel, since that administration has some effect on the hostel, but a specific proportion is difficult to decide upon. Even more remote from the actual

Table 3.2 Unit costs of services, Reading 1972/73 (£)

Service	Unit of measurement	Staff costs	Overhead costs	Transport	Items provided	Contributions	Net unit costs	Annual cost to Social Services Dept. of providing one unit of each service
Home help	hours per week	0.503	0.121	—	—	−0.03	0.594	30.90
Meals-on-wheels	meals per week	—	0.50	0.024	Food 0.22	−0.089	0.205	10.70
Luncheon club	person p.a.	—	1.50	11.40	Food 11.40	−2.6	21.70	21.70
Day centre	visits per week	0.461	—	0.218	—	−0.043	0.636	33.10
Residential care	person p.a.	n.a.	n.a.	n.a.	n.a.	n.a.	837	837
Sheltered accommodation	person p.a.	n.a.	n.a.	n.a.	n.a.	n.a.	47.70	47.70
Aids and adaptations	person p.a.	n.a.	n.a.	n.a.	{ Adaptations 51.80 Aids 25.00	−23.3	53.50	53.50
Telephone	person p.a.	n.a.	n.a.	n.a.	n.a.	n.a.	20.90 (4.40 additional cost in first year only)	20.90
Holiday	person p.a.	n.a.	n.a.	n.a.	n.a.	n.a.	19.70	19.70
Centre for the deaf	person p.a.	11.70	28.90	n.a	n.a	n.a.	40.60	40.60

Source: Reading (1973), pages 19, 47, 48

environment, how much of the salary of a local Director of Social Services can be allocated to any of his establishments? This tends to become a matter of local costing practice and, in some places, indirect costs tend to be allocated to a particular establishment in the same ratio that its direct costs are to the direct costs of all establishments of that type. In others allocation is carried out simply on the ratio of its beds to the total beds'.

They arrived at figures for Group Home/Adult Training Centre costs of £31.51 per person per week for 1974/75 compared with £27.62 for 1973/74 (14.1 per cent growth rate) when social worker and home help costs are included, and £24.80 per person per week for 1974/75 compared with £21.69 in 1973/74 (14.3 per cent growth rate) when those additional costs were excluded.

The social services budgets of local authorities vary considerably, but it is felt worth while to give an idea of the breakdown of preliminary budgetary estimates as provided to two Social Services Committees (Buckinghamshire and Hillingdon) for the year 1976/77 to show what information on administrative costs is readily available.

The Buckinghamshire study

The total budget of Buckinghamshire Social Services, amounting to £6.28 million for 1966/67, is broken down under four heads: fieldwork (14.8 per cent), residential care (51.9 per cent), support services (33.1 per cent), and research and development (0.2 per cent).

Under *fieldwork*, 75.6 per cent of the cost is for salaries and employment expenses, and 15.1 per cent is for administration recharged from the Administration Holding Account. The remaining 9.3 per cent covers transport, establishment expenses, agency services and miscellaneous expenses less income; over half of this is for travelling, subsistence and conference expenses under establishment expenses.

Under *residential care* it is hard to isolate people with disabilities as a percentage of the occupants of the various homes for the elderly. The provision of homes for the younger physically handicapped, blind and deaf through support to other agencies costs 3 per cent of the residential care budget (i.e. 1.6 per cent of the total budget, or £980,000). The provision of homes for mentally handicapped adults costs the authority 1.6 per cent of the residential care budget (0.9 per cent of the total budget, or £565,000).

Provision in Buckinghamshire for these categories of clients is by local authority financial support to other agencies. Where the local authority itself runs residential accommodation, the costs are broken down into employment costs, capital and maintenance costs, supplies and services, establishment expenses, miscellaneous expenses and debt charges, less any income. The cost of administration recharged from the Administration Holding Account for all the residential care accommodation constitutes 13.8 per cent of the residential care budget (7.1 per cent of the total budget).

With *support services* the day care provision for the younger physically handicapped and mentally handicapped is again through other agencies, partially supported by the local authority. The expenses of day care establishments are broken down in the same way as for residential care establishments, with the addition of transport costs. The costs of home help provision account for 30.7 per cent of the support services budget (10.2 per cent of the total budget). Other services for the chronically sick and disabled – including aids and adaptations, television, telephones, talking books, recreational services and holidays – constitute 2.3 per cent of the support services budget (0.8 per cent of the total budget). The administration costs recharged from the Administration Holding Account amount to 16.2 per cent of the support services budget (5.4 per cent of the total budget).

The gross costs (excluding income) for the Administration Holding Account amount to £960,300 (15.3 per cent of the total budget). Of this sum £518,320 (54 per cent) is for salaries and employment costs, £195,300 (20.3 per cent) is for central establishment charges, £110,890 (11.5 per cent) is for the apportionment of expenses of administrative buildings, and £77,550 (8.1 per cent) is for other establishment expenses. The remaining £58,240 (6.1 per cent) is for building maintenance, movables, supplies and services, debt management expenses, Regional Planning Committee expenses and miscellaneous expenses. These expenses are recharged to the individual sections already mentioned.

The Hillingdon study

The most comprehensive study so far undertaken into local authority social services costs is *An analysis of social services costs in Hillingdon* (June 1976). This study went beyond the detailed budget figures in trying to attribute the administrative and supervisory costs more specifically to different services. The figures are based on revised estimates of the 1975/76 social services budget for the London Borough of Hillingdon. It was estimated that costs for 1976/77 would be 10–15 per cent greater.

The total estimated budget of Hillingdon Social Services for 1976/77 was put at £5.64 million of which central establishment charges constituted £472,010 (8.4 per cent), social workers £843,789 (15.0 per cent) and the Administration Holding Account £478,502 (8.5 per cent). The costs of individual residential homes, day care institutions and other services are not aggregated under division heads as for Buckinghamshire. They are, however, broken down into employment costs, premises, supplies and services, transport and plant, establishment expenses, agency services and debt charges in approximately the same way.

Of the total net expenditure in 1975/76 of £4.79 million on social services, it was estimated that 54 per cent (£2.59 million) was spent on the elderly and physically handicapped and 14 per cent (£670,000) on the mentally handicapped. There were 206 past or current cases of mentally handicapped people and 1,500 current cases of physically handicapped, excluding 521 blind and partially sighted and 199 people who were deaf or hard of hearing.

The major difficulty in trying to allocate administrative costs lay within the figures for the Administration Holding Account (£441,097) and central establishment charges (£433,640). The Administration Holding Account includes the salaries of central office staff and their travel expenses, less sundry income. Some of the staff were 'allocable' to services, but 16 others (director, director's secretary, four assistant directors, three central typing staff, four research staff and three training staff) were 'unallocable', and accordingly their costs had to be allocated to different services. The additional expenses beyond the salaries and their associated on-costs (employment costs) of £393,079 were £48,018 (*12.2 per cent* of the salary on-costs), making a total net cost of £441,097. Because it was not possible to allocate these additional expenses to particular staff according to any more precise criteria, they were allocated on the basis of 12.2 per cent across the board as shown in Table 3.3.

Table 3.3 Social Services' salaries costs in a London borough (£'000)

	1. Salary costs and on-costs	2. Total costs (1) + 12.2%
'Unallocable' (Directorate; central admin.; typing; training and research)	152.6	171.2
Allocable to services:		
Residential services administration	15.9	17.8
Day services administration	28.5	31.9
Meals service organisers	7.4	8.3
Student unit organiser	9.7	10.9
Playgroup organisers	6.3	7.0
Home help clerks	3.9	4.4
Occupational therapy clerks	8.8	9.9
Principal social workers	25.2	28.3
Team administration	108.6	121.9
Voluntary services liaison officers	9.6	10.8
Fostering and adoptions	16.3	18.3
Balancing item	0.3	0.4
Total allocable	240.5	269.8
Total	393.1	441.1

Source: Hillingdon Cost Study, June 1976, Appendix 1

This having been accomplished, it was necessary to allocate all those costs which were 'unallocable' to service sections, namely:

	£
Administration Holding Account 'unallocable', including share of 'own' overhead	17,227
Central establishment charges for offices etc.	433,640
Research and publicity	4,450
	609,317

Although central establishment charges could have been related to divisional salaries, and other expenses to total divisional expenditure, it was decided that the differences in methods were unlikely to be great, so they were simply allocated as a percentage of *gross* service costs, which in 1975/76 amounted to £5.85 million, including receipts from clients, payment from other local authorities and other sundry income; this was considered more appropriate than using *net* service costs. Accordingly £609,317 as a percentage of £5.85 million was *11.6 per cent*. In consequence 11.6 per cent was systematically added to *all* costs incurred by divisions, *and* to all allocated central office overheads.

Upon this basis, and with an additional increase of 4.1 per cent on the salaries of social workers for incidental employee and establishment expenses (recruitment, etc.) excluding travel, the total costs of the social work/fieldwork section were estimated at £951,000. The breakdown of these expenses is shown in Diagrams 1 and 2 (pages 107 and 108–9). The numbers of staff in each group are shown in terms of whole-time equivalents (w.t.e.).

The difficulty lies in trying to allocate these staff and their associated costs. Of the specialists, 5.5 w.t.e. basic grade specialists were working for the blind or deaf, while the other 4.5 were not working with handicapped people. One of the two senior specialists also worked with the blind and deaf. Unfortunately the only study of staff work patterns so far undertaken, except for a more recent one on occupational therapists, was carried out in January 1973 into social worker work patterns, in which the only kind of work broken down by client type was that of visits to clients. At that time, following a CSDP survey the number of visits to handicapped people formed a greater proportion of social worker visits, and accordingly could not safely be used to estimate mid-1976 work patterns.

The Hillingdon study also attempted to analyse the cost of different services under section 2 of the Chronically Sick and Disabled Persons Act for 1975/76. These include home helps, television, transport for voluntary organisations and for services of the Social Services Department, aids and adaptations, holiday homes, meals-on-wheels and telephones. The total direct budget cost was put at £926,700, with extra overhead and supervision costs of £302,400. Thus, these administrative costs represented about a quarter of the overall costs. Unfortunately, some items do not include the central administration costs, and the direct budget costs in some cases include wages, salaries and on-costs that strictly speaking should be included in the administrative costs.

The study analysed three sorts of unit cost:

cost *per unit of service* (e.g. the cost of providing one week in residential accommodation per person);

cost *per client* serviced for the entire duration of care (e.g. cost per home help case); and the

cost *per worker* (e.g. the cost of a social worker per year).

Diagram 1

Salary costs of social work/fieldwork in the London borough of Hillingdon: 1975–1976

Costs in £ thousand.

Total cost: £951

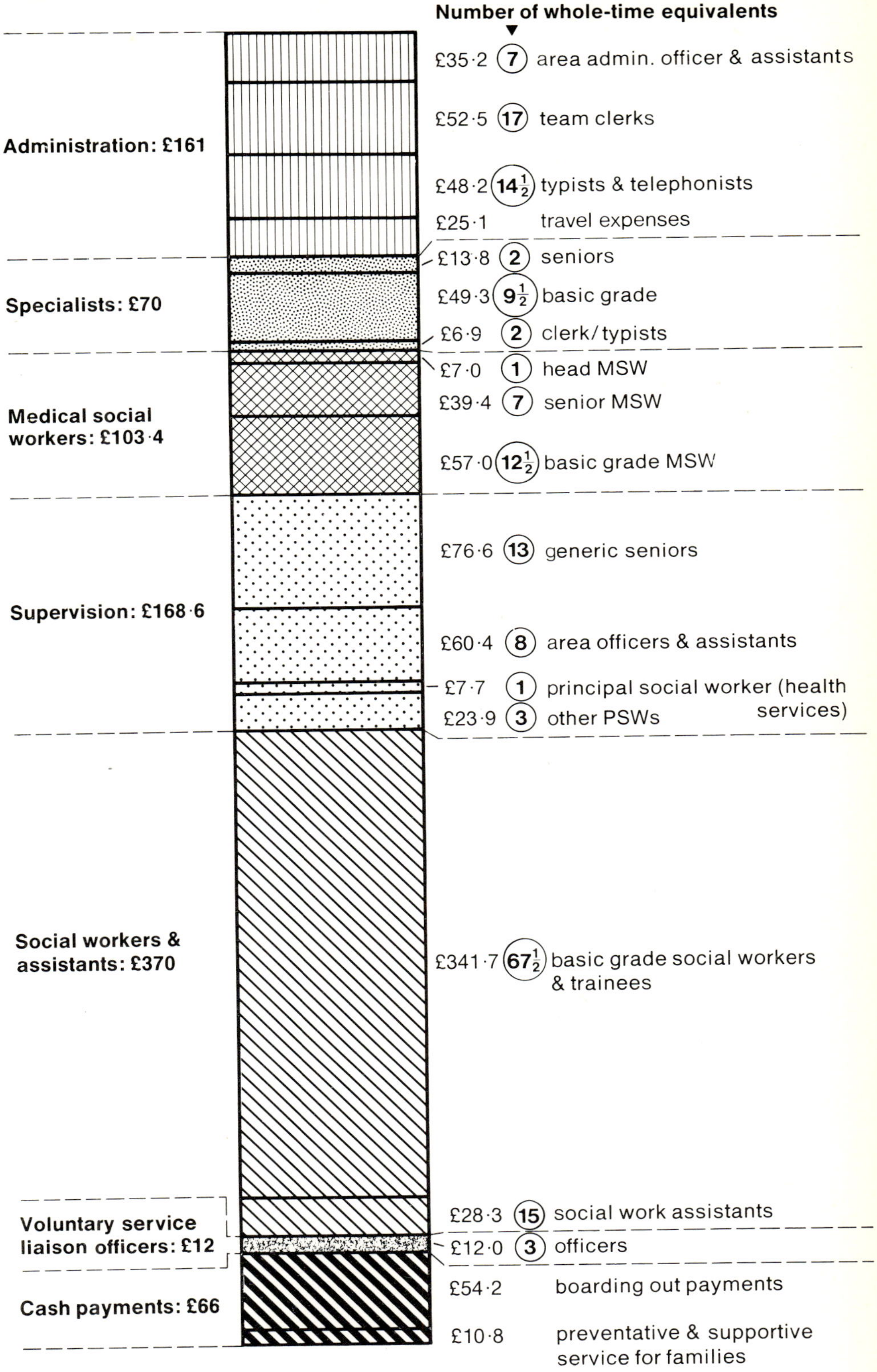

Source: Hillingdon Cost Study, 1976

Number of whole-time equivalents

Administration: £161
- £35·2 (7) area admin. officer & assistants
- £52·5 (17) team clerks
- £48·2 (14½) typists & telephonists
- £25·1 travel expenses

Specialists: £70
- £13·8 (2) seniors
- £49·3 (9½) basic grade
- £6·9 (2) clerk/typists

Medical social workers: £103·4
- £7·0 (1) head MSW
- £39·4 (7) senior MSW
- £57·0 (12½) basic grade MSW

Supervision: £168·6
- £76·6 (13) generic seniors
- £60·4 (8) area officers & assistants
- £7·7 (1) principal social worker (health services)
- £23·9 (3) other PSWs

Social workers & assistants: £370
- £341·7 (67½) basic grade social workers & trainees
- £28·3 (15) social work assistants

Voluntary service liaison officers: £12
- £12·0 (3) officers

Cash payments: £66
- £54·2 boarding out payments
- £10·8 preventative & supportive service for families

107

Diagram 2

The annual cost of social service workers in Hillingdon: 1975-1976

Excluding office accommodation cost

Central overhead

Management

Supervision

Basic grade

Direct support

Area support

Social worker: £8440

£1072 Share of central overhead & central establishment charges

£688 1/30 of an area officer and assistant area officer* & share of principal social workers

£1126 1/5 of a senior, of which senior's casework is £225

£4394 One trained social worker, whole-time

£578 1/5 of a team clerk

£582 1/30 share of area admin. officer & assistant, telephonists, typists etc

Occupational therapist:
£8938

- **£931** Share of central overhead & central establishment charges
- **£454** 1/14 of a head occupational therapist
- **£1032** 2/7 of a senior occupational therapist
- **£4085** One occupational therapist, whole-time
- **£829** 2/7 of a team clerk
- **£1025** 2/7 of a technician
- **£582** 1/30 share of area admin. officer & assistant, telephonists, typists etc

*Responsibilities include home helps and occupational therapists as well as social workers

Home help:
(whole-time)
£3127

- **£398** Share of central overhead & central establishment charges
- **£28** 1/200 of principal home help organiser
- **£348** 1/25 of home help organiser & assistant
- **£2272** One home help; whole-time equivalent
- **£58** 1/50 of a clerk
- **£23** 1/750 of area admin. team (telephonists, typists etc)

Discussion of the unit cost of individual *services* has been included later in this chapter. Analysis of costs of a *client* is difficult because of the inadequacy of accurate guidelines on turnover rates and referral rates. Calculations are possible, for instance, for clients of the Home Help Service, who receive on average eighteen months of provision, for which the total cost is assessed at around £200 each. But where clients receive individual items of service or where there are considerably fluctuating servicing demands, unit costs are difficult to establish.

The unit cost *per worker* can be established quite easily. Unless work patterns are analysed under different types of work, however, no analysis can be made of the proportionate cost of these workers for individual types of work or providing for different client groups. From Diagram 1 the unit costs, including overheads and administrative costs, of different workers as whole-time equivalents can be calculated as shown in Table 3.4.

The three bars in Diagram 2 show the breakdown in allocated costs which constitute the total costs of social workers, occupational therapists and home helps. The average cost per day of a social worker was put at £41, of an occupational therapist at £43, and of a home help at £14.

In these unit cost calculations, however, no attempt was made to assess the unit cost *per application* for benefit, which can be important for certain cash benefits

Table 3.4 Unit costs per worker per year in the Social Services Department of a London borough

Worker	Unit cost per worker per year 1975/76 (£)
Social worker and trainee	5,060
Social work assistant	1,890
Generic senior (supervisory)	5,890
Area officer's assistant (supervisory)	7,550
Principal social worker (supervisory)	7,900
Head and senior medical social worker	5,800
Basic grade medical social worker	4,525
Typist and telephonist	3,325
Team clerk	3,090
Area administrative office assistant	5,030
Voluntary service liaison officer (VSLO)	4,000
Clerk/typist to specialist	3,450
Basic grade specialist	5,190
Senior specialists	6,900
Social worker[1]	8,440
Occupational therapist[1]	8,938
Home help[1]	3,127

[1] These three were calculated separately within the Hillingdon study (1976)

and high-demand services such as telephones. Where a considerable proportion of time is taken up in administering unsuccessful claims for benefits or services it would be useful to know such unit costs.

An appraisal of the costs of administration of individual local authority services is set out below.

Rent Rebates and Allowances

From the study of Rent Rebates and Rent Allowances conducted by Charles Legg and Marion Brion an analysis of the costs of administering the Rent Rebates and Rent Allowances scheme was made. When the Rent Rebate and Allowance schemes were introduced under the Housing Finance Act 1972, central government did not attempt to estimate the administrative costs of the schemes as there was little evidence on which to base such estimates. The Act did, however, provide that one of the contributions from the General Rate Fund to the Housing Revenue Account should be 'the local authority's costs of administering their rebate scheme', that 'a local authority's costs of administering their rebate scheme under Part II of this Act for any year shall be arrived at by the local authority in accordance with such formula as the Secretary of State shall from time to time determine', and that 'Before making any such determinations the Secretary of State shall consult with such associations of housing authorities as appear to him to be concerned and with any housing authority with whom consultation appears to him to be desirable'.

In 1972 the sum of £1 per rebated tenant per year was arrived at for this cost, and this figure remained until 1974/75 when inflation led to a renegotiation and Circular 66/75 settled on higher rates of £4 for districts and £6 for metropolitan districts and the London authorities. The formula used was defined in Circular 124/72 as follows:

'The formula is £1 per annum times the average number of tenants whose rent is subject to rebate ... on a day convenient for the authority in each of the relevant periods in a financial year, divided by the number of relevant periods. For 1973/74 the relevant periods are those commencing on 1st April, 1st July, 1st October and 1st January in each year.'

The costs of administering the Rent Allowance scheme are met directly out of the General Rate fund.

The raw data used in Legg and Brion's study came from 1974/75 revised estimates in which often the formula figure for rebates was available and integrated into the rent accounting system at some point. The costs that are associated with adjustments to the property register or to rent collectors' strips are never analysed separately by local authorities because they form part of a whole mass of adjustments which are made at regular intervals. Four sample areas and three extra London boroughs supplied the information: Gateshead, Hammersmith, Southend, Stoke, Lambeth, Lewisham and Redbridge.

District salary costs were analysed for processing staff. A full-time staff equivalent of 36 hours per week was used. Supervising staff were included, often allocated on a percentage basis. Knowing how far up the administrative 'tree' to proceed, and establishing the extent of responsibility of different workers, presented some problems. The greatest problem existed where the administration of the two schemes was integrated, or where either was integrated with another scheme, such as Rate Rebates. It was concluded that in their samples where Rent and Rate Rebates were integrated, each Rent Rebate took twice as much time as a Rate Rebate.

The other costs included (*a*) 'establishment' costs of printing, stationery, computer costs, through to a proportion of the overhead costs of the local administration, (*b*) building costs relating to the cost and maintenance of offices and (*c*) Giro costs for Rent Allowances. Rent Allowance Giro and printing costs are reliable and standard, but other costs differ according to different accounting practices and the difficulties of allocating costs to a small part of the service. The 'standardised total costs' that Legg and Brion arrived at did not take regional differences into consideration, but did allow for the differences between manual and computerised systems, by adding a multiplier to direct salary costs of 40 per cent for manual systems and 53 per cent for computer systems.

The costs per tenant and per calculation made are set out in Tables 3.5 to 3.8. Table 3.7 shows the considerable variations in the cost of administration per tenant. Two of the cheapest systems (Stoke and Southend) have five points in common:

a. the operation is computerised;

b. staff are paid at similar salary levels;

c. processing is done on a six-monthly batch system;

d. Rent and Rate Rebates are processed together;

e. publicity does not exceed the statutory minimum.

This last point needs to be borne in mind when considering the efficiency of the system in relation to the tenants and take-up.

Legg and Brion also concluded that the costs of recalculation at too-frequent intervals did not result in any saving, and pointed out that the significant cost of nil assessment should be borne in mind when assessing publicity costs which result in positive assessments rather than negative ones.

Taking the four sample areas only, it was calculated that the average cost of administering Rent Rebates was about £8–£13 per tenant in receipt per year. This constitutes about 6 per cent of the amount of benefits paid out, and if central government costs (including publicity) are also added it would amount to about 6.5 per cent to 7 per cent of the amount of benefit paid out. Legg and Brion did, however, consider that their sample was liable to produce a slightly lower

Table 3.5 Administrative costs of Rent Rebates per tenant in receipt, 1974/75

	Gateshead	Hammersmith	Southend	Stoke	Lambeth	Lewisham	Redbridge
Average number of tenants receiving benefit	6,700	2,842	1,849	3,526	5,300	3,126	2,003
Combined with Rate Rebate	no	yes	yes	yes	no	no	no
Costs of staff directly involved	£5.75	£5.08	£4.88	£2.50	£4.65	£12.23	£4.96
Costs of other staff, printing etc.	£2.45	£4.33	£0.42	£2.31	£4.42	£3.05	£1.66
Costs of buildings	£0.65	£2.51	£1.61				£0.79
Total	£8.85	£11.92	£6.92	£4.81	£9.07	£15.28	£7.40
Standardised total cost	£8.05	£7.77	£7.47	£3.83	£7.11	£17.11	£7.59

Source: Legg and Brion (1976), page 158

Table 3.6 Administrative costs of Rent Rebates per calculation made, 1974/75[1]

	Gateshead	Hammersmith	Southend	Stoke	Lambeth
Average number of tenants receiving benefit	6,700	2,842	1,849	3,526	5,300
Combined with Rate Rebate	no	yes	yes	yes	no
Estimated number of calculations[1]	6,700	4,575	3,185	9,110	17,000
Ratio of calculations (to tenants in receipt)	1:1	1:1.61	1:1.72	1:2.58	1:3.20
Cost per calculation made	£8.84	£7.40	£4.02	£4.81	£2.82
Ratio of wage earners to pensioners at September 1974	1:0.88	1:0.5	not known	1:1.36	not known

[1] The number of calculations made includes all fresh and renewal applications which were processed through the computer or had manual calculations done, including nil assessments; but in most cases this number has to be estimated or reached by indirect means

Source: Legg and Brion (1976), page 159

Table 3.7 Administrative costs of Rent Allowances per tenant in receipt, 1974/75

	Hammersmith	Southend	Stoke	Lambeth	Lewisham	Redbridge
Average number of tenants in receipt of allowances	1,479	1,060	342	2,000	675	506
Combined with Rate Rebate	yes	no	yes	no	no	no
Direct staff costs	£11.89	£7.25	7.72	£9.86	£21.14	£15.26
Administration	£12.06	£1.83				£5.06
Buildings	£5.87 } £19.39	£3.01 } £8.14	} £9.47	} £11.71	} £5.28	£2.44
Giro and post	£1.46	£3.30				
Total	£31.28[1]	£15.39	£17.19[1]	£21.57	£26.42	£22.76
Standardised total cost	£18.19	£11.09	£11.81	£15.09	£29.60	£23.35

[1] Including processing of Rate Rebates

Source: Legg and Brion (1976), page 161

Table 3.8 Ratio of tenants in receipt of Rent Allowances to number of calculations made, 1974/75[1]

	Hammersmith	Southend	Lambeth
Average number of tenants receiving allowances	1,479	1,060	2,000
Combined with Rate Rebate	yes	no	no
Estimated number of calculations	4,185	3,143	7,500
Ratio of tenants in receipt to calculations	1:2.83	1:2.96	1:3.75

[1] The number of calculations made includes all fresh and renewal applications which were processed through the computer or had manual calculations done on them, including nil assessments; but in most cases this number has to be estimated or reached by indirect means
Source: Legg and Brion (1976), page 162

figure than a wider sample might yield. They estimated that the **total national cost of the administration of the Rent Rebate scheme in 1974/75 was about £6.7 million**.

The administration of the Rent Allowance scheme was more expensive, and based on Stoke and the three London boroughs in which the schemes are not integrated with the Rate Rebate scheme, they arrived at an average administration figure for London authorities of £22.79 per tenant in receipt per year and £15.84 for out-of-London authorities. This constitutes between 13 per cent and 19 per cent of the amount of benefit paid out, and if central government costs are also added, about 20 per cent of the amount of benefit paid out. They estimated that the **total national cost of the administration of the Rent Allowance scheme in 1974/75 was £2.65 million**.

Legg and Brion were keen to emphasise that efficiency measured just in terms of costs is a very limited way of assessing the validity of different types of administration, although it needed to be included. They prepared several lists of 'improvements' and how these would be affected by different objectives and cost considerations. These are set out in Table 3.9.

Holidays

In 1969 the net cost to local authorities for subsidised holidays was £574,000, of which £200,000 (34.8 per cent) was estimated to be for the physically handicapped and their relatives (about £13,775 for the relatives), and £374,000 (65.2 per cent) for the elderly. The average rate-computed unit costs of holidays to local authorities ranged from £12.02 per week per head for physically handicapped in voluntary centres to £3.72 per week per head for physically handicapped in hotels and boarding houses, and from £8.35 per week per head for relatives in other schemes to £3.50 per week per head for relatives in hotels and boarding houses.

Table 3.9 Administrative 'improvements' related to their objectives and effects on cost

Likely to reduce cost but to affect quality of service	Likely to improve either take-up or quality with minimal disbenefits to the other objectives	Likely to improve quality of service with possible increase in cost
Reduction in use of area offices	Recommended maximum times for processing and regular checking for delays	Increasing the number of offices at which advice on application is offered to tenants
Reduction in staff time allocated to advice	Combination of application and processing for rent and rate benefits	Ensuring adequate privacy for tenants receiving advice
Reduction in home visiting	Processing Rent Rebates, Rent Allowances and Rate Rebates in the same department and to the same standard	Identification of and provision for training of processing, administrative and advisory staff
Abolition of use of 10% discretion		
Reduction in level of checking for staff errors	National advice service to local authorities on all aspects of the schemes	Improved code of practice for dealing with Rent Allowance and eligible rents
Use of crude estimators for allowable rents		'Simplification' of schemes generally
More rigorous checking of tenants' information	Greater computerisation and mechanisation (so long as adequate attention is paid to service to tenants)	Central government research on comparative effectiveness of advertising
	Greater standardisation of procedures for checking tenants' information	Monitoring of improvements with local authorities
	Improved communication between central and local government and within local authorities	Abolition of change of circumstances provisions
	Increased training and exchange of information for 'middle level' administrators	Central government research on development of new model form
	Improvement of application forms	Improved procedures for renewal
	Abolition of distinction between 'capital' and 'cash'	
	Rent Allowances to be renamed Rent Rebates	
	Clearer allocation of responsibility for publicity between central and local government	

Source: Legg and Brion (1976), page 196

The Reading study found that in 1972/73 its Social Services Department spent £19.70 on average per person per year for holidays, but did not give any breakdown of the administrative component in this cost.

In Hillingdon in 1975/76, £13,000 was estimated to have been spent on holidays and £141,000 on a holiday hotel. The revised estimates of direct budget costs for 1975/76 were £138,600 spent on 'facilitating the taking of holidays', with a supervision and overhead and central administration cost of £17,200. This means that for every £1 spent on administration, £8.06 was spent on holiday provision.

In 1974/75, local authorities in England and Wales spent £47.62 million on subsidised holidays, an average of £19.53 per person per year. In London boroughs £6.77 million was spent on such holidays, an average of £22.61 per person per year. In the metropolitan districts £10.51 million was spent on holidays, an average of £17.23 per person per year. In the counties £30.34 million was spent, an average of £15.05 per person per year.

The cost of resident escorts' pay for the London Borough of Wandsworth in December 1975 was the normal salary of council staff, plus a recognition grant of £35 per week for officers-in-charge and £25 per week for assistants. When external recruits were used their pay was £56.38 and £38.35 per seven-day week for officers-in-charge and assistants respectively.

Using Hillingdon's ratios of administrative cost to benefit cost, it can be estimated that the cost of administering holidays in England and Wales in 1975/76 was between £310,000 and £320,000, and the **cost of administering holidays for the disabled was probably between £110,000 and £120,000**.

Day care

The Hillingdon Study (1976) calculated unit costs for their centre for younger physically handicapped people. The total net unit cost per client per week in 1975/76 was put at £17.16 (i.e. about £900 per client per year). Of this sum, about £115 was for administration. Thus for every £6.83 spent on actual day care provision (excluding transport) £1 was spent on administration. If these rates are applied to figures for England and Wales, **the estimated expenditure on administering day care centres for younger physically handicapped people in 1976/77 was probably between £1.18 million and £1.20 million**.

Transport

The costs of local authority transport have been increasing markedly in recent years, and attention is now being focussed on them. The Hillingdon transport study looked at the local authority transport provision for 489 clients in Hillingdon in November 1974, to analyse the most cost-effective methods of use and to cost the need for future provision. Some costs per person per mile for different types of vehicle are given in Table 3.10.

A breakdown of the capital and running costs of different local authority vehicles are set out in Table 3.11.

Table 3.10 Costs per person per mile of different 'alternative transport' facilities, November 1974 (pence)

Type of vehicle	Full load		Average load
Special borough coach (10 seater)	5.2		5.8
Special borough coach (16 seater)	3.6		6.3
Borough minibus	3.8		4.2
Hired minibus (10 seater and borough escort)	4.9		5.3
Hired coach (Adult Training Centres only)	2.5		3.0
	1 client	2 clients	3 clients
Volunteer's car	3.0	1.5	1.0
Hired car	28.0	14.0	9.0

Source: Hillingdon Transport (1975), page 25

It is estimated that about 70 per cent of the clients are handicapped, and that about 60 per cent of the trips made are made by handicapped people, who in general use tail-lift vehicles. Accordingly, averaging the total running costs for the vehicles for which those costs are available and which are also used by handicapped people, one arrives at an average figure of 54.5p per mile total cost. In addition, 26,320 concessionary bus passes were issued in Hillingdon in 1974/75, of which 398 were for registered physically handicapped and 64 were for registered blind people.

Meals-on-wheels

In 1971 the local authority expenditure on meals-on-wheels was estimated to be around £2.50 million per year, yet up to that time no study of the comparative costs of different methods of preparing and delivering meals-on-wheels had been published.

In 1970/71 it was calculated that the transport cost of delivering a meal was 8.3p in Leicester (paid staff), 16.0p in Lewisham and 9.0p in Kensington (volunteer drivers only). These costs constituted about a third of the total costs of the service.

In 1970/71 amongst London boroughs the net expenditure per meal ranged between 22.3p and 33.7p, and between 17.3p and 24.7p in boroughs surveyed outside of London. The average cost was put at about 24p per meal, and about 27p per meal on average in London boroughs.

The Warwickshire study of the meals-on-wheels service (1975) assessed the delivery costs of meals at 2p per meal using community methods, 10p per meal using a chef mobile kitchen, and 13p per meal using school kitchens.

Table 3.11 Costs for different local authority vehicles

1	2	3	4	5	6	7	8	9	10	11
Vehicle	Running costs[1] (£ per week)	Staff costs[2] (£ per week)	Depreciation[3] (£ per week)	Total cost per week (£) (2 + 3 + 4)	Average mileage per week (miles)	Average running costs per mile (pence)	Average running costs + staff costs per mile (pence)	Total cost (including depreciation) per mile (pence)	Average total cost per mile by vehicle type (pence)	Average total cost per year (52 weeks) (£)
Bedford V.A.S. T/L (capacity 16)										
Vehicle A	32.70	132.70	19.20[5]	184.60	297	11.0	55.7	62.2	} 56.9	9,600
Vehicle B	33.70	132.70	19.20	185.60	425	7.9	39.2	43.7		9,650
Vehicle C	28.10	132.70	19.20	180.00	278	10.1	57.8	64.7		9,360
Ford Transit Minibus (capacity 10)										
Vehicle A	21.80	132.70	8.10	162.60	442	4.9	35.0	36.8	} 38.2	8,455
Vehicle B	19.70	132.70	8.10	160.50	339	5.8	45.0	47.3		8,350
Vehicle C	18.50	132.70	8.10	159.30	458	4.0	33.0	34.8		8,285
Vehicle D	14.80	132.70	8.10	155.60	458	3.2	32.2	34.0		8,090
Commer K.C. T/L (capacity 10)[4]										
Vehicle A	29.10	132.70	11.70	173.50	333	8.7	48.6	52.1	52.1	9,022

[1] Includes fuel, oil, tyres, tubes, repairs and maintenance, insurance, road tax and depot overheads (April–December 1974)
[2] Staff costs at November 1974 (including on-costs and average overtime payments)
[3] Depreciation over 7 years on a straightline basis, based on November 1974 costs
[4] All data based on the 16 weeks up to 31 March 1975 as Commer came into service in December 1974
[5] Engineer's department estimate of November 1974 capital cost, on the cost in April 1974 of £6,358
Source: Hillingdon Transport (1975)

In 1972/73 Reading Social Services Department estimated an average net unit cost per meal of 20.5p for meals-on-wheels. This is made up by a cost of 22.0p for the food, 2.4p for transport and 5.0p for overheads, less contributions from recipients of 8–9p: a cost per year of £10.70p for the provision of one meal per week.

The borough of Hillingdon had a revised estimate of £58,600 for the cost of meals provision in 1975/76. In addition, the overhead and supervision cost was put at £12,400. Of this figure £7,400 was for the salary and on-costs of a meals service organiser. At these rates, for every £1 spent on administration, £4.73 went on actual provision of meals-on-wheels.

Home Help Service

In 1973, it was estimated that about £35 million per year is spent on the Home Help Service in England and Wales. The cost of travel for the home helps was a substantial proportion of this cost, amounting in some rural areas to as much as 50 per cent of the cost of provision.

For 1972/73 Reading Social Services arrived at a net unit cost for a home help per hour of 59.4p, consisting of 50.3p for staff and 12.1p for overheads, less contributions of 3p (although this study unfortunately does not provide a breakdown of the costs of supervisory and field staff). This constituted an annual cost of £30.90 for a home help for one hour per week.

Leicester Social Services Department assessed their Home Help Service following a survey in October 1975. They concluded that it would be uneconomic to administer accounts of £1 per month or less, and that under this criterion it would only be economic to assess for payment 38 per cent of the elderly and chronic sick population. The total Home Help Organiser time per effective assessment was likely to be 30 minutes per client, and to cater for this it would necessitate the employment of another Home Help Organiser throughout the year at a total cost of £4,219 per year. The additional costs of clerical staff, at £3,123 per year per person, were estimated to be £4,747 per year, and the additional costs for the Treasurer's Department to maintain the estimated 880 accounts, £7,392 per year. The cost of Central Office assessments was put at £7,095 per year, and of reassessment officers at £8,545. The total annual cost of such an assessment scheme would have been £31,998. The minimum expected income from the scheme was estimated to be £48,277, giving an annual return of £14,279.

The costs of the Home Help Service provided in the Hillingdon study (1976) lend themselves most easily to analysis. For 1975/76 the total cost of the Home Help Service for Hillingdon was put at £483,000, of which £394,000 (81.6 per cent) was for the home helps' wages and on-costs, £27,000 (5.6 per cent) for family aides, £37,000 (7.7 per cent) for organisers, £5,000 for clerks, £6,000 for management, £8,000 for transport and £6,000 for other items. At the time there were 1,899 home help clients, of whom about 90 per cent were estimated to be disabled in some way. This represents 1,709 people. If one leaves out the cost of the family aides and counterbalances this by omitting the £6,000 for 'other items' as their administrative cost involved, one is left with a total cost of £450,000, of which £402,000 (89.3 per cent) is for home helps and transport and £48,000 (19.7 per cent) is for administration. The average cost of home helps and their transport per client is accordingly about £212 per year, and the cost of administration per client is about £25 per year. This represents a cost of £1 in administration for every £8.5 spent actually supplying the service. Hence the estimated cost of administering the Home Help Service for disabled clients in Hillingdon in 1975/76 is about £43,200 per year.

The cost of a full-time home help, including overheads and apportionment of other workers' costs, was put at £3,127 per year. Of this, £2,272 was for the home help, £398 for a share of central overhead and central establishment charges, £28 for a 0.5 per cent share of a Principal Home Help Organiser, £348 for a 4 per cent share of a Home Help Organiser and assistant, £58 for a 2 per cent share of a clerk and £23 for a 0.13 per cent share of the area administration team. This worked out at a total cost per day of £14 for each home help.

An idea of the allocation of Home Help Organisers' time to different jobs can be obtained from the study of work patterns undertaken in March 1975 in Hillingdon, in which the duties undertaken were recorded for each day in half-hour units and calculated as percentages of total working time as shown in Table 3.12.

Table 3.12 Work patterns of Home Help Organisers and their staff (percentages)

	Organiser	Assistant organiser	Organiser/ clerks	Average of team organisers
Visits to clients	14	22	13	16
Visits to home helps	4	4	1	3
Telephone	22	16	14	17.5
Planning, etc.	25	31	62	39
Meetings	19	9	3	10
Courses	3	10	1	5
Training	2	0	0	1
Other travel	1	0	0	0
Other contacts	7	4	3	5
Informal discussions	3	4	3	3.5

Source: *Home helps*, Hillingdon (1975), Appendix C

Some recent studies have found that Home Help Organisers spend an inordinate amount of time on administration. The Warwickshire study (1975) found that they were spending the equivalent of two days a week on administrative matters. Abbas Baba's study in Birmingham (1975) also found that 'many Home Help Organisers in Birmingham spend a considerable proportion of their time on clerical work', mainly charges, financial assessments, preparation of accounts and the collection of home help service fees.

In Buckinghamshire in 1976/77, of the gross cost of £669,510 for the Home Help Service £533,620 (79.7 per cent) was for the salaries of home helps and £45,580 (6.8 per cent) for the salaries of the Home Help Organisers. The employment costs of both amounted to £53,090 (7.9 per cent). Of the remaining costs, £36,370 (5.4 per cent) were for travelling and subsistence expenses, and £850 (0.2 per cent) for other establishment and miscellaneous expenses. These excluded other administration costs and overheads.

Using the ratios given in the Hillingdon study, the **cost of administering the Home Help Service in England and Wales in 1975/76 for people with disabilities was probably between £8.88 million and £9.50 million**.

Residential accommodation

In 1970/71, 116,000 people over 65 years of age were being accommodated in local authority homes for the elderly and disabled; most of these would be classed as mildly disabled. A further 8,300 disabled people under 65, most of whom were nevertheless over 50, were accommodated in other homes.

Besides their own homes, local authorities contribute to the costs of accommodating disabled people in voluntary homes, usually to the amount it would cost them for Part III accommodation (about two-thirds of the actual running costs). Contributions for capital costs are rare.

The study *Care with dignity* (EIU, 1973), examining a sample of nine homes for the physically handicapped, found that the average capital cost per place was £6,660, with a range of averages between £4,140 and £12,160. Average weekly running costs were estimated at that time as £18–£20 per person. According to another source the national average cost of local authority residential accommodation in 1973 was £18.82 per week (National Spinal Injuries Centre Report, October 1975, page 2).

In 1975/76, the total net cost per week per client at the Bourne Hostel for handicapped adults in Hillingdon was about £51.06, including capital and running costs and total administration overheads. This makes an annual cost per client of about £2,655, of which about £400 per year is for administration, £763 per year is for the servicing staff and £558 per year is for running costs. Thus for every £6.64 spent on supplying and servicing residential accommodation about £1 went on administration. If these ratios are adopted **the probable cost of administering residential accommodation for physically handicapped adults in 1975/76 was £1.61 million to £1.65 million**.

Aids and adaptations

A study of the administration of the provision of aids and adaptations by London boroughs is at present being undertaken by Ursula Keeble at the London School of Economics. Although a very comprehensive analysis of the administrative system and the overall costs of supply of different aids and adaptations, the work does not include a cost analysis of the administration.

Preliminary work, however, has included a comparison of the cost of installations using direct labour and using contracted labour. One borough found that over a period of one year most single items billed against the Social Services vote by another borough department were *twice as expensive* as the same item costed in a control experiment using private builders and surveyors.

The Hillingdon Study (1976) analysed collectively the costs of provisions for access, aids and adaptations in the borough of Hillingdon in 1974/75. Their total cost was put at £344,000. Of this £145,000 was for adaptations, but only £75,000 of this was a cost of Social Services. Aids cost £48,000 and access £50,000. Amongst the administration staff, the time of senior occupational therapists (OTs) is spent primarily on access and major adaptations, that of other OTs on aids, minor adaptations and some major adaptations, and that of OT aides on adaptations and aids, particularly in follow-up. A more detailed breakdown of the work pattern of each is not available. The one-off nature of adaptations leads to high administrative costs. It was calculated that for an adaptation costing £1,000, another £836 is spent in staff time and incidental expenses. In 1975/76 in Hillingdon, 2,877 aids were supplied or financial assistance towards them given and 831 adaptations were made.

Thus the average cost of each aid to the Social Services Department was £16.75 and that of each adaptation £90.25. The administrative costs to the Social Services Department for aids, adaptations and access were £22,000 for senior OTs, £43,000 for other OTs, £7,000 for OT aides, £3,000 for travel, and £26,000 for clerks, technicians, storekeepers and other administration staff. Allowing for the probable allocations of the time of each, one arrives at administration costs of about £62,700 for adaptations (£75.45 per adaptation) and £37,500 for aids (£13.08 per aid). Thus for every £1.20 spent on adaptations another £1 was spent on administration and for every £1.28 spent on aids another £1 was spent on administration. This probably means that in 1975/76 **about £1.39 million was spent on the administration of adaptations by Social Services Departments and about £940,000 on the administration of aids**.

Mention has been made in earlier chapters of the complexities of finance relating to major adaptations. In this connection the recent experience of Hillingdon is significant. There can be considerable benefit to the Social Services' finances if Improvement Grants are secured – an amount exceeding £13,000 spread over twenty-three recent applications was estimated. But the additional administrative cost of securing such a grant is high. It is estimated to involve additional OTs' time costing approximately £80 per case and to involve staff in some *seventeen* further procedures to process the grant application (as distinct from arranging for the application itself). The extra work for the Social Services and Borough Architect's Departments in making these applications is so great that a ruling was made that an application for an Improvement Grant should be entered only when the total cost of the adaptation was likely to exceed £150, and it has since been suggested that this limit be raised to take account of the administrative cost involved. If the limit on the twenty-three cases considered in 1976 had been £500, *nine* would have been excluded; the loss in grants would have been £1,064 and the saving in administration £720 in OTs' time alone.

The costs to clients of using the system

The cost of administering the system is not confined to the administrators, but includes the cost to the people who are potential and actual recipients of the various benefits and services. These costs include such items as the time spent in finding out about benefits and services, applying, being assessed, attempting to correct errors on the part of the administration, obtaining medical evidence and collecting payments.

For some clients a direct cost is involved – in the form of postage and stationery – which sometimes is insignificant but which may be greater if a telephone has to be used or journeys need to be made to administrative offices. This last item can be particularly costly for a handicapped person who has mobility difficulties which give rise to extra costs, especially if he or she has to be escorted by an able-bodied helper who may be forfeiting earnings as well as incurring costs himself.

Many of the better Social Services Departments do recognise the mobility constraints on people with disabilities, and try to overcome them by improving the communication links with the people concerned, either by increasing the use of the telephone or by arranging more visits. These arrangements themselves, however, involve an extra cost.

Efforts were made in the course of this study to get people with disabilities to assess these direct extra costs, but retrospective assessment proved difficult for several reasons.

First, many people do not keep a systematic record of their dealings with administrative departments, although some more wary individuals do keep copies of letters sent to administrative departments and letters received. This practice was considered essential by some of those interviewed: experience had taught them to be sure that they could if necessary refute incorrect statements and produce evidence of errors on the part of the administrative departments. Very few people, however, keep a record of *all* their telephone calls or journeys.

Secondly, there are considerable variations in the capabilities of different individuals to deal efficiently with a complex system or with the anomalies it produces, resulting in a need for more – or less – repeated or lengthy communication, depending on the articulateness of the client and on the particular members of the administration with whom he or she is dealing.

Thirdly, the needs of varied individuals in varied circumstances with varied disabilities are such that it is not possible to standardise the costs of administering different benefits and services incurred by potential or actual recipients. Such direct costs need to be calculated by claimants monitoring their own communications in finding out about and obtaining different benefits and services as they go along, and this was not possible within the scope of the present study. The methodological problems of such an exercise do not recommend it, especially considering that often small sums only are involved – even though these may bulk relatively large in a small budget. It might only be worth doing in the case of benefits and services that have been proved to have necessitated long and complex communications between potential and actual recipients and administrative departments.

The comment of one articulate disabled recipient of a number of benefits and services, when approached to sort out his communications on different benefits and services to provide material for analysis, reflects the difficulties of conducting such a study and its doubtful usefulness. He said:

'I would like to help because of all the time and effort I have had to spend in dealing with administrators in the past. Other disabled people I know have also wasted a lot of time and money on protracted correspondence with administrators. It was bad enough at the time, but now to go through it all again would be tedious, and I don't know how much use it would be to you anyway. Why can't people recognise that the problem is there without going into the minutiae, and get on with changing the system rather than losing themselves in small details?'

Besides the direct costs, there are the opportunity costs associated with the time used by clients to obtain benefits and services, and the loss of income from spending this time. There is no lack of awareness among administrators that about 65 per cent of people with disabilities are over retirement age, that accordingly they would not be likely to be in full-time work, and that their opportunity costs in terms of income lost would thus be negligible. There is, however, a tendency to assume that this applies to *all* clients. The people most affected by such an assumption are those with disabilities who are nevertheless in full- or part-time employment, and the associates and relatives of people with disabilities obliged to spend their time in trying to secure for them the benefits and services to which they are entitled.

In addition, there is a steadily increasing number of voluntary groups providing advice and assistance to people with disabilities – in addition to paid Welfare Rights Officers – all of whom are effectively helping to stop gaps in the existing system; yet they are performing functions that either should not be necessary or should be performed by the administrators concerned. The work of these voluntary groups involves a considerable cost in time and resources.

The difficulties of measuring opportunity costs were encountered by Mavis Hyman in her recent pioneering study of *The extra costs of disabled living*. She looked at the opportunity costs of income given up or the time expended by those who assist the disabled person in day-to-day care. She felt (page 42) 'in general, opportunity costs appeared to be the most difficult to isolate and cost', because:

a. help in daily living activities was staggered over a day, being seen as a full-time job by some and hardly noticed by others;

b. accompaniment on outings could not be seen as for the sole benefit of the disabled person;

c. some care was highly specific with no 'going rate' of remuneration;

d. it was difficult to isolate the different roles of attendants; and

e. the question of financial loss to attendants of the disabled was sometimes extremely hypothetical.

As a result of these difficulties she simplified these costs to an estimate of £1 an hour for *all* personal services directly related to disability.

People with disabilities require *additional* time for such activities as self-care and travel; but this was not taken into account as *average* time scales for particular activities were not known. This was the major difficulty encountered in this part of our study. Mavis Hyman met with the same problem, and was not able to establish any such time scales from the limited number of interviews undertaken; and we were not in a position to monitor these activities in order to make any assessment. As Mavis Hyman concluded:

'The point can only be made that there was considerable cost in time, in energy and in organisation incurred by the disabled person, but this could not be quantified.'

It is, however, worth drawing attention to these costs, to which the administrators in Social Services Departments and the people who create the benefits and services seem often to be oblivious. We had to beware, however, of devoting too much time to the effort to obtain specific itemisation of these costs, as the difficulties are considerable and the results would scarcely justify the effort required.

In some ways a greater cost, in human terms, is the emotional and mental stress felt by potential and actual recipients of benefits and services and the people who assist them. One person with a disability who was interviewed, and who has struggled on a number of issues regarding benefits and services, said that although he had four different points that he wished to take up with the Attendance Allowance Board, he was intending to deal with only one point at a time, as he 'couldn't stand the thought of the stress it would cause [him] if he tried to tackle all of them at once'. If somebody as dynamic as this individual felt such a pressure, it is hard to convey any real understanding of the degree of stress caused to others who are less articulate, less literate and less active, to those with a mental handicap, and to hard-pressed partners of the most severely handicapped, themselves often elderly and close to the limit of their physical resources.

It is hoped that some impression of these aspects of administrative cost will emerge from a reading of Chapter 7, which deals with the effects of the system upon clients as they are seen in individual case histories. In part, these costs may be inescapable – since obviously it is necessary to establish just what it is that each person requires – but much of the needless stress and difficulty is certainly related to *the multiplicity of means-related benefits*.

The costs of duplicating assessment procedures

The ever-increasing number of means-related benefits has multiplied the problem of duplicating assessment procedures. Attention to these problems is comparatively recent; for instance, during the last few years considerable attention has been given to the combining of assessment for Rate Rebates and Rent Rebates.

A review of the different combined assessment schemes undertaken is provided in Chapter 6. One of the major findings of that review is the inadequacy of cost analysis within such schemes. While those who have carried out the studies and experimented with reforms have recognised the considerable waste caused by duplicating assessment, they have not established the full extent of that waste by cost analysis; they have usually preferred to concentrate their attention and their limited resources on rationalising the system. In many ways it is better that they should do so. When resources are limited it is more important to make the necessary reforms than to create further waste in the process of demonstrating their desirability in detail, when even a cursory appraisal makes this clear. Nevertheless, a degree of more precise cost data and analysis is desirable; hence our recommendations in Chapter 6.

Unfortunately, however, for our present study, there is negligible cost data now available on assessment procedures. It is hoped that the cost analysis of the current Inverclyde Project will offer some comparative data on these procedures. Some local authorities have reviewed the assessment costs of individual benefits and services, but usually these enquiries have been designed to find at which point it is economically worthwhile to introduce assessment for such services (often for charging purposes) rather than to examine the cost of allowing such assessments to duplicate each other.

We have already described some of the difficulties in arriving at costs of different workers' time in relation to the administration of benefits. In addition, efforts to isolate the time spent on assessment for each benefit or service have been rare. The isolating of such costs for individual benefits and services is difficult enough, but isolating the costs of overlapping assessments is still more complex, particularly where only parts of the assessment procedures overlap.

Consider, for instance, an assessment for the Home Help Service (and this is a straightforward assessment compared with others – see, for example, the comments on assessment for adaptations on page 122). Each assessment takes on average half an hour of a Home Help Organiser's time, and the cost in respect of that time alone is over £10. If we take into account travel and other on-costs and the time – frequently more than equal to the Organiser's time – spent by the applicant in preparing financial and other data, the true cost must be at least three times that figure. It is not necessary to enter into more precise calculations to realise the economic implications of such situations as that outlined in the Welsh study of housing and education benefits (quoted on page 192) where staggered and repeated claim times, dictated by the administrative system, necessitate people with school-age children having to be assessed afresh at least six times each year. There are still many boroughs where there has been no resolving of the need to be separately assessed, on different principles (as when details of income are required sometimes on a weekly, sometimes on a monthly, sometimes on an annual basis), by four or five different offices – for instance, the Housing Department for rent benefits, the Treasurer's Department for Rate Rebate, the Home Help Organisers for their service, by another officer of the Social Services Department for help with holidays, and by yet another if there is a child seeking a day nursery place; all this is in addition to details and medical certification (now doctors' statements) required by the Department of Health and Social Security and the income tax authorities.

Accordingly we suggested that while the recommendations in Chapter 6 should be followed and the costs of assessments for services and benefits should be measured and compared and the overlapping components isolated, at the same time regard should be given to orientating such study of assessments towards actually eliminating unnecessary work and not merely creating more.

The costs of providing unwanted benefits and services

Even from the limited number of case histories available to us, it is clear that too often people with handicaps discover that the only benefits or services available to them are ones which either they cannot make use of, or which do not offer an acceptable alternative to the services they really want, save in the impersonal view of 'the system'.

For example, entitlement to a concessionary bus pass or to financial help towards the cost of public transport is no 'alternative' to a personal vehicle if you cannot travel on a bus without danger or acute discomfort, or without an escort, and if buses are the only form of transport in your area. This may not have any measurable *economic* consequences (apart from the wasted paperwork behind the infuriating annual arrival of the bus pass!), and its consequences in frustration are not the subject of this section of the study. There are, however, many instances when there is a substantial economic consequence of providing such false alternatives. Many of the most glaring and currently the most topical examples lie in this field of mobility.

Take, as an example, a male worker of 38, married, with no children; because of a disability, he becomes unable to use public transport. By giving up work, at 1975 benefit rates, he would have become eligible to draw a basic £18.00 per week Unemployment Benefit for himself and his wife; eventually, on Invalidity Pension, he would have drawn £22.90. Compare this with his position if he had been able to remain in continuous work at the 'average male manual worker' level usually used for sample calculations (though, since manual work is, in the nature of the proposition, unlikely, it is also worth looking at the average pay for clerical and administrative workers, given here in parentheses). Earning gross pay of £60 (£70) and allowing for income tax and National Insurance, he would have had a net income of just over £42 (£48). The Exchequer, meantime, would have gained £17.70 (£21.70) in tax and National Insurance contributions *plus* the cash – £18 or £22.90 – not being paid out in benefits. In round terms, the cost to the state of *not* getting this man to work comes out at £2,000 a year.

Yet this expensive 'alternative' is the opposite of what the recipient wanted. Moreover, as time progressed, continued living on the low income from benefits would probably bring such a household into the still more expensive care of the Supplementary Benefit system since there would otherwise after a time be nothing available for major items of expenditure.

Or take the numerous cases where unsuitable aids are supplied. Most people with disabilities know of instances where repeated efforts have failed to secure for them a genuinely suitable aid or appliance, not because these do not exist, but because of administrative problems: either the specification is not clearly relayed to the issuing officer or the particular type of aid most suited to the client's needs is not at the time included in the range permitted under the system – for example, when a Queensway powered wheelchair was not provided through the appliance service even to people to whose needs it is ideally suited and to whom it can restore a measure of independence. The argument that cost limits the available range is indefensible in such cases.

The *direct* waste may be considerable – for example, something like £100 worth of hoist (plus the administrative cost of supplying it) sitting in a garden shed because the hoist is of a type designed for the large polished floor of a hospital ward and is virtually unusable in the small, carpeted bedroom for which it was supplied. The ultimate economic consequences may be much larger: the need for which the hoist was allocated is not met, a husband, wife or perhaps elderly parent continues to lift a severely handicapped person unaided, and before long the disabled person and the partner may be costing *at least £150 a week* – the one in residential care, the other occupying an acute bed in a hospital as a result of damage to the heart or back, or possibly of a hernia, with only the small saving in benefits not paid to meet the handicapped person's needs to offset against the cost of the consequences.

Even the smallest of these false alternatives can be ridiculously expensive. Repair for a long-reach 'Helping Hand' aid (cost of the new, complete aid in 1976 under £3) was asked for by telephone by one interviewee. Repair was 'not worth-while', was the response: a new aid would be supplied. The type required was carefully explained over the telephone. A *month* later an officer arrived from the county authority (return journey 32 miles) to deliver a *short-reach* aid. Because of the client's particular handicap, this was of no use at all. The specifications were again explained, and this time not only was the name and number of the model given, but the damaged aid itself was shown to the visiting officer. A further month passed, and an officer called again (another 32 miles) without prior notification, and the client was out. The aid was left at the house, but this one too was useless, since it was without the retaining clip essential for its use by anyone with a weak grip. The client telephoned and suggested the officer merely collect it (32 miles again) and forget the whole thing.

Using the figures given earlier in this chapter (though these are for a different borough, and one which is probably above average in efficiency), we know that the purely administrative element in the cost of dealing with an application for an aid averages £13. In this case the officer made three calls, at a distance of 16 miles from base, the client made several useless telephone calls, and the net result was five or six pounds of expenditure on two aids for which there was no user. Perhaps the most telling point, however, lies in the fact that when the client in desperation rang the manufacturer direct, a completely satisfactory repair was carried out within three weeks and cost 'about £3'. This has to be compared with the administrative cost, over a period of more than two months, of the abortive effort to obtain a low-cost but vital aid. The reason for this client's application to the local authority was the perfectly correct advice: 'you are entitled to get this through the local authority'. Many other applicants would have difficulty in financing a £3 repair and would have a struggle to recover the cost (e.g. from the Supplementary Benefit officers) when this service is theoretically available via the local authority.

Clearly there is no way in which one can assign a total sum to the cost of this problem, and there will remain an irreducible minimum of such wastage in any system so vulnerable to human error and the changing condition of some applicants. It is not often realised, however, how large may be the cost of the wastage factor arising from false alternatives under the existing system. It is nevertheless possible to use a little guesswork in order to obtain a very rough idea of the size of the problem.

Even if it is assumed that some such experience befalls only *one in a hundred* of disabled people in a year (and our experience suggests that this is an over-generous view of the true situation), that amounts to 35,000 such cases. For some (perhaps 10 per cent) the wastage element may be in tens of pounds. At the other end of the scale, particularly in the present situation regarding mobility, are the cases such as the first example quoted above, where unwilling recipients have heaped upon them a wastage in excess of £1,000. In between are those costing, like our example of the useless hoist, several hundreds of pounds, and probably these form the largest group. Even if the *average* cost were only £100, and this is probably an unduly optimistic figure, the sum involved would be £3.5 million (at 1976 prices). The real figure may well be twice as much. In other parts of this chapter we have dealt with the legitimate costs of administering real services. Here we are talking about the wasteful expenditure of millions of pounds to achieve no desired end. Anything which can help to reduce this sum will release resources for the genuine help of disabled people.

Summary

Table 3.13 presents estimates based on the studies cited earlier, of the administration costs of different benefits and services as a percentage of the net expenditure on these benefits and services, estimates of the total administrative costs for each, and the total administrative costs that can be allocated to providing these benefits and services for people with disabilities in 1975/76. With inadequate data on the proportion of adults with disabilities amongst the recipients of each benefit, and on the proportion of administrative time that this group occupies, however, it has often been difficult to isolate the cost of administration that can be apportioned to this group of clients.

The estimated administrative costs for 1975/76 of central government *cash benefits* (allowing for inflation, and using the data provided on central government administration) are £270–£290 million for National Insurance benefits, £22–£25 million for Industrial Injury and Industrial Disablement payments, £6–£7.5 million for War Disablement Pensions and £275 million for payments from the Supplementary Benefits Commission (by no means all concerning people with disabilities).

Table 3.13   The estimated administration costs of benefits and services for adults with disabilities, 1975/76

Benefit	Administration costs as % of total net expenditure on benefits	Total administration[1] (£ million)	Administration costs of benefits received by people with disabilities (£ million)
National Insurance Benefits	4.0	270–290	22–25
Industrial Injury Benefit / Industrial Disablement Pension	10.3	22–25	22–25
War Disablement Pensions	4.2	6–7.5	6–7.5
Family Income Supplement	7.1	1	0.07
Supplementary Benefits	11.8	190	15–35 (minimum) 45–60 (probably)
Adaptations[2]	45.0	0.14–0.15	0.14–0.15
Rent Rebates[2]	6.1–6.5	7.5–8.5	n.a.
Rent Allowances[2]	11.6–16.0	2.8–3.5	n.a.
Holidays[2]	11.0	0.31–0.32	0.11–0.12
Day-care centres – Younger physically handicapped centres[2]	12.8	1.18–1.20	1.18–1.20
Meals-on-wheels[2]	17.5	n.a.	n.a.
Home Help Service[2]	10.5	9.85–1.00	8.88–9.50
Residential accommodation for handicapped adults[2]	13.1	1.61–1.65	1.61–1.65
Aids[2]	43.9	0.94–0.95	0.94–0.95

[1] Including overhead and central establishment charges for local authority personal social services
[2] England and Wales only
Source: EIU estimates

The proportion of net expenditure on cash benefits absorbed by administration is about 4 to 5 per cent, but is as high as 7.1 per cent for FIS, 10.3 per cent for Industrial Injury benefits, 11.8 per cent for Supplementary Benefits and 11.6–16.0 per cent for Rent Allowances.

The cost of administration of *services* usually represents between 10 and 15 per cent of net expenditure, except in the administration of aids and adaptations which incurred a very high administrative expense of around 43–45 per cent. These figures indicate how much less is the cost of administering cash benefits than services, although it must be borne in mind that the costs given here for the administration of cash benefits paid by central government do not cover all the overhead and central administration costs in the same way that the figures for local authority benefits do.

The total net expenditure by local authorities in England and Wales on personal social services, and on social services for adults with disabilities, are set out in Tables 3.14 and 3.15 respectively, which are both based on data from the Chartered Institute of Public Finance and Accountancy (CIPFA). In some of the categories of residential accommodation and day care institutions it is difficult to isolate expenditure on people with disabilities from that on other clients, such as the elderly.

From the CIPFA data it is estimated that expenditure by local authority Social Services Departments on fieldwork staff in England and Wales in 1975/76 was £117.94 million, and on administrative and research staff £108.81 million. By adding the 11.6 per cent universal overhead figure derived from the Hillingdon study, 12.2 per cent for staff charged to the Administration Holding Account, and 4.1 per cent for social workers and occupational therapists (assuming that they represent about 40 per cent of the fieldwork costs), a total administrative cost is reached for fieldwork staff of about £145–£150 million, and total administrative cost for administrative and research staff of about £135–£140 million.

Although it is not possible to arrive at a precise figure for the total cost of administration of the existing system of benefits and services for disabled people, it is clear that, when central and local government provisions are considered together, the aggregate figure must be in excess of £300 million per year. It has been estimated that there are 3.5 million people with disabilities in this country, though not all of these in fact receive benefits at present; this total can thus be regarded as an administration cost of £1.65 per disabled person per week, or £85.70 per annum. To people on very limited incomes this is a sufficiently large sum to make them want to be sure none of it is being wasted – and there is all too much evidence that the way the system operates at present can indeed give rise to administrative costs which are not achieving their intended ends.

The major conclusion of this part of the study is that, because of the way in which cost data are compiled and aggregated, it is not possible to make a comprehensive analysis of the costs of administration for all the different benefits and

Table 3.14 Expenditure of local authorities in England and Wales on personal social services, 1973/74 to 1975/76 (£'000)

	London boroughs (31)			Metropolitan districts (32)			Counties of England and Wales (47)			All authorities of England and Wales (110)		
	73/74	74/75	75/76[1]	73/74	74/75	75/76[1]	73/74	74/75	75/76[1]	73/74	74/75	75/76[1]
Total expenditure met from rates and rate support grant	87,480	143,930	177,190[2]	90,550	135,920	180,790[2]	163,240	304,740	364,440[2]	341,270	584,590	722,430[2]
Expenditure on field-work staff[3]	12,862	23,688	29,414	12,486	19,061	26,938	26,131	51,939	61,590	51,480	94,676	117,942
Expenditure on administrative staff and research and development[3]	15,522	25,963	31,185	10,899	19,766	23,683	23,969	48,086	53,937	50,387	93,771	108,805

[1] CIPFA estimates
[2] Calculated from net expenditure per 1,000 population and actual population
[3] Calculated from expenditure per 1,000 population and actual population for 1973/74 and 1974/75, and from estimated percentage of net expenditure on fieldwork for 1975/76
Source: CIPFA statistics

Table 3.15 Expenditure of local authorities in England and Wales on personal social services for adults with disabilities, 1973/74 to 1975/76 (£'000)

	1973/74	1974/75	1975/76[1]
Residential care of the elderly	72,742	123,544	156,770[2]
Residential care for younger physically handicapped	4,326	7,635	12,320[2]
Residential care for mentally handicapped adults	5,942	9,634	12,502[2]
Day care centres/clubs for:			
elderly	3,719	7,004	9,339
younger physically handicapped	4,595	7,385	9,216
mentally handicapped	478	555	836
multi-purpose (18–64 year olds)	1,188	2,499	3,509
Home Help Service	42,255	74,069	93,987
Meals service for pensioners	3,455	6,745	8,555
Sheltered housing	2,604	2,615	4,338
Telephones	1,258	2,381	3,055
Aids	1,137	1,905	} 5,186
Adaptations	1,627	2,715	
Holidays	1,554	2,381	2,850
Laundry	85	n.a.	n.a.
Travel concessions for people over 18 years	n.a.	3,619	5,369
Total number of handicapped persons [3] ('000)	561.7	779.2	864.5

[1] CIPFA estimates
[2] Calculated from number of resident weeks times net cost per resident week
[3] Includes deaf, blind, partially sighted, hard of hearing and general classes; figures are for the end of the financial year
Source: Data based on CIPFA Personal Social Services Statistics

services under review, still less to estimate with any accuracy the proportion of each that should be allocated to people with disabilities. Accordingly, because of the difficulties encountered in trying to arrive at adequate cost analysis, it is recommended:

1. That central and local government authorities responsible for the benefits concerned undertake to review – preferably jointly but otherwise individually – the cost data available and the methods used in their compilation, to determine whether figures can be isolated to give a clearer breakdown of expenditure by client groups and services together, and to follow this by making analyses of those data along the lines indicated.

2. That where the compilation of cost data is inappropriate at present for the analysis of expenditure by client groups and services together, the system for compiling cost data be reviewed and modified (though with a watchful eye to

the additional cost of changing the system) in order to make it easier in future to compile data which can be used as a guide both for internal planning and testing the efficacy of individual services, and to provide more accurate guidelines for policy-makers, and for people and organisations involved with particular client groups. (Organisations such as the Chartered Institute of Public Finance and Accountancy (CIPFA) or the Personal Social Services Council may be able to assist the reviewing of these systems.)

3. That indices of local authority and central government wage and administration costs be established to aid planning and to provide more accurate bases for estimates of expenditure in an inflationary economy.

Having made these recommendations, we wish to re-emphasise that it would be better to use available resources in modifying the existing administrative structure where this is clearly inappropriate and to reduce the duplication of administrative procedures, rather than to carry out a highly detailed analysis of the costs of the different administrative systems for benefits and services. Nevertheless, there is a far from adequate degree of accuracy of data at present obtainable in analysing the costs of administration for different services and benefits, and some of these inadequacies could be overcome by means of a comparatively small allocation of resources to research into the matters raised by our recommendations.

Chapter Four

Take-up of benefits and services

In Chapter 3 we considered the cost of the complex system of services and benefits available to people with disabilities. In this and the subsequent chapter we examine the effectiveness of this system in reaching the people for whose needs it has been assembled. An important test of the success of a service or benefit is its 'take-up', that is, the number of people who claim it expressed as a percentage of the number considered to be eligible. 'Non-take-up' is the complementary figure, the percentage of the eligible group who do not claim it.

Several qualities of a benefit are tested by measurement of take-up, and success in achieving a take-up approaching 100 per cent depends on a number of factors. The existence of the benefit must be known to those eligible, to their advisers and to the associated administrative officers. The method of application and the criteria of eligibility must be easily understood. The benefit must be real, in that the successful claimant must be materially assisted. The effort involved in claiming the benefit must not be disproportionately large. Finally, its award must not be followed by immediate, compensating reduction in one or more other benefits – a not uncommon sequence under the present system.

There is a wide range of take-up for the different benefits that are currently available. At one end of the scale, the Old Person's Pension was claimed by 156,000 people (by the end of 1971), although the estimated eligible population was only 150,000. At the other extreme, in a study carried out in Wandsworth less than 4 per cent of one group eligible for free medical prescriptions on low-income grounds were found to be claiming it.

Exploration of non-take-up is a particularly difficult area of social research. Some potential respondents show a reticence towards organisations or individuals trying to find out details of their private lives; others, for a variety of reasons, tend to fall outside the major communication channels which facilitate both the take-up of benefits and the related social research.

Factors affecting non-take-up of benefits

Non-take-up of a benefit may have more than one cause. People with disabilities in particular, may not consider themselves to be 'handicapped', and accordingly may eschew contacts in which they are labelled as such; or, because of the strong determination to be self-reliant that is common in this group, they may not wish to have anything to do with either the benefits or the people enquiring about them. This characteristic of handicapped people is illustrated by the experience, in the 1971 survey, of the Office of Population Censuses and Surveys. In preparing *Handicapped and impaired in Great Britain* (henceforward referred to as the '1971 OPCS Survey'), researchers found that, of their two interview sample sets of 15,096 and 2,640 potential respondents, 421 refused to be interviewed, and refusals were made by others on behalf of a further 227. The reasons for these refusals were examined, and are set out in Table 4.1.

The most common reason given for refusal was that respondents felt that their impairment was not sufficient to warrant an interview: almost two-thirds of these respondents were people who had arthritis or rheumatism or who had difficulty with kneeling or bending, or both. In over a quarter of the refusals either no specific reason was given, or refusal was inferred from the fact that the subject broke two or more appointments.

Another common cause of non-take-up is the potential claimant's ignorance of the benefit. This, also, can be a particular problem for people with disabilities that limit their mobility, social contact, literary skills or contact with the media.

Table 4.1 Reasons for people refusing interviews about handicap

Reason for refusal	Refusal by subject (%)	Refusal by other (%)
Not sufficiently handicapped to need being interviewed (but not saying that not handicapped at all)	24	12
Embittered by disability or does not like talking about disability	4	13
Says does not want any help or care	13	9
Too ill or not well enough	6	6
Dislikes surveys or answering questions	10	6
Too busy, not interested	11	11
Subject dead: proxy refused interview	—	11
No specific reason given, indirect refusal by breaking appointments	26	26
Other reasons	6	6
No. on which % based	421	227

Source: OPCS Survey (1971), page 247

There may be misunderstandings on the part of potential claimants regarding eligibility criteria, and confusion and difficulties regarding the relevant initial application forms and procedures.

Even when contact with the authorities has been established other reasons may come into play: pride and fear of stigma, negative responses from officials, difficulties in going through the application procedure, or discouragement by initial refusal of a claim, even though an appeal would be likely to succeed. Some potential claimants will have already developed a strong dislike of officialdom caused by the rejection of past claims or by former negative contacts with officials.

Even when these considerations do not restrict take-up, the claimant may be doubtful as to whether either the amount to be received, or the quality or utility of the service sought, merits the effort involved in claiming, or whether perhaps another benefit might prove more appropriate. Moreover, general attitudes of self-reliance and independence may lead to non-take-up by the people who are eligible for and in need of the benefits.

Efforts are made from time to time by both central and local government to establish the numbers eligible for different benefits, and to ensure that those eligible are fully aware of and encouraged to apply for them. But such efforts have often proved ineffective, and the initiative is too often left in the hands of ill-informed potential claimants.

Handicapped people outside the welfare system

The question of the numbers of sick or disabled people who were outside the welfare system altogether, or who were only receiving part of their possible entitlement, was an important concern of the Chronically Sick and Disabled Persons Act 1970, especially in its first section.

The 1971 OPCS Survey discovered considerable numbers of handicapped people outside the welfare system who may have been entitled to benefits. It estimated that there were 1,129,000 people in Britain who were handicapped and needing some support, and that of these 157,000 were very severely handicapped, 356,000 were severely handicapped and 616,000 were appreciably handicapped. This compared with 260,000 people registered as disabled on local authority registers for England and Wales at 31 March 1971. By 31 March 1975, the numbers of people on these registers had increased to 594,268, with an additional 138,630 registered as blind or partially sighted, and 46,330 as deaf or having impaired hearing, a total of 779,228. A considerable shortfall still remains between the number of people who have disabilities and the number who are registered as such with local authorities, although the gap is diminishing each year.

Local authority registers The 1971 OPCS Survey showed that only 17 per cent of those classified as very severely and severely handicapped claimed knowledge of local authority registers of the handicapped, compared with 21 per cent of those with appreciable handicaps. The higher percentage in the latter group was attributed to its lower age, and it was concluded that 'knowledge of the register is more likely to depend on younger age than on degree of handicap'.

This study also found that only just over 2 per cent of impaired people interviewed thought they were on local authority registers, while just over 5 per cent of them actually were. Of those who said they had never heard of the register, 5 per cent were actually registered, as were 4 per cent of those who knew about the register but maintained that they themselves were not registered. In comparison, half of those who claimed to know of the register and to be registered were found not to be so. It was clear that a proportion of respondents were uncertain whether they were or were not on the register, that some people were put on the register without their knowledge, and that some people confused the local authority register with the Department of Employment register.

The main benefit of registration as seen by the respondents was the supply of aids for mobility. The main reason for non-registration by those claiming to know of the existence of the register was that they did not consider themselves to be handicapped. A very small proportion claimed to be too independent, or to dislike 'authority'. Of those who had not heard of the register, 70 per cent said that they would still not have asked to be registered as they did not consider themselves in need. Although this is probably a *bona fide* justification for many of the respondents in this survey who were impaired rather than handicapped, it may also reflect a desire for independence that was not made explicit.

The proportions of people with different degrees of handicap who are on local authority registers (general classes) are shown in Table 4.2.

Table 4.2 Severity of handicap, related to registration with a local authority

Degree of handicap		% registered	No. on which based
Very severe	1 + 2	13.9	101
	3	18.7	551
	(1 − 3)	(17.9)	(652)
Severe	4	9.0	410
	5	11.7	1,010
	(4 − 5)	(10.9)	(1,420)
Appreciable	6	6.7	2,457
All handicapped (1 − 6)		11.8	4,529

Source: OPCS Survey (1971), page 44

Severity of handicap did not by itself seem to affect registration among elderly people, but there were large differences between the rates of registration for elderly and non-elderly people with the same degree of handicap. Of very severely handicapped people, only 9 per cent aged 65 years and over were registered, in comparison with 39 per cent for 50–64 year olds and 47 per cent for 16–49 year olds. In the severely handicapped group the differences between the age groups were smaller: 9 per cent registration for people of 65 and over, 14 per cent for 50–64 year olds and 18 per cent for 16–49 year olds.

Taking the very severely and severely handicapped groups together, 16 per cent of those living alone and 16 per cent of those living with a spouse (whether or not there were children in the household) were registered, compared with 8 per cent for those who were widowed and living with an unmarried child and 3 per cent for those living with married children.

Mobility also seemed to be an important consideration. Table 4.3 shows that those who could get out with an escort had a greater likelihood of being registered.

Geographical variations in registration were less marked. In 1971, the proportion of very severely and severely handicapped respondents registered was between 11 and 17 per cent in the country as a whole, with figures of 9 per cent in Scotland and 7 per cent in the northern region of England.

Registration of handicapped people with local authorities is itself not necessarily of value. However, the 1971 OPCS Survey did show that while only 12 per cent of the estimated handicapped were registered, 40 per cent of the registered used one or more of the services, and that registered people were more likely to be getting a service than non-registered ones. Of those who were registered, 25 per cent more of the very severely handicapped, 40 per cent more of the severely handicapped and 33 per cent more of the appreciably handicapped had an on-going service compared with those with a similar degree of handicap who were not registered. The details are set out in Table 4.4.

The largest disparity between the registered and non-registered was to be found in the greater number of registered people visited by social workers, and it was assumed that welfare departments often did not know of the existence of handicapped people unless they were registered. Fifty-three of the 87 people in categories 1 and 2 of the severely handicapped people who were not registered were visited by a district nurse, and this suggests the possible usefulness of a closer liaison between health and welfare workers. The proportions of people with different degrees of handicap receiving help from both health and welfare services are set out in Table 4.5.

John Hagget reported a study in the Wirral in which it was found that a large number of people who might be classified as handicapped were not registered as such, even though they were receiving services. This state of affairs was thought to arise because specialist officers were apt to treat their responsibilities to

Table 4.3 Severity of handicap and mobility, related to registration with a local authority

	Degree of handicap							
	Very severe		Severe		Appreciable		All handicapped 1–6	
	% reg.	No. on which % based	% reg.	No. on which % based	% reg.	No. on which % based	% reg.	No. on which % based
Bedfast	10	116	—	—	—	—	10	116
Housebound and chairfast	13	179	(7)	54	—	8	12	241
Other housebound	16	146	12	318	9	370	12	834
Gets out if accompanied	28	171	17	294	13	319	18	784
Gets out on own with aids or difficulty	(10)	30	12	419	9	788	11	1,237
Gets out with no aids or difficulty	—	8	3	335	2	968	2	1,311
All handicapped	18	652[1]	11	1,420	7	2,457[1]	10	4,259[1]

[1] Final column includes two very severely and four appreciably handicapped people whom it was not possible to classify for mobility
Note: brackets denote number not percentage
Source: OPCS Survey (1971), page 46

Table 4.4 Severity of handicap and use of services, related to registration with a local authority (percentages)

	Degree of handicap							
	Very severe 1–3		Severe 4–5		Appreciable 6		All handicapped 1–6	
	Reg.	Not reg.	Reg.	Not reg.	Reg.	Not reg.	Reg.	Not reg.
Home help	18	13	31	16	25	10	25	12
Meals-on-wheels	5	4	14	4	10	3	10	3
District or male nurse	48	39	19	13	10	7	23	13
Health visitor	19	10	13	6	13	4	14	5
Social worker	27	7	25	4	17	3	22	4
Occupational therapist	9	1	5	2	9	1	8	1
Physiotherapist	8	2	4	2	7	1	6	1
Chiropody	21	16	31	15	12	12	21	13
Visitor for the blind	2	2	—	1	—	2	—[1]	2
Attends local authority centre for the physically handicapped	7	—[1]	15	1	16	1	13	1
Voluntary societies	2	1	1	—[1]	2	1	2	1
In sheltered employment	3	1	3	—[1]	4	1	3	1
Other service	2	2	3	1	1	1	2	1
None of these services	16	41	21	61	37	70	26	63
No. on which % based	117	535	155	1,265	164	2,293	436	4,093

[1] Less than 0.5 per cent
Source: OPCS Survey (1971), page 52

Table 4.5 Severity of handicap, related to use of services irrespective of registration (percentages)

	Degree of handicap				
	Very severe		Severe	Appreciable	All handicapped
	1 + 2	3	4 + 5	6	1–6
Home help	17	13	17	11	13
Meals-on-wheels	2	4	5	3	4
District or male nurse	58	37	12	8	14
Health visitor	18	11	7	4	6
Social worker	8	11	7	4	6
Occupational therapist	1	3	2	1	2
Physiotherapist	2	3	3	1	2
Chiropody	17	17	17	12	14
Visitor for the blind	4	1	1	2	2
Attends local authority centre for the physically handicapped	—	2	3	2	2
Attends centre for the mentally handicapped	—	—	—	—	—
Voluntary societies	—	1	1	1	1
In sheltered employment	—	1	1	1	1
Other service	2	2	1	1	1
None of these services	26	39	57	68	60
No. on which % based	101	551	1,420	2,457	4,529

Source: OPCS Survey (1971), page 50

individual clients in isolation, and also because of the lack of common criteria for the registration of the handicapped. Registration of the people receiving services would have doubled the numbers on the register.

Stage 1 of a study conducted in Newcastle in 1972 took the form of a postal survey, and revealed that 41.4 per cent of the 5,119 respondents had been previously unknown to the Social Services Department; the percentage range between different wards ranged from 31.7 to 50.3 per cent. Only 8.6 per cent maintained that they did not wish to be registered with the local authority; 11.7 per cent did not answer.

Stage 2 of this study consisted of a door-to-door survey; it discovered an incidence of 18 per cent of households with chronically sick and disabled members, compared with 5.9 per cent recorded from the Stage 1 postal survey. Of the 423 respondents interviewed in Stage 2, only 24.6 per cent had returned the postal questionnaire from Stage 1. Of the Stage 2 interviewees, moreover, only 7 per cent of those with a sensory disorder had responded to the postal questionnaire, compared with 42 per cent of those suffering from disorders of the central nervous system. Those with a high self-care (low dependence) score were more likely to have replied than those with a low one (high dependence). Proportionately, more replies reported children, the very old and those living alone (presumably often because someone able-bodied replied for them); men were slightly more likely to have replied than women.

Met and unmet needs

The crucial issue, however, is not so much the percentages of the estimated handicapped population taking advantage of the benefits provided, but the shortfall in take-up from the point of view of 'need' as defined by the handicapped themselves, or by people qualified to assess their 'needs'. Some local authorities, in complying with the Chronically Sick and Disabled Persons Act 1970, have borne these considerations firmly in mind when organising their surveys of the handicapped.

The Social Policy Research Report (1973) on the implementation of the Chronically Sick and Disabled Persons Act showed that two authorities kept no register of disabled people as such; one recorded clients according to their needs, and the other was in the process of computerising records of clients by needs rather than by disability. A number of other authorities also expressed a dislike of categorising people according to their impairment rather than according to their needs for services.

The 1971 OPCS Survey tried to get some idea of how far the very severely handicapped saw their needs as being met. Of these people, 12 per cent said that they had applied unsuccessfully for help; nearly a quarter of them had applied for financial help to the (then) Ministry of Social Security, one-fifth had asked for a home help and one-fifth for mobility aids. Other unmet requests had been for meals-on-wheels, chiropody, clothing and bedding, rehousing, transport, social visiting and institutional accommodation (the last was a particularly common request of people who felt they were a burden to their families). The usual reasons given for refusing aid were that the applicant did not qualify or that no service was available, although one in four of those refused said that no reason was given. One in five of the very severely handicapped thought the Social Services should do more to help them.

Who is left out?

Although increasing attention has been paid to the non-take-up of specific benefits in recent years, it has not focussed on particular client groups, except where a benefit such as the Attendance Allowance is designed to meet a specific need. The take-up of different benefits amongst handicapped people has not been thoroughly studied, and, of the surveys conducted by local authorities under the Chronically Sick and Disabled Persons Act 1970, only one or two have tried to focus on the take-up of specific benefits and services. Accordingly, considerations of take-up peculiar to handicapped people or to certain groups of handicapped people are still often shrouded in hearsay and conjecture.

In the London Borough of Newham, however, efforts have been made during the last few years to assess the types of disabled people who get left out of the system, using the annual 'flood studies' which make a 100 per cent coverage of the area of the borough which is below flood level. The number of disabled people known by the Newham Social Services Department doubled as a result of surveys carried out after the Chronically Sick and Disabled Persons Act. Non-take-up cases were found to be predominantly of two types. One category consisted of those people, such as the very elderly, who were experiencing a long-term and gradual disablement. For many of them, disability had begun prior to the introduction of the present system of benefits, or they were unaware of the benefits because these had not been available when they were younger and more likely to absorb information about them. Also, because they had experienced no abrupt cut-off point, such as having to retire early from work, these people had not been brought into sudden awareness of the constraints of disability. Many of them did not think of themselves as 'disabled' but as just suffering from 'old age'. This self-evaluation appears all too often to be reinforced by doctors with whom such people may occasionally come into contact. The second principal category of non-take-up cases was found to consist of people – almost always men – of working age with a family, who had suddenly become disabled (by a stroke, for instance, or by coronary thrombosis) and who had been unable to come to terms with the fact of their dependence in place of being the breadwinner, especially where the social mores and peer-group attitudes reinforced the importance of the role of the provider.

Take-up of cash benefits

Studies of the take-up of individual benefits have increased in the last few years, but there have been few studies of take-up of individual cash benefits by people with different degrees of handicap. In the 1971 OPCS Survey, Amelia Harris and her associated workers looked at the entitlement to Supplementary Benefits of impaired people in Great Britain. A few of the surveys conducted by local authorities in compliance with the Chronically Sick and Disabled Persons Act 1970 looked at the needs of these people for specific benefits, but only one of these (the 1972 Newcastle Stage 2 Survey) looked specifically at awareness and take-up of certain benefits. In this report, however, it is often not possible to differentiate between lack of knowledge of a benefit and non-response because of non-applicability; also the numbers of respondents taking up some of the benefits were so small that some of the take-up percentages appear distorted. The overall impression was that a large proportion of handicapped people knew of the benefits that were more generally available, but it was doubted whether 'full use is being made of special Supplementary Allowances, Attendance Allowances and Family Income Supplements' (page 72).

The remainder of this section reviews one by one the benefits for which attention has been given to take-up, giving specific information on take-up by people with disabilities where it is available.

Supplementary Benefits

Concern over the take-up of Supplementary Benefits by the disabled has been much more explicit than for other benefits. At the time of the OPCS Survey the Department of Health and Social Security wanted information about handicapped people with low incomes, particularly those who appeared to be entitled to Supplementary Benefits and who were not claiming, as well as about people only marginally above the Supplementary Benefit level. Therefore provision was made within the OPCS Survey to collect and analyse data on these areas. The survey work was conducted in 1968 and 1969 but the analysis was not published until 1972.

It was found that 26.4 per cent of the handicapped in the sample were receiving an income less than their assessed 'requirements'. This percentage was greatest amongst the very severely handicapped (categories 1 to 3), for whom it was 39.7 per cent. Of the impaired people in the sample 29.9 per cent were receiving Supplementary Benefit, 51.9 per cent were ineligible because their income was over the benefit level, 7.8 per cent were excluded because the relationship of their income to the benefit level was unknown, and 3.1 per cent were ineligible for other reasons (mainly for being full-time workers, married women whose husbands were in full-time work, or full-time students) despite their incomes being below the benefits level. This left 916 people (7.2 per cent) who might have been considered eligible, including 44 people who might have been considered eligible if certain 'disregards' applied.

Sex differences amongst the potentially eligible group of impaired people did not appear significant. Age differences were: just over 2 per cent of those aged 16 to 49 appeared to be eligible non-claimants, whereas the proportion was 5 per cent for the 50–64 age group, over 10 per cent for the 65–74 age group, and 8.5 per cent for those over 75. Degree of handicap also had some significance. Among the 16–49 age group, for all degrees of handicap the number potentially eligible regularly constituted about 3.3 per cent, whereas people with severe and very severe handicaps (categories 1–5) in the 50–64 age group constituted 6.5 per cent; for all groups of people classified as handicapped and between 65–74 years the figure was about 9.5 per cent. Among people over 75, however, there was a markedly higher proportion (10.5 per cent) of very severely handicapped people potentially eligible for Supplementary Benefits. People with mobility problems were especially common amongst non-claimants, as were widows, particularly those aged 65 or over.

Besides the methodological problems of estimating the likely national entitlement of impaired people to Supplementary Benefit, the researchers were faced with the difference between those who would have been likely to have claimed and those who would not.

It was estimated that 70,000 people in Britain were entitled and willing to claim, and 100,000 people were entitled but not willing to claim. Some of the major reasons given for non-claiming were that people believed themselves above the limit, or more often that they could 'manage' without. In some cases this appreciation that they were able to manage was the result of support from others, in others that they could 'scrape along'. It was concluded that

'People's ideas of an adequate income may vary according to the style of life they have been used to in the past. In some cases and in some areas individual old people who have been used to low wages and plain living may genuinely be able to manage without claiming benefit. However, in some cases there was a suggestion that things had had to be given up' (page 28).

The Newcastle Stage 2 Survey (1972) showed that 88 per cent of the chronically sick and disabled knew of Supplementary Benefits, and 64.1 per cent had received them, compared with 66.9 per cent who had applied at any time.

In November 1974 it was estimated that 2.68 million people were in regular receipt of Supplementary Benefits, which constituted an estimated take-up of 73 per cent. At the same time 260,000 sick and disabled people were receiving Supplementary Allowances out of a provision for 385,000 (i.e. 67.5 per cent). At December 1974 it was estimated that there were 550,000 people over pensionable age (in 450,000 families) who were not claiming Supplementary Benefit although their incomes were below the Supplementary Benefit level, and 850,000 people under pensionable age (in 470,000 families) in similar circumstances. Of these 850,000 people, 360,000 (in 130,000 families) were normally in full-time work, and were only temporarily sick or unemployed. The number who had been sick or disabled for more than three months was estimated to be 60,000 (in 20,000 families), compared with 110,000 (in 40,000 families) at December 1972. The reduction in the number of people in this category resulted from the introduction of overlapping benefits or their uprating, rather than from a reduction in need.

The survey by Audrey Hunt, *Families and their needs* (OPCS, 1973) was oriented to families in general rather than to people with disabilities, but it showed the extent of ignorance among different groups regarding Supplementary Benefits and other forms of financial assistance. In response to the question of what kinds of financial help are available to people in need, 21–32.6 per cent of fatherless families, 31.3–46.4 per cent of motherless families, and 32.7–44.6 per cent of two-parent families said that they did not know. Moreover, 29–44 per cent of single mothers did not know that they could receive Supplementary Benefit if they did a part-time job.

A study of the take-up of Supplementary Benefit amongst the elderly in Coventry in 1973 found that, out of 1,104 pensioners, 512 were in receipt of a Supplementary Pension, 299 knew they were ineligible and 281 had never applied. After the survey, 115 (just over 10 per cent) were referred to the DHSS and almost all of them were successful in obtaining help. This study concluded that the main reasons for not applying for a Supplementary Pension were dislike of 'charity', feelings of humiliation and resentment at having to undergo a means test, and the unfriendly attitude of the DHSS.

It is difficult to determine the extent of non-take-up of Supplementary Benefit by potentially eligible people with disabilities. According to the Family Expenditure Survey, the provision of alternative benefits in recent years has reduced those eligible to 60,000 people, but if the conclusions of the Amelia Harris study (OPCS, 1972) still apply, perhaps only 30,000 of these people would be willing to claim. The statistics, however, leave much to be desired as an accurate assessment.

Additional Supplementary Benefit Allowances

Knowledge and, accordingly, take-up of additional Supplementary Benefit allowances has been low in the past, partly because they have not been widely publicised by the Supplementary Benefits Commission. The onus of responsibility has been left firmly upon the potential claimant, and there has been little effort to make him aware of these allowances.

The Newcastle Stage 2 Survey (1972) showed that 42 per cent of the chronically sick and disabled sample were eligible for allowances and knew of them, but that only 12.8 per cent had applied at some time, and only 10.4 per cent had received them.

Coventry Community Development Project studied 'discretionary' payments in 1972 and 1973. The 1972 study, looking at Supplementary Benefit claimants under pensionable age, found that 75 per cent of respondents had not heard of Exceptional Circumstances Additions (ECAs) and that 95 per cent had not heard of Exceptional Needs Payments (ENPs). It was estimated that 25 per cent of respondents were eligible for ENPs but not claiming them, and 7.5 per cent were in a similar position regarding ECAs. The 1973 study looked at retirement pensioners claiming Supplementary Benefit, and estimated that 83 per cent of respondents had insufficient knowledge to make a reasonable application for an ENP, despite earlier publicity and information on discretionary payments.

The Grassmarket study in Edinburgh (1975) revealed that, amongst the single and homeless, a considerable number were not receiving the dietary supplements to which they were entitled. A major difficulty seemed to be that proof of illness is usually required by the DHSS before the dietary allowance is awarded, but only a low proportion of these people were registered with a doctor. (A recent Lothian Health Board survey showed that less than 40 per cent of the Edinburgh lodging-house population were permanently registered with a doctor inside the city.) Laundry allowances were also rarely awarded, although the need appeared to be present, particularly with the high incidence of enuresis (incontinence of urine) among this group. Many people were unaware of special allowances and payments, and those who did know were reluctant to claim, either because of hostility at the local DHSS offices to claimants for these benefits, or because of low expectations amongst these claimants.

In November 1974 there were 70,000 sick and disabled people claiming Exceptional Circumstances Additions out of a total of 260,000 sick and disabled claiming Supplementary Benefit. If the Coventry study can be used as a guide, this would mean that there may be about 20,000 sick and disabled people who are receiving Supplementary Benefits and are eligible for Exceptional Circumstances Additions, but who are not receiving them.

Family Income Supplement (FIS)

When the Family Income Supplement was introduced in 1971, the government set itself a target of an 85 per cent take-up rate. It was officially estimated that 165,000 people would be eligible, but in 1972 this figure was revised downwards to 140,000.

Up to the end of 1973 the highest number of recipients for any one quarter of the year was 106,000 (at 25 September 1973), and in many of these three-month periods the take-up did not exceed 50 per cent. More recently, official estimates have maintained that a two-thirds take-up was achieved in 1973 and a three-quarters take-up in 1974. These estimates have been greeted with some scepticism, as the numbers in receipt of FIS declined from 95,000 at the end of 1973 to 70,000 at the end of 1974 and 61,000 at the end of 1975. In April 1976, when the take-up was 59,000, Mr Orme, Minister for Social Security, said in the House of Commons:

'Estimates of the number of families eligible to receive FIS are based on limited information using the Family Expenditure Survey and are subject to wide margins of error'.

In 1974 there was also a drop in the number of claims for FIS, to 148,021 for the year, compared with 167,996 in 1973. It is difficult to ascertain whether the initial estimates of the numbers eligible for the benefit were much too high, or whether there still remains a marked non-take-up.

It is also difficult to know how many of these recipients and potential recipients are people with disabilities. In July 1972 a survey was conducted of two-parent families who were receiving FIS. They constituted 60,000 of the 95,000 currently receiving the benefit. In this sample, 7 per cent of the breadwinners were registered as disabled with the Department of Employment, representing about 4,200 recipients. In 1975 the number of two-parent families receiving FIS was about the same as the number of one-parent families doing so. The Newcastle Stage 2 Survey (1972), which was conducted just after FIS was introduced, found that the benefit was both known and applicable to only 14.2 per cent of the chronically sick and disabled respondents; only 1.7 per cent had ever applied for it and less than 1 per cent had received it.

Old Person's Pension

The take-up rate for the Old Person's Pension, payable to people over 80 years old, is very high. It was originally estimated that 150,000 pensioners would be eligible for this pension, and by the end of 1971 156,000 claims had been made. Evidently any distaste pensioners may have for some means-tested benefits does not extend to *all* benefits.

Free prescriptions

Knowledge about free prescriptions appears more widespread amongst people with disabilities than that about some other benefits. The Newcastle Stage 2 Survey (1972) showed that 97 per cent of the chronically sick and disabled sample knew of free medical prescriptions; 84.4 per cent had applied for them at some time, and 82.3 per cent had received them. 'Season tickets' for prescriptions were known to only 25 per cent; only 3.6 per cent had used them, but most of this group would qualify for free prescriptions.

In Molly Meacher's study in Islington (1972), however, 67 per cent of her sample were unaware of free prescriptions, 5 per cent were aware but thought themselves ineligible, 12 per cent were aware and considered themselves eligible but did not claim, and only 16 per cent claimed. Problems of form-filling and arranging visits, failure to recognise eligibility, and ignorance of the procedure for claiming seemed to be the three main reasons for the low take-up.

In reviewing the publicity regarding these benefits chemists were found to be generally helpful, but in some matters they were confused themselves. Post offices were not providing the requisite literature, and clerks in out-patient dispensing departments seemed unaware of exemptions, though they had been aware of the distress caused by prescription charges to some people. Often general practitioners prescribed only one item to low-income recipients although they regarded two or more items as necessary.

A high proportion of prescription charge waivers are passported through Supplementary Benefits or Family Income Supplement. In 1971, out of an estimated 990,000 people in receipt of free prescriptions, 865,000 were estimated to be receiving them on grounds of receipt of Supplementary Benefit and 62,000 on grounds of receipt of Family Income Supplement. When take-up of the passporting benefits is inadequate, of course, the low level of take-up is transferred to the prescription waivers.

During 1971, the government ran an extensive advertising campaign which increased the number of people receiving non-passported free prescriptions from 20,000 to 69,000. This number has, however, fallen markedly since then, and by 1975 it was down to 13,000, while the number of refunds made on grounds of low income declined from a peak of 17,000 in 1972 to only 5,000 in 1975. No official estimate has ever been given of the numbers eligible for free prescriptions on the grounds of low income.

Michael Meacher made estimates, based on the Islington survey, that by the end of 1971 the take-up rate was 49 per cent. This level also appears to have dropped again since. The Wandsworth People's Rights study showed the disparity of take-up between the different categories of claimants. Only 3.7 per cent of those eligible on a direct means test had claimed free prescriptions compared with 76.8 per cent of those who were passported, and 96.7 per cent of those claiming on grounds other than low income.

The Salop study 1975/76 (see page 187) found that, prior to the introduction of its single multi-purpose form, the non-take-up for free prescriptions was 67 per cent. After its introduction non-take-up fell to 42 per cent for those particularly concerned with Social Security benefits, but for people more specifically concerned with housing and education benefits it was nearly 80 per cent. Thus in this area the take-up of free prescriptions has increased only slightly since 1972. The respondents who had not claimed free prescriptions gave as reasons for not claiming: never heard of benefit (12–14 per cent); did not know enough about it (about 30 per cent); did not think they were entitled (about 35 per cent); and too much trouble or not worth it (about 20 per cent). Only a few gave the reason that they did not accept charity or that they were managing to pay without help.

The difference between the Newcastle study and the others is difficult to explain, except that a high proportion (64 per cent) of Newcastle respondents had received Supplementary Benefits, and so they would have been passported.

Free dental and optical treatment

The Newcastle Stage 2 Survey (1972) found that, of the chronically sick and disabled sample, 92 per cent knew of free dental and optical treatment, and that 67.4 per cent had received the benefit at some time, compared with 71.1 per cent who had applied for it at some time.

But, as with free prescriptions, Molly Meacher's study (1972) indicated a different situation in Islington where the take-up for free dental treatment was only 6 per cent. Fifty-eight per cent of the sample were unaware of the benefit, 10 per cent were aware but considered themselves ineligible, while 26 per cent were aware of the benefits and considered themselves possibly eligible but still did not claim. A basic problem was found to be resistance to visiting a dentist at all, as well as problems of form-filling and arranging visits, failure to recognise eligibility and ignorance of the procedure for claiming. Following the government advertising campaign in 1971 the take-up of exemption from optical charges increased from 48,097 to 180,000 between March and October 1971, and exemption from dental charges from 24,771 to 110,000 over the same period.

The Salop study in 1975/76 showed that non-take-up by people primarily inquiring about Social Security benefits was about 17–18 per cent for free dental treatment and 10–11 per cent for free optical treatment, but that for people primarily inquiring about housing and education benefits the corresponding figures were 61–82 per cent and 60–78 per cent. This appears to reveal some improvement in take-up of these benefits compared with earlier studies. In the Salop study the samples of respondents who had at no time claimed free dental or optical treatment were small, because take-up is fairly high. Of those who had not claimed for free dental treatment, about 65 per cent either did not know enough about it or did not think they were entitled. Amongst non-claimants of free optical treatment about 40 per cent felt they were not entitled, about 15 per cent did not know enough about it, and about 15 per cent were unaware of the benefits.

Since October 1974, the statistics for claims for remission from dental and optical charges have not isolated claims made by people in receipt of FIS or Supplementary Benefit. The total numbers of those receiving free dental treatment have fallen from a peak of 441,000 in 1972 to 366,460 in 1975, and those receiving free optical treatment from 808,000 in 1972 to 564,143 in 1975.

Rent Rebates and Allowances

In 1972 and 1973 considerable concern was expressed regarding the non-take-up of Rent Rebates and Rent Allowances for which the intention had been that the take-up should be 100 per cent. A study commissioned by the Birmingham City Council indicated that of those entitled to claim rent benefits, 50 per cent of council tenants and almost 80 per cent of private tenants in unfurnished accommodation failed to claim in 1973. During the 1972/73 period it was estimated that only 10 per cent of those entitled to do so actually claimed Rent

Allowances. Peter Taylor-Gooby estimated (November 1975) that in 1974 local government distributed £135 million in rent benefits, while a possible £120 million went unclaimed.

The Birmingham study drew attention to the inadequacies of the Department of the Environment's official estimates of eligibility for take-up of Rent Rebates based on Family Expenditure Survey data; for the period under review the Department estimated take-up by council tenants at 70 per cent, compared with Birmingham's own estimate of 50 per cent. The study also found that among council tenants take-up was lowest (33 per cent) for the 35–44 age group, but was as high as 93 per cent for the age group of 65 and over, and that this was partly because Supplementary Benefit recipients are passported to Rent Rebates. The Birmingham workers concluded (page 23) that 'among pensioners generally – at least those in municipal housing – there was more awareness of their right to Rent Rebate facilities than among other groups'. They also felt that misunderstandings and low expectations were of greater importance in non-take-up than direct feelings of stigma, although clear distinction between those two was not possible. Amongst the council tenants who were eligible but not claiming, the reasons given for non-take-up were:

did not know how to apply (54 per cent);
did not like asking for help (54 per cent);
objected to revealing details of circumstances (57 per cent);
preferred to manage without (41 per cent);
felt others in greater need (13 per cent);
expected rebate to be too small to be worth applying for (25 per cent).

Amongst pensioners in unfurnished accommodation, the take-up of Rent Rebates and Allowances was high (71 per cent) if people passported by Supplementary Benefits are included, but otherwise was much lower (35 per cent).

Amongst non-claiming private tenants, ignorance of how to apply and objections to revealing details of circumstances seemed more important reasons for non-take-up than amongst council tenants. Ignorance of eligibility was also common, particularly ignorance of the dependence of eligibility on such things as the number of a claimant's children and the amount of his income that is spent on rent, rather than on any absolute income levels. Amongst private tenants, ignorance of Rent Allowances was particularly marked. The researchers also concluded that 'the elderly were more likely than other tenants to feel that claiming for rebates or allowances incurred a loss of pride, self-respect or independence; that they 'would rather manage without' was a very commonly offered (and unprompted) reason why they had not considered applying and why they thought others did not apply (page 97). The Haringey Action Research project conducted in 1973 and 1974 found that retirement pensioners responded to publicity better than other groups.

During the first half of 1975, according to official estimates, 70–75 per cent of all those eligible were receiving a Rent Rebate, but only 30–35 per cent of eligible tenants of unfurnished premises were receiving a Rent Allowance, and only 10 per cent of those in furnished accommodation. The only indication that the official estimates may be more accurate than in 1973 is the Salop study 1975/76, which showed that only between 2 and 7 per cent of eligible respondents who were primarily enquiring about housing benefits had not claimed; and only 18–20 per cent of others who were eligible but were primarily concerned with educational and Social Security benefits had not taken up Rent Rebates and Allowances. The number claiming Rent Rebates in April 1976 was officially estimated at 930,000 compared with 844,000 in April 1975, while the number in unfurnished accommodation claiming Rent Allowances increased from 150,000 in April 1975 to 180,000 in April 1976. The number in furnished accommodation claiming Rent Allowances in 1976 was estimated at 11,000.

It appears from these studies that people with disabilities might be amongst those who are more likely to claim Rent Rebates and Allowances, since older people and people on Supplementary Benefit tend to claim more readily than others, and to be more aware of these benefits. The Newcastle study (1972) looked at the take-up of Rent Rebates by the chronically sick and disabled. At that time, however, Rent Rebates in Newcastle only applied to tenants in local authority housing, although other tenants were due to become eligible in 1973. The survey showed that almost all of the chronically sick and disabled council tenants were aware of Rent Rebates, and that about a quarter of them had applied at some time, but that only about a fifth of them were currently receiving them. It is difficult to compare the likelihood of eligibility of the chronically sick and disabled with other groups; but if the Birmingham study is correct in its assumption that 60 per cent of council tenants (including those receiving Supplementary Benefits) are eligible for Rent Rebates and Allowances, then the proportions of the disabled taking up the benefits may be low, even though their awareness of the existence of the benefit may be high. Unfortunately the depth of study into the circumstances of people with disabilities is far from adequate as far as this benefit is concerned.

Rate Rebates

There has been more research into non-take-up of Rate Rebates than for some other benefits, but hardly any of it looks specifically at non-take-up by people with disabilities. Molly Meacher's study of Rate Rebates in Islington (1972) was the first systematic study of the effectiveness of this benefit.

Rate Rebates were introduced in 1966, and at first the take-up rates were higher than they have been since, mainly because of the initial publicity. In 1966/67, 859,000 Rate Rebates were granted: since then the numbers have stabilised at between 785,000 and 810,000 (about 50 per cent take-up), but in 1972/73 (partly because of the government publicity campaign) they increased to 905,423, of which 85 per cent were taken up by people who were wholly or partly retired. Those receiving rebates represented 5.4 per cent of all domestic ratepayers in England and Wales, 7 per cent of all owner-occupiers, 3.2 per cent of all local authority tenants and 2.3 per cent of other indirect private ratepayers (mainly private tenants). The highest percentage of Rate Rebate recipients were found in seaside resorts and the lowest percentage in the poorest areas of the country.

In 1972/73, before the advertising campaign, the overall take-up rate was only 12 per cent. After the campaign it increased to 19 per cent. Amongst eligible retirement pensioners it increased from 15 to 23 per cent. Pensioners who were private tenants were found to be much less likely to claim than other types of occupiers.

Before the advertising campaign, 82 per cent of respondents had been unaware of rebates, and 6 per cent had been aware but not claiming. (The control study had similar findings.) After the campaign, 39 per cent were still unaware of rebates; 25 per cent were aware but thought the scheme irrelevant to themselves, while 17 per cent were aware and realised that the rebates were relevant to themselves, but still did not claim.

Awareness was increased by the advertising campaign, but the degree of understanding of the eligibility criteria increased only from about 10 to about 20 per cent. After the campaign, still only 15 per cent of eligible non-claimants realised that £1,000 savings does not automatically preclude eligibility, 27 per cent realised that tenants may be entitled to the rebate, only 40 per cent knew where to claim, and only 18 per cent were clear on general knowledge of the eligibility criteria.

The most frequently cited reason for failure to claim Rate Rebates, once full awareness of entitlement had been established, was the low value of the potential gain, particularly where the size of the accommodation and hence the rebate was small (over half of the cases), where three or more adults lived in one household, thus reducing the reckonable rate upon which a Rate Rebate was calculated (about a third of cases), and where the income of the householder only slightly exceeded the eligibility limit, resulting in a very small rebate.

Fears of the administrative performance associated with applying, and limited articulateness, presented some problems and, amongst elderly people, questions of stigma also arose. Follow-up interviews showed that 5 per cent of householders entitled to rebates would not claim because of their anxiety about upsetting the landlord or their fear of local officials.

One interviewer concluded that a number of people rendered themselves ineligible because of their strong desire for self-sufficiency which drove them to extra work despite the hardship this caused, and that it is because so many families are so self-reliant and so concerned to be responsible for their own economic needs, even at the cost of many hours of overtime, that so few families are among those in the sample of persons eligible for Rate Rebates (Molly Meacher, *Rate Rebates* 1972, page 69).

In Kirklees, a campaign to improve the take-up rate of Rate Rebates from the existing level of 34 per cent had a small but significant effect, but council initiatives in combining Rate and Rent Rebate procedures were found to be more effective in increasing take-up than the publicity campaign.

A new national Rate Rebate scheme was introduced in April 1974, based on the same needs allowances and general principles of calculation as the rent benefit scheme. In 1974/75 it was estimated that 3.50 million ratepayers were eligible for a Rate Rebate, of whom about 2.45 million (70 per cent) claimed.

The work in Kirklees in 1975 indicates a low take-up of Rate Rebates by private tenants who pay their rates inclusively with rent to their landlords. The Salop study 1975/76 indicated that the non-take-up of Rate Rebates was between 10 and 32 per cent, and, if these figures are reliable, it would appear that actual take-up rates and official estimates now correspond more closely.

The Newcastle Stage 2 Survey (1972) found that about 60 per cent of the chronically sick and disabled in their sample were both eligible for and knew of Rate Rebates although only 9.9 per cent had received the benefit at any time, compared with 14.2 per cent who had applied at any time. These differences were assumed to be the result of many respondents currently receiving Supplementary Benefit, thus automatically making them eligible for Rate Rebate.

Peter Taylor-Gooby estimated in 1975 that local government distributed £85 million in Rate Rebates during 1974, and that a possible £60 million went unclaimed.

As no comparative studies of take-up of Rate Rebates have been undertaken since the introduction of the new scheme in April 1974 and none of the recent surveys of chronically sick and disabled persons has looked at take-up of this benefit, it is difficult to assess the present extent of non-take-up of Rate Rebates by people with disabilities.

Educational benefits

Molly Meacher's study (1972) found that 68 per cent of those eligible for free school meals and 37 per cent of those eligible for school clothing allowances were receiving them. Six per cent of those eligible for free school meals were unaware of the benefit, 11 per cent were aware but thought themselves ineligible, and 15 per cent were aware, realised the benefit was relevant to themselves but still did not claim. For school clothing allowance, 40 per cent of those eligible were unaware of the benefit, none were classified as aware but believing themselves ineligible, but 23 per cent were aware, realised the benefit was relevant to themselves, yet still did not claim.

All the families who were unaware of free school meals were non-British, and had severe language problems. Altogether 16 per cent of eligible families were foreign. Of the British non-claimants, half did not realise they were eligible, but half would not claim because of stigma, a desire for independence or a dislike of form-filling. Among the non-claimants nearly one-third were single-parent families and a further two-fifths were two-parent families who had suffered sickness and unemployment for the whole 26 week period studied. It was felt that these two groups had been missed out in promotional campaigns.

The comparatively high take-up for both these benefits is attributed partly to the value of the benefit, which makes it worth claiming, partly to families being put off less by questions of stigma or diminished independence and partly to the direct contact which most parents have with authorities in the field of education, which may help to overcome ignorance or language problems. Officially the national take-up of free school meals has been estimated at 80 per cent, but this has been challenged, particularly as children who do not take school dinners at all are not included in the base for the estimate (in Kirklees this constitutes 35 per cent of the school children). After families claiming Family Income Supplement and Supplementary Benefits were passported for educational benefits in 1971 the take-up improved in some areas.

Parents with disabilities have not been analysed separately from the point of view of take-up. In 1972, however, it was found that of the families with sick men in them who were receiving Supplementary Benefit, 32 per cent were not claiming free school meals; this was the highest percentage of non-claimants amongst the groups isolated. The numbers in receipt of free school meals have fluctuated from year to year. They fell from 850,000 in 1972 to 750,000 in 1974, and rose again slightly in 1975 to 784,000 (9.3 per cent of pupils).

In some areas recipients of free school meals are also reviewed for school clothing grants. The Educational Welfare Officers who decide on the allocation of school clothing grants often have close contacts with the Supplementary Benefits Commission, and may at times try to secure its support in the form of Exceptional Needs Payments for clothing under the 1966 Social Security Act.

In his article of November 1975, Peter Taylor-Gooby maintained that in 1974, local government distributed £30 million in free school meals and clothing grants, and that £15 million went unclaimed.

Attendance Allowance

The Attendance Allowance was introduced in 1971, and was at first paid only to people who needed round-the-clock attendance. In 1972, a lower (two-thirds) rate was introduced, payable to people needing attendance by day *or* by night. By 30 June 1976, the allowance was being paid to 230,000 handicapped people of all ages (130,000 at the higher and 100,000 at the lower rate).

The Family Fund study

In 1974, the Family Fund Research Project studied the take-up of Attendance Allowance by families with handicapped children who were in contact with the Family Fund. It found that these families had heard about the allowance mainly through the press, television and radio (26 per cent), relatives and friends (17 per cent), social workers (17.6 per cent) and voluntary societies (10 per cent). The limited official publicity for this benefit was criticised by some of the respondents, even though £180,000 had been spent on it in 1973/74.

The study looked at 92 individual non-applicants for the Attendance Allowance, and it concluded (page 4) that non-application was

'the product of a set of complicated interactions between social class, family composition and handicap types which needs further investigation, the question being further complicated by age-related differences in the attendance needs of different handicaps and the stresses these impose on families at different times'.

Almost half of the non-applicants had not known of the Attendance Allowance before being asked by the members of the research project. Of those that had known, 37 responded to being asked why they had not applied; 21 of them wrote that they did not think they were eligible, 9 that they did not know how to apply or where to get or send forms, and 5 that they had been told that they were probably ineligible. Two were opposed to the benefit.

Differences between the applicants and non-applicants for the Attendance Allowance for children in relation to applications for a variety of other benefits were not statistically significant; but fewer non-applicants had contacts with other families who had applied for Attendance Allowance. The researchers concluded (page 79) that despite the comparatively high number of agencies with which they were in contact, the non-applicants had a surprising gap in their knowledge of the Attendance Allowance and had been prevented from applying by ignorance of its existence or its eligibility criteria, by failure to identify themselves as potential recipients or by their inability to cope with the details of obtaining, completing and returning application forms. It seemed that non-applicants were distinguishable from applicants by their lesser knowledge of helping agencies and by a less successful record of contact with them, and that they also were less knowledgeable about other possible sources of help in financial crisis, although no one of these differences was particularly important.

An unwillingness to apply was recognised in families of children with certain diseases or handicaps, particularly deafness or heart disease (Tables 4.6 and 4.7). These families were less likely to be awarded the benefit than those with a spina bifida child, but the difference in success in application was not in itself big enough to justify non-application, and it was concluded (page 80) that

'deaf children and others with the handicaps that figure prominently in the non-applicant population, have a better chance of success than many of their parents believe, and should be encouraged to apply and helped with reviews and appeals'.

The Family Fund researchers concluded that better publicity was needed, and that it could perhaps best be concentrated through hospitals, welfare clinics and special schools, and that social workers, doctors and health visitors should be encouraged to assume more responsibility for communicating information about this and other benefits to likely recipients. They also considered (page 81) that

'supplies of application forms could perhaps be made available in the places where there is publicity together with information about criteria, and help with completing application forms and preparing review submissions'

Table 4.6 Attendance Allowance applications and non-applications for children, related to handicapping disorders

Handicap	No. of people applying	% of total	No. of people not applying	% of total
Cancers	18	78.3	5	21.7
Haemophilia	26	44.1	33	55.9
Mental illness	725	90.6	75	9.4
Mental subnormality	1,965	88.9	246	11.1
Cerebral palsy	1,491	90.1	163	9.9
Epilepsy	164	83.7	32	16.3
Other central nervous system diseases	54	83.1	11	16.9
Congenital heart disease	72	59.0	50	41.0
Cystic fibrosis	45	60.0	30	40.0
Digestive diseases	14	58.3	10	41.7
Kidney/bladder	10	45.5	12	54.5
Blindness	139	57.4	103	42.6
Deafness	112	33.0	227	67.0
Muscular dystrophy	246	86.3	39	13.7
Bone diseases	67	79.8	17	20.2
Spina bifida	1,848	93.4	130	6.6
Other congenital malformations	187	62.5	112	37.5

Source: Family Fund Research Project Report (November 1974), Appendix page xiii

Table 4.7 Attendance Allowance awards to handicapped children, related to handicapping disorders

Handicap	Total applications	High rate	%	Low rate	%	Refused	%	Pending	%
Haemophilia	26	8	30.8	5	19.2	5	19.2	8	30.8
Mental illness	725	539	74.3	120	16.6	17	2.3	49	6.8
Mental subnormality	1,965	1,411	71.8	326	16.6	60	3.1	168	8.5
Cerebral palsy	1,491	1,132	75.9	195	13.1	45	3.0	119	8.0
Epilepsy	164	120	73.1	26	15.9	7	4.3	11	6.7
Congenital heart disease	72	35	48.6	17	23.6	7	9.7	13	18.0
Blindness	139	82	59.0	27	19.4	13	9.4	17	12.2
Deafness	112	52	46.4	23	20.5	13	11.6	24	21.4
Muscular dystrophy	246	178	72.4	31	12.6	9	3.7	28	11.4
Bone diseases	67	48	71.6	9	13.4	5	7.5	5	7.5
Spina bifida	1,848	1,499	81.1	184	10.0	37	2.0	12	15.1
Other congenital malformations	187	103	55.0	2	15.0	31	16.6	25	13.4
Total	7,042	5,207		991		249		595	

Source: Family Fund Research Project Report (November 1974), Appendix page xii

but that

'until we know more about the prevalence of severe handicap among children the size of the non-application problem cannot be measured.'

The researchers prompted 41 non-applicants to apply for the allowance, of whom 25 were successful, while decisions on a further 8 were still pending at the time of their report.

By April 1974, 50,000 applications for Attendance Allowance had been made on behalf of children. By June 1975 22,247 children were receiving the high rate and 14,281 the lower rate; the official estimates had been 10,000 and 50,000 respectively. It was estimated that another 42,000 severely disabled children existed, who either were not technically eligible, or were eligible but had failed to apply, or had been turned down and had failed to ask for a review. The Family Fund researchers suggest (page 3 of their 1976 report) that 'at least 10 per cent of families with very severely handicapped children known to them are eligible for and have not applied for the Attendance Allowance', and that since the Family Fund may attract 'claimers', this proportion may be even greater in the community at large.

They also compared the regional take-up of Attendance Allowance with Family Fund applications in each region on the assumption that, if there were marked differences, these were more likely to be due to variations in factors affecting take-up than to variations of severe handicap prevalences. Their results are set out in Table 4.8; they show that although there is a fairly strong relation between the two sets of data for most regions, more claims are made to the Family Fund from some regions, such as Scotland, than for the Attendance Allowance.

They also found that the Northern Region, Yorkshire and Humberside, Manchester and South London have a significantly greater proportion of payments at the higher rate, compared with the West Midlands, South West, Merseyside and Northern Ireland, which have a greater proportion at the lower rate. This suggests that some regional differences exist in the criteria for eligibility.

Estimates for all ages of the numbers eligible for Attendance Allowance have been too low, and successful applications have been much more plentiful than was expected. By June 1976, almost five years after the higher-rate benefit was introduced, the numbers seemed to have stabilised, perhaps because they already contained a good proportion of those eligible, or there may have been a decline in applications attributable to a decrease in publicity. New awards for the lower-rate benefit were still being made at a steady rate, indicating perhaps that the non-take-up for the lower-rate benefit was still considerable.

The long period of time needed to secure a full take-up reflects inadequacy in the publicity and in the administrative structure deployed to deal with the

Table 4.8 Attendance Allowance awards to handicapped children, related to geographical region

| Region | Population under 16 | Attendance Allowance June 1975 ||||||| Percentage receiving higher rate | Family Fund June 1975 ||
| | | Higher rate || Lower rate || Total || | | |
			Per '000 pop.		Per '000 pop.		Per '000 pop.			Per '000 pop.
Northern	847,017	1,610	1.90	804	0.95	2,414	2.85	66.69	1,649	1.95
Yorks and Humberside	1,184,603	2,096	1.77	1,257	1.06	3,353	2.83	62.51	2,006	1.69
E. Midlands and E. Anglia	1,299,494	2,097	1.61	1,397	1.08	3,494	2.69	60.02	2,285	1.76
London N.	1,316,475	1,930	1.47	1,190	0.90	3,120	2.37	61.86	2,019	1.53
London W.	1,388,253	2,001	1.44	1,350	0.97	3,351	2.41	59.71	2,221	1.60
S. Western	941,925	1,340	1.42	948	1.01	2,288	2.43	58.57	1,609	1.71
Wales	685,285	1,247	1.82	877	1.28	2,124	3.10	58.71	1,665	2.43
W. Midlands	1,348,817	2,099	1.56	1,668	1.24	3,767	2.79	55.72	2,290	1.70
N. Western (Manchester)	749,117	1,745	2.33	945	1.26	2,690	3.59	64.87	1,526	2.04
Scotland	1,462,080	1,817	1.24	1,121	0.77	2,938	2.01	61.84	2,651	1.81
N. Western (Merseyside)	1,059,672	1,939	1.83	1,401	1.32	3,340	3.15	58.05	2,052	1.94
London S.	1,397,052	2,326	1.66	1,323	0.95	3,649	2.61	63.74	2,509	1.80
N. Ireland	483,855	1,103	2.28	785	1.62	1,888	3.90	58.42	1,501	3.10
All regions	14,163,645	23,350	1.65	15,066	1.06	38,416	2.71	60.78	25,983	1.83

Source: Family Fund Report (February 1976), page 4

benefit. The eventual high take-up of Attendance Allowance compared with some other benefits appears to have stemmed less from official publicity than from the widespread publicity of certain disputed cases and from publicity by disability organisations and by individuals concerned with welfare rights.

Mobility Allowance

From the time claims for Mobility Allowance were first taken up (January 1976) to August 1976, over 53,000 claims were made, but of these only 37,000 were from people in eligible age groups. By 9 September 1976, 25,000 awards had been made to people between 15 and 50 years old. Thus out-of-phase claims (i.e. claims by people in age bands not yet eligible to claim) and claims by ineligible age groups account for 16,000 out of the total. This considerable incidence of incorrect claims may partly be explained by ignorance on the part of potential recipients of the claiming procedure and the eligibility criteria.

It may also, however, reflect the efforts of older claimants to secure the allowance before they become ineligible by reaching retirement age. In addition, some claimants may feel that their need is pressing and immediate, especially if they are struggling to hold down a job, but incur considerable cost in travelling to work.

It was originally estimated that by the end of the three-year phasing-in period 150,000 people would have been eligible for Mobility Allowance, of whom 50,000 would have been beneficiaries under the Invalid Vehicle Scheme. On 31 December 1975 there were estimated to be 40,000 people with three-wheelers supplied by the DHSS or with Private Car Allowances instead, and many of these may opt for Mobility Allowance at a later stage. It is not clear, however, how many of these people are above or approaching retirement age.

One DHSS civil servant involved with Mobility Allowance maintained that 'we have no indication as to how many might claim' out of those eligible for the allowance.

Take-up of local authority services

House adaptations

Part 2 of the 1971 OPCS Survey reported that the proportion of people having had housing adaptations was greater for every type of adaptation for people who were on the local authority register than for people who were not. Moreover, for all adaptations, except for the replacement of coal fires, a much higher proportion of people who were registered had had free adaptations compared with unregistered people.

It was also found that four out of every five people who said they would like adaptations had not attempted to obtain them. Their reasons are set out in Table 4.10; the main reasons are 'cost' and 'never bothered', but some of the other answers are more vague. Of those registered, 13 per cent 'did not like to

Table 4.9 Summary of take-up of cash benefits

Benefit	Estimates of numbers eligible	Take-up	Take-up rate	Sources
Sickness Benefit		about 4.5 million claims per year for claims of 2 weeks duration or more		*Financial provisions for handicapped people in the UK*, Sept. 1976 (*FPHPUK*) p.8
Invalidity Benefit		450,000 (Sept. 1976)		*FPHPUK* p.8
Invalidity Allowance		337,500 (Sept. 1976)		based on information in *FPHPUK* p.8
Non-Contributory Invalidity Pension		129,000 (June 1976)		*FPHPUK* p.8; letter from B McGinnis, July 1976
Industrial Disablement Pension		430,000 (Sept. 1976)		*FPHPUK* p.11
Unemployability Supplement		11,500 (Sept. 1976)		*FPHPUK* pp.10–11
Special Hardship Allowance		140,000 (Sept. 1976)		*FPHPUK* pp.10–11
Exceptionally Severe Disablement Allowance		1,400 (Sept. 1976)		*FPHPUK* pp.10–11
Constant Attendance Allowance		9,500 (Sept. 1976)		*FPHPUK* pp.10–11
War Disablement Pensions		320,000 (end of 1975)		letter from B McGinnis, July 1976
Family Income Supplement	165,000 (1971) original DHSS estimate	71,000 (Dec. 1971)	43% (1971)	CPAG Nov. 1974; Ruth Lister
	140,000 (1972) revised DHSS estimate	100,000 (June 1972)	71% (1972)	CPAG Nov. 1974; Ruth Lister
	93,000 (1974) presumed revised DHSS estimate based on alleged take-up rate	70,000 (Dec. 1974) 59,000 (April 1976)	75% (1974)	CPAG *Poverty*, summer 1976 Hansard, 30.6.75 Hansard, 29.4.76
Retirement Pension		8 million (of which about ⅓ of those aged 65–74 and ½ of those aged 75 and over are handicapped)		*FPHPUK* p.9
Old Person's Pension	150,000 (original DHSS estimate)	156,000 (end of 1971)	104%	CPAG Nov. 1974; Ruth Lister

Benefit	Estimates of numbers eligible	Take-up	Take-up rate	Sources
Attendance Allowance (higher rate = HR) (lower rate = LR)	HR 50,000 (original DHSS estimate) HR (children only) 10,000 LR (children only) 50,000 (original DHSS estimate)	HR 117,726 (end of 1974) HR 127,000 (Sept. 1976) LR 69,441 (end of 1974) LR 94,000 (Sept. 1976) HR 22,247 } (June 1975) LR 14,281 }		DHSS, *Social Security statistics 1975*; *FPHPUK* p.9 Family Fund Research Project Report, Feb. 1976
Invalid Care Allowance		3,000 (Sept. 1976)		*FPHPUK* p.9
Mobility Allowance	150,000 (original DHSS estimate; includes 50,000 then receiving help through the Vehicle Service)	25,000 (Sept. 1976) (benefit being phased in)		*FPHPUK* p.10 letter from D M Woolley, Sept. 1976
Supplementary Benefit	70,000 outstanding impaired people eligible and willing to claim (1969) 100,000 outstanding impaired people eligible but unwilling to claim (1969) 60,000 sick and disabled for more than 3 months eligible but not claiming (Dec. 1974)	260,000 sick and disabled (Nov. 1974)	73% (overall) (Nov. 1974)	CPAG *Poverty*, summer 1976 Amelia Harris Part III study, 1972
Exceptional Circumstances Additions (ECAs)		70,000 sick and disabled (Nov. 1974)		CPAG *Poverty*, summer 1976
Free prescriptions		990,000 (1971) of which 865,000 passported through Supplementary Benefit; 62,000 passported through FIS; 63,000 non-passported 13,000 non-passported (1975)	49% (end of 1971) (estimate from Islington study)	CPAG Nov. 1974; Ruth Lister CPAG *Poverty*, summer 1976 Molly Meacher (1972)
Remission of dental (DC) and optical charges (OC)	OC 48,097 (Mar. 1971) (excluding those passported) OC 180,000 (Oct. 1971) (excluding those passported) OC 808,000 (1972)			Molly Meacher (1972) CPAG Nov. 1974; Ruth Lister

Benefit	Estimates of numbers eligible	Take-up	Take-up rate	Sources
	OC 564,143 (1975) DC 24,771 (Mar. 1971) (excluding those passported) DC 110,000 (Oct. 1971) (excluding those passported) DC 441,000 (1972) DC 366,460 (1975)			CPAG *Poverty*, summer 1976
Rent Rebates		844,000 (April 1975) 930,000 (April 1976)	50% (council tenants) (1972–73) 40% (private tenants in unfurnished accommodation) (1972–73) 70% (council tenants) (1972–73) 70–75% (first half of 1975)	Birmingham study (1975) Haringey study (1976) Official estimate
Rent Allowance		'unfurnished' tenants 150,000 (April 1973) 180,000 (April 1976) 'furnished' tenants 11,000 (April 1976)	10% (1972–73) 30–35% ('unfurnished' tenants) (first half of 1975) 10% ('furnished' tenants) (first half of 1975)	CPAG *Poverty*, summer 1976 Official estimates
Rate Rebates	3.5 million (1974/75) (official estimate)	2.45 million (1974/75)	12% (Islington study, 1972)	Molly Meacher (1972)

163

Benefit	Estimates of numbers eligible	Take-up	Take-up rate	Sources
Free school meals		750,000 (1974) 784,000 (1975)	34% (Kirklees study) (1975) 70% (1974/75) (official estimate) 68% 1972 80% 1975 94% 1976	Batley study (1975) CPAG *Poverty*, summer 1976 Molly Meacher (1972) Official estimate Salop study (1976)
School clothing grants			37% (1972) (Islington study) 45% (1976) (Salop study)	CPAG *Poverty*, summer 1976
Employment Grants		313 (1975/76)		

164

Table 4.10 Reasons for handicapped people who wanted housing modifications not applying for them, related to registration with a local authority (%)

Reason	Registered	Not registered	All
Moving	3	5	5
Impracticable (dwelling condemned, etc.)	6	8	8
Has not the space	2	3	3
Not really necessary	4	5	5
Necessity has only just arisen	7	1	2
Never bothered and does not know why	22	28	27
Intends to ask	7	4	4
Not owner or tenant	1	4	4
No use asking landlord	2	4	4
Does not like to ask	13	3	3
Would make too much mess	—	1	1
Too occupied in other ways	1	1	1
Cannot afford the cost	24	30	29
Says authorities are no good	13	10	10
Does not know where to go	5	5	5
Does not know what is available	3	3	3
Other answers	4	4	4
No. on which % based	163	1,789	1,952[1,2]

[1] Excludes seven not answering
[2] Percentages add to more than 100 as more than one reason may be given
Source: OPCS Study (1971), Part 2, page 102

ask' for adaptations, which suggested that they felt they were already making too great a demand on the authorities, or that the authorities were discouraging.

Rehousing

The Newcastle Survey (1972) found that 30 per cent of the chronically sick and disabled respondents stated that they would have liked to move but were unable to, but that only 15.8 per cent of these had applied to Newcastle council for rehousing within the preceding five years. The reasons for non-take-up were not studied.

Judith Buckle's study (1971) attempted to analyse the non-take-up of rehousing. She found that 18 per cent of very severely disabled, 20 per cent of severely disabled (group 4) and 28 per cent of severely and appreciably disabled (groups 5 and 6) wanted to move. Only 38 per cent of these 'potential movers' had become 'active movers', however, by applying for local authority rehousing, and 23 per cent of these 'active movers' had not applied within the last five years. Efforts to be rehoused in non-local authority housing were not analysed.

The reasons why 'potential movers' did not apply for local authority rehousing are set out in Table 4.11. It shows that 29 per cent did not want local authority housing (presumably they wanted private housing) and that 29 per cent maintained that they had not bothered, but 15 per cent also felt they were ineligible and 12 per cent felt that the waiting list would exclude them. The study tried to isolate reasonable demands for rehousing from others. They accepted the following reasons as valid for reasonable demand:
a. the accommodation is being demolished;
b. the accommodation is in bad condition or lacks amenities;
c. the impaired person cannot manage the stairs or steps;
d. the impaired person is unable to manage because of the house itself;
e. the impaired person lives alone and is too far from relatives.

Only 56 per cent of people who desired to move were considered under these criteria to have reasonable demands.

Of the 'active movers', 23 per cent had been offered accommodation and refused. The reasons given for their refusal are set out in Table 4.12. 'Difficult access to shops' and 'dislikes area' are two major categories of reasons given, but other reasons were quite varied, and a considerable number of people were concerned about room size, access or stairs.

It has been suggested that the availability or non-availability of adaptation can affect demands for rehousing. However, the cross-categorisation of adaptations with demands for rehousing did not reveal any significant differences. This may be in part because, even with adaptations, the housing still presented difficulties, so that adaptations were seen as a second-best or stop-gap while hoping for rehousing.

It has been found in recent years that where housing has been specially provided for disabled people, suitable tenants have sometimes not been forthcoming, or the accommodation has been refused by those considered suitable. This non-take-up often reflects an inadequacy in the matching of proposed accommodation with the people who are likely to use it, and also a lack of communication between the administration and potential clients at early stages in the planning. Questions of mobility, access, proximity to hospital, social links and employment constraints all contribute to non-take-up, particularly when the people needing housing feel that if they accept accommodation which is inadequate for their needs, although better than what they have, they may prejudice their chances of being rehoused somewhere more suitable in the future.

Telephones

The 1971 OPCS Survey found that 74 per cent of handicapped respondents did not have telephones, and 69 per cent of the very severely handicapped, 36 per cent of the severely handicapped and 26 per cent of the appreciably handicapped felt they could not use telephones. The two major causes of inability to use telephones appeared to be hearing impairment and very restricted mobility. It was considered, however, that some people without telephones over-estimated their inability to use one.

Table 4.11 Reasons for handicapped people not applying to local authority for rehousing related to age-group (%)

Reason	Age group 16–29	30–49	50–64	65–74	75 and over	All ages
Does not want local authority housing	36	35	29	26	27	29
Wants to move out of area	10	8	7	5	8	7
Thinks ineligible	19	16	16	15	10	15
Waiting list	9	15	11	12	13	12
Not well enough	—	1	1	4	2	2
Cannot afford it	5	8	10	11	7	9
Has not bothered	26	24	30	33	27	29
Waiting to be rehoused	—	3	4	2	3	3
Has to move	—	—[1]	—[1]	1	—[1]	—[1]
Will apply	2	2	3	2	2	2
Reluctant to apply	—	1	1	—	2	1
Does not want to leave area	2	2	2	3	6	3
Does not want to leave family	7	3	3	4	7	4
Dislikes estates	—	1	—[1]	1	—	1
No pets allowed	—	—	—[1]	—	3	1
Other answers	4	4	4	4	4	4
No. on which % based	57	338	646	574	252	1,867

[1] Less than 0.5 per cent
Percentages add to more than 100 as more than one reason may be given
Source: J Buckle (1971), page 14

Table 4.12 Reasons for refusing accommodation offered to handicapped people by local authorities (%)

Reason	%
Flat in multi-storey block	9
Stairs/too many stairs	9
Access to shops difficult	21
Too far from family	11
Dislikes area	24
Dislikes heating system	2
Too expensive	7
Too small	7
Other answers	15
No. on which % based	262

Percentages add to more than 100 as more than one reason may be given
Source: J Buckle (1971), page 113

In the Newcastle Survey (1972), 46 per cent of handicapped people maintained that they would like a telephone in the Stage 2 interviews, although a much smaller number had expressed the same desire in reply to the Stage 1 postal questionnaire. One of the justifications for installing telephones has been the need for people to attract attention in an emergency. In the Stage 2 Survey, however, 73 per cent of chronically sick or disabled people said that they were able to attract attention in an emergency, although 36 per cent felt an alarm would be useful. The desire for a telephone by people with disabilities is not always tied closely to emergency need; where telephones are available the demand is considerable. The difficulties lie more in the assessment of eligibility, in the feasibility of alternatives and in supply, than in take-up.

Meals-on-wheels

The Newcastle Stage 2 Survey (1972) showed that almost 99 per cent of the chronically sick and disabled were aware of what the meals-on-wheels service provides, but less than 6 per cent had received its help. Two-thirds of the sample currently receiving the service wanted more help, and one-sixth of them felt the service could be improved. Thirty-one people, about 7 per cent of the sample not getting the service, wanted it. Of these 31 people, 16 could prepare their meals without difficulty, and 10 could do local shopping without difficulty; but 11 were totally dependent on others for shopping and 5 of them needed help with shopping. Non-take-up does not appear to be a major problem regarding meals-on-wheels; greater difficulties seem to arise because of the restricted availability of the service, and in decisions whether it is the most appropriate service for a particular person's need.

Home helps

The basic study on home helps is still the survey conducted by Audrey Hunt and Judith Fox in 1967, *The Home Help Service in England and Wales* (1970). This survey found that 94 per cent of housewives in the sample selected had heard of the Home Help Service, if the service was included in the list of welfare and health services provided by their authority. The extent of knowledge of the Home Help Service on the part of those who had no personal experience of it was found to be much lower amongst people over the age of 65 years, and amongst men responsible for most domestic tasks (referred to as 'male housewives' by Hunt and Fox). Of 57 people found in their general survey to be in need of the service (need being defined by the current level of provision within the service), 14 were chronically sick. Of the 57, 21 said they did not want any help in spite of their difficulties (9 were already receiving help from family or friends outside the household, but 12 were not). The reasons for this non-take-up were not explored further.

The Newcastle Stage 2 Survey (1972) showed that over 95 per cent of the chronically sick and disabled sample knew about the Home Help Service and what it provides, and that about 20 per cent had at some time received help from it. A third of those receiving help maintained they would like more help, but the questioning appears to have been loaded. Satisfaction with the service appeared to be high, although again the questioning seems loaded. Forty-one people (about 12 per cent of the sample) who were not getting a home help would have liked one; of these, 14 were living alone. Of the 41, 19.5 per cent could do everyday domestic tasks without difficulty, 41.5 per cent could only do them with difficulty or special aids, 26.8 per cent could not do them without someone's help, and 12.2 per cent were totally dependent on others for this help. Reasons for non-application and refusals were not given.

Certainly the problems of adequate provision of home helps seem to be greater than those of take-up. Ignorance of the benefit does not appear a great problem. The Hunt and Fox study suggested that deliberate non-take-up did exist but gave hardly any indication of how common this is among people with disabilities. More recent studies give no further information concerning non-take-up.

Day centres

The non-take-up of local authority day centre places for handicapped people was explored in the 1971 OPCS study. The main reasons for non-attendance among the impaired were lack of knowledge of centre availability, severely limited mobility or a work commitment.

In attempting to discover the reasons for non-attendance of those who knew of the local centre, and who could get there if they wished, respondents were asked whether the reason for their non-attendance was because they did not consider themselves physically handicapped or for some other reason. This questioning, not surprisingly, threw up a response by 27 per cent of the handicapped that they were 'not physically handicapped'. Even 17 per cent of the severely and very severely handicapped made such a claim, and it was most strongly asserted by women. The other main reasons given for non-attendance were 'not interested' or 'too ill/too tiring'.

Holidays

The 1971 OPCS Survey showed the percentages of handicapped people who had been offered holidays during the preceding two years, but had not taken them up: 10 per cent of very severely handicapped, 9 per cent of severely handicapped and 8 per cent of appreciably handicapped. Of holidays offered to handicapped people and refused, 68 per cent had been offers from family or friends, and only 10 per cent had been offers from official bodies. The reasons given for refusal of holidays offered by the official bodies were not always easy to analyse, but are summed up in Table 4.13.

Table 4.13 Reasons for refusing holidays offered to handicapped people by official bodies (%)

Reason	%
Financial	5
Disability/health	24
'Don't want to go alone'	18
Prefer own home	23
Difficulty in getting about in holiday home	2
'Don't want to be a nuisance'	2
Others, don't knows, vague or irrelevant	30

Source: OPCS Survey (1971), page 161

Chapter Five

Non-take-up of benefits: a major problem

The preceding chapter looked in detail at the take-up rates of a wide range of services and cash benefits, varying from the near-complete to the negligible. There are wide disparities between the take-up rates for different benefits administered by the same department, and there are significant variations in the take-up of the same benefit administered by different authorities and in the take-up by age group, by severity of handicap and even by kind of handicap.

A benefit that achieves only a very low take-up is clearly a failure. For some benefits much effort has been invested in attempts to improve take-up. On the other hand, it has on occasion seemed to be a deliberate policy to avoid efforts to achieve good take-up in order to avoid the consequent cost and associated budgetary embarrassment.

The analysis of reasons for non-take-up has shown several contributing factors and we end this chapter with six recommendations for the improvement of the general practice of benefit administration.

Publicising benefits

The first and most critical requirement for good take-up is that those eligible must know of the existence of the benefit. Administrative difficulties, inadequacy of benefit and plain refusal to apply are secondary features. We therefore first discuss the questions of ignorance of benefit and the use of publicity to correct it.

Despite the emphasis placed on the publicising of available benefits in the Chronically Sick and Disabled Persons Act 1970, and despite subsequent efforts of some local authorities and central government publicity departments, as well as the activities of voluntary groups, social workers and welfare rights workers, there still seems to be widespread ignorance of the existence of certain benefits, of criteria for eligibility and of application procedures, and this ignorance constitutes a major reason for non-take-up.

In 1972, Molly Meacher estimated that of the non-take-up of the means-tested benefits she was reviewing, 72 per cent was due to ignorance of the benefits, of the income limits or of the claiming procedure, and 27 per cent of respondents had failed to claim benefits because they were confused by, or unaware of, the eligibility criteria.

Since 1970, some local authorities have produced booklets and posters and conducted campaigns on the radio or in the local press: some booklets, such as the ones produced by the London Borough of Camden, have been well designed and encouraging to potential applicants. On the other hand, some local authorities have been reluctant to publicise some of their benefits because they feel that the supply cannot match an increased demand. This has particularly been a consideration since government cuts directly affected the extent of provision of benefits and services.

Some of the new Welfare Rights Officers have tried to extend the knowledge of benefits by producing guides or kits for use not only by health workers, social workers and voluntary workers, but also by potential recipients. Strathclyde has produced one such guide which helps to disentangle the benefits.

The Department of Health and Social Security and the Department of the Environment have both made various efforts to publicise certain benefits, but, considering the expenditure involved, the results have not been spectacular. Approaches have been at best pedestrian, and have done little to stimulate interest or to clarify the sometimes complex eligibility criteria and application procedures, or even to try to overcome stigma. They rarely try to 'sell' their product.

Preparing publicity

Publicity within the DHSS is the responsibility of the Information Section, which is divided into a press section and a publicity section. The publicity section works in close collaboration with the Central Office of Information (COI) which advises on leaflet and poster design. Most of the publicity, however, is subcontracted to a firm of consultants, which in 1976 was the firm Doyle, Dane and Bernbach. When new benefits are to be introduced the section concerned provides the publicity department with information on the type of expected claimants, estimates of those eligible, details of the take-on period and information regarding eligibility. The staff of the publicity department in their turn determine the groups to whom they need to direct their publicity and decide which media to use. They tend to embark on short-term countrywide campaigns, using national media rather than local, but sometimes concentrate on specialist magazines and journals (particularly for people with disabilities). Usually their assessment is made six months or more before the benefit is to appear, for budgeting purposes. Sometimes the publicity department is restricted by delays brought about by amendments to the legislation in Parliament, which can disrupt the planning of campaigns and slow down the provision of accurate publicity.

The most effective publicity campaigns are thought to be those which are conducted at the time of introduction of a new benefit or at the time of an uprating of an old one, which use both television and national press coverage. The DHSS tends not to use the regional press. Publicity through family doctors and other types of social and health workers has been found to be disappointingly ineffective.

Once the brief is ready it is passed to the advertising agents who prepare material which is vetted by the publicity department, by the department concerned with the benefit, and sometimes even by the Minister and Secretary of State. Alf Morris, Minister for the Disabled, is reported to have taken special interest in the publicity for the Mobility Allowance.

Of the DHSS benefits under review, publicity campaigns have been conducted for Family Income Supplement, Non-Contributory Invalidity Pension, Old Person's Pension, Attendance Allowance, Invalid Care Allowance, Mobility Allowance, Supplementary Benefits and free prescriptions. Printing of the leaflets is undertaken by HMSO. Since April 1976 the DHSS Information Division has prepared its material in such a way that analysis of printing costs for specific benefits by HMSO should be easier in the future.

Publicity distribution

The strategy adopted is benefit oriented. Thus, where Supplementary Benefit is concerned it is based on the belief that most of the target group already come into contact with the Social Security system, and relies heavily upon this network for communicating with them. For such benefits posters are displayed and leaflets are supposed to be available at every local Social Security office. The Welfare Rights Officers' Group, however, concluded from its national survey that

'the general standards of publicity in local offices are extremely poor – in many cases the manifest lack of care and effort involved creates a standard of publicity so poor that it may be seen by the public as an added stigma upon the benefits which that publicity aims to produce'.

This is a reflection more on the distribution of the publicity than on the publicity itself. For benefits that are oriented to people in work, who do not necessarily come into contact with the Social Security system, direct mailing and national advertising techniques have been used. More recently, however, direct mailing to existing recipients has been used less, partly because it is felt that this may encourage too many abortive claims and so cause additional administrative work.

Some leaflets are supposed to be available at all post offices in the country. The DHSS pays the 1,600–1,700 Crown post offices a market-rate fee for displaying posters and also covers the costs of displaying both posters and leaflets. The Post Office usually assigns members of its staff to be responsible for these materials; it has occasionally threatened to charge a commercial price for this work. The 23,000 sub-post offices are paid a nominal sum for their efforts, but few of them display posters satisfactorily. It has been estimated that only 75 per cent of post offices actually stock leaflets, although the trend is meant to be improving. The Welfare Rights Officers' Group concluded from its survey that there was a serious failure by the Post Office to perform the functions expected of it.

The only instance of market research on this publicity appears to have been that by Leo Burnett in October 1973 when this firm was the Department's advertising agency. It covered Supplementary Benefit and FIS leaflets as well as the research carried out by the Central Office of Information in April and May 1975 on alternative versions of FIS commercials. From the latter it was concluded that it was better to use a direct information approach ('here are the extra things you can buy with FIS') rather than an 'advocate' approach in which the benefit is discussed with an audience.

Publicity campaigns

Some of the more systematic efforts to increase knowledge of benefits and subsequent take-up have not had the positive results that had been hoped for. In 1971, for example, a special publicity drive on Rate Rebates was carried out by the Department of the Environment in the London Borough of Islington, and it was monitored by the Child Poverty Action Group. The campaign consisted of a complete household coverage by leaflets giving details of the benefits, eligibility criteria and application procedures. Effective distribution was somewhat limited in that the leaflets were delivered to many multi-occupied buildings only through the one main door. Advertisements were also placed in the national and local press and on hoardings throughout the borough. Direct ratepayers also had a note on their rate accounts giving details of the possibility of claiming a Rate Rebate and of the application procedure. No television advertising was included, but the Director of the CPAG appeared on television at the time and talked of Rate Rebates, and this had an effect on response.

The publicity appeared to increase knowledge of the existence of Rate Rebates quite substantially, but it had only a limited effect on knowledge of eligibility criteria and application procedure. During the half-year following the campaign, monitoring of the applications for Rate Rebates showed that out of 500 new claims, 279 were successful. Of the 500, however, 150 followed enquiries about concessionary bus fares for retirement pensioners, which had been advertised immediately before the Rate Rebate campaign, and 65 were made as a result of the notes included on the back of all rate accounts. Among the remaining 23 per cent who could therefore be said to have claimed as a result of the campaign, the leaflet seemed to be the most important source of information: some 42 per cent had read it. The effect of newspaper advertising seems to have been minimal. Less than half the householders who had learnt of rebates from hoardings had grasped the main point 'that if you pay rent, you probably pay rates and may therefore be entitled to a Rate Rebate', whereas 60 per cent of those who had heard from leaflets or newspaper advertisements had absorbed this idea. Of those respondents who had heard of Rate Rebates via personal contacts but had not seen any part of the campaign, only a third realised that tenants might be eligible for Rate Rebates, or knew how to apply.

Awareness that people with even substantial savings might not be precluded from eligibility for Rate Rebates was increased from 3 to 22 per cent (in the wider control survey), and to 15 per cent for eligible non-claimants. The awareness of tenant eligibility for Rate Rebates increased from 10 to 37 per cent, and to 41 per cent for eligible tenants. Knowledge of where to claim increased from 37 to 54 per cent, although the increased knowledge was hardly apparent amongst the lowest-income families. Nevertheless, despite this increase in knowledge post-survey ignorance was still marked: 27 per cent of eligible householders remained unaware of the benefit and three-quarters of those with savings still felt that the possession of capital precluded eligibility, while more than half of the eligible tenants still believed that they were ineligible because they lived in rented accommodation.

The Batley Welfare Benefits Project, which began in 1972, attempted to use a variety of publicity methods to increase knowledge and take-up of means-tested benefits. A publicity leaflet for Rent Rebates is distributed annually by law to council tenants. Publicity is put in local newspapers at appropriate times. Private landlords are required to insert particulars of Rent Allowances in rent books under pain of an £80 fine. The visiting collectors to whom many council tenants pay rent are also an important point of contact.

It was found that leaflets for Rent Rebates and Allowances quickly became out of date, and in June 1973 a campaign to publicise rent benefits began, consisting of leafletting, mailing publicity to private tenants, newspaper coverage, talks to field workers and the production of special cards and carrier bags. But there was little impact on take-up. Similarly, there was disappointingly little effect from the Rate Rebate campaign of leaflets distributed to owner-occupiers and council tenants, postal leaflets distributed to compound-rated properties, and posters in Gujerati; the subsequent small but significant improvement in take-up was considered to be due to the council's initiative in combining Rate and Rent Rebate application procedures rather than to the publicity campaign. As with rent benefits, private tenants are the least aware of the Rate Rebates. The Batley authority's publicity for FIS only appeared to influence an eighth of new claims that were made in the following six months.

In 1973 and 1974 an action research project was undertaken for the Department of the Environment in the London Borough of Haringey. Some quite imaginative publicity increased take-up, but only from 8 to 25 per cent, and three-quarters of eligible tenants still had not applied for Rent Allowances. Distribution of literature effected an increase in take-up of 24 per cent, and personal advice accounted for a 12 per cent increase. The most successful activity was the direct mailing of the Department of the Environment leaflet *There's money off rent*, which produced a 40 per cent increase in the take-up rate. Recall of publicity and information was uniformly low: less than 40 per cent of respondents recalled the relevant experiment and a quarter of all tenants interviewed said they had never heard of Rent Allowances. Of the eligible non-applicants who had heard of Rent Allowances, only 17 per cent correctly recognised their eligibility.

Seven types of promotion were tried: a housing rights stall, a housing rights caravan, a door-to-door canvasser, three different leaflet mailings, and one door-to-door leaflet delivery in nine different areas (including two as controls). But even amongst those who were aware of the different types of publicity, attention to the content was not particularly forthcoming. It was felt that the transmission of any information depends on the consciousness of the recipient, and the content must be seen to have some significance for the life of the intended recipient. The delay of several months between the publicity exercises and recall seems to have limited the findings of the research.

Tentative estimates for the publicity cost per successful applicant ranged from an average of £6.90 for direct mailings of *There's money off rent* to £431 for the Rent Allowance caravan, with an overall average of £32 per successful applicant. The main preliminary conclusion of the study has been that it is possible to improve the take-up of Rent Allowances, but the extent of improvement is so small that a high level of take-up is probably unlikely to be achieved (*Haringey Rent Allowance Project Report*, page 21).

In recent years the Department of the Environment has made much more widespread efforts to overcome ignorance of housing benefits. It spent £612,000 on mass-media advertising in 1972 and 1973, and a more limited advertising campaign, primarily on hoardings and radio, was undertaken in 1975; it also tested different leaflets. Despite these efforts the changes in take-up have not been particularly marked.

The Salop Study (1976) looked at the sources of information for potential recipients of a variety of benefits. It was found that for housing benefits about 60 per cent of cases either received leaflets or claim forms, or absorbed information from the media. For educational and Social Security benefits about 60 per cent learnt of them either from an official other than one at the benefit office, or from friends, relatives or neighbours. No secondary tracing of how these sources were informed of the benefit has been made in this or any other study. A DHSS official concerned with publicity held that such secondary tracing would not merit the effort involved.

Molly Meacher concluded in her study (page 31) that

'because the section of society to whom means-tested benefits are geared are un-accustomed to dealing with complicated reading matter and because their ability to grasp the many details involved is limited, advertising campaigns, however good, are unlikely significantly to increase awareness among those most in need'.

A number of the advertising campaigns conducted by local authorities and central government have either been ineffective or produced only a temporary take-up increase which has not been sustained. In addition the cost of some of these campaigns has been high relative to the low yield in increase in claimants, while they may also have stimulated abortive claims that increased the burden on the administration. In 1974 there were 715,000 abortive claims for Supplementary Benefits, while for FIS there were as many as 76,787 rejected claims, as opposed to 72,349 that were accepted.

Failure of publicity

Ignorance of benefits, of criteria for eligibility and of application procedures are important reasons for non-take-up. Some people do not absorb publicity simply because they feel that it does not apply to them or that the groups to whom it does apply must be abnormal. The non-absorption of benefit information may be closely related to questions of stigma (discussed later in this chapter), and even where there is encouraging publicity for individual benefits, the over-riding ethos of stigma still tends to nullify its effects. Information on complex conditions of eligibility and application procedures is difficult to convey to the general public, and particularly to some members of low-income groups, whose literary competence may be far below that of the people who devise and administer their benefits, and the 'necessity' to include considerable information on criteria for eligibility for some benefits, particularly for those which are means-tested, tends to make many leaflets cumbersome and off-putting.

Publicity material usually receives very little advance testing by market research before its introduction to the public, and there has been little effort to test alternative outlets for the distribution of publicity material. The Salop study (1976) tried out different outlets with some success, and post offices and housing benefit offices were test-used for publicity for educational and Social Security benefits. The high take-up rate for the Old Person's Pension, despite limited publicity, shows that a system of non-means-tested benefits might be much more appropriate, and might bypass a need for costly publicity.

Publicity for the different benefits remains, however, a very secondary matter to the main problem of appraisal of the nature of the benefits themselves.

Application forms

Non-take-up may not be directly attributable to difficulties with application forms, but such difficulties do quite often appear to contribute to the problems that potential recipients encounter in trying to claim. The Department of Health and Social Security has paid a little more attention to the design of forms in the last few years, but it still seems to be reluctant to design forms that are oriented to the client's rather than the administrator's needs.

In 1974, workers at Brunel University reviewed Rent Allowance application forms obtained from 100 out of 113 local authorities. Of these 100 authorities, 26 used the standard forms of the Chartered Institute of Public Finance and Accountancy. When duplications were eliminated there remained a sample of 66 different Rent Allowance application forms then in use. The forms were analysed for 'acceptability' or 'unacceptability' on five counts:
a. print size – unacceptable if a form contained any large sections set in 8-point or smaller type;
b. instructions and answer space – unacceptable if there was one major fault in instructions or answer space;
c. difficult content – unacceptable if more than two questions had difficult content;
d. comprehensibility – unacceptable if 20 per cent or more of questions on the form were likely to be difficult for tenants to understand;

e. overall impression – unacceptable if there were two or more 'negative points'.

The results are set out in Table 5.1.

Table 5.1   Analysis of acceptability of 66 Rent Allowance forms by five criteria

Item	Acceptable	Not acceptable
a. Print size	50	16
b. Instructions and answer space	4	62
c. Difficult content	45	21
d. Comprehensibility	26	40
e. Overall impression	19	47

Source: 'A form of trial', *Housing Monthly*, August 1975

The most common faults under the second heading were: failing to provide any instructions, providing 'Yes/No' answers without instructions about deleting, failing to provide sufficient space for answering, and muddled layout. 'Difficult questions' included those which asked for more detailed information than average, or for information which fieldwork has shown to lead to difficulties for tenants. Some of the comprehensibility problems arose from actual printing errors, but the major difficulty arose from bureaucratic language and involved sentence construction. Bureaucratic language mainly consisted of the use of words in a special legal sense, or of the use of difficult terms when everyday words would be suitable. Involved sentence construction is often introduced, perhaps because the legal branches of an authority are involved with the drawing up of application forms. Unnecessary difficulties were introduced by the posing of 'dual questions' which cannot be answered logically, such as: 'Is the dwelling your normal place of residence? If not, does your spouse live there and pay the rent? Yes/No'.

They concluded that 'whatever the complications of the schemes there are many errors on the forms which could be put right'.

Some multi-purpose forms used in combined assessment schemes are reviewed in Chapter 6. Some schemes, particularly the Liverpool project, have paid great attention to form design.

The most comprehensive work on this critical matter of form design and wording has been undertaken by Pat Wright and Phil Barnard of the Medical Research Council's Applied Psychology Unit in the University of Cambridge. In 1975 they tested five local authority forms in use for Rent Rebates and Allowances. Particular difficulties were found with sentences containing many negatives, unfamiliar words, 'Yes/No' questions and awkward layout. In their article 'Just fill in this form – review for designers' (1975), they reviewed the main points on which form designers need to concentrate attention. Their major injunctions to form designers are:
use short, active affirmative sentences;

use familiar words;
ask questions about one thing at a time;
organise temporal sequences;
beware of ambiguities;
use headings;
consider alternatives to prose (presumably verse is not to be considered);
provide adequate answer space;
choose appropriate print;
clarify the general structure and layout for easy appreciation by the reader.

The only work on application forms directed specifically to people with disabilities is the study carried out in 1976 in Lambeth Directorate of Social Services on *Cash benefits for the disabled*. A draft 'NI 220' form was tested for joint application for Attendance Allowance and Mobility Allowance. The test revealed a number of design difficulties, but it did not go into the depth of analysis that has been used in Cambridge.

How has central government responded to the need for greater attention to the design of application forms? The Department of the Environment is incorporating some of Wright and Barnard's work in their guidelines on Rent and Rate Rebates and Rent Allowances circulated to local authorities. But form design by both central and local government remains conspicuously amateurish. Her Majesty's Stationery Office set up a special Form Design Unit in 1973 but the unit has no power to call in any forms before they go to the public: it has a staff of only three, and much of their time is spent in producing new forms, primarily for internal use. The Civil Service Office runs three-day courses in form design, which concentrate on printing techniques and the omission of the worst howlers; it did not hear of the work of Wright and Barnard at the Cambridge unit until 1975.

The Central Office of Information has five qualified research officers who plan the control surveys, but their work is vetted by the Survey Control Unit of the Office of Population Censuses and Surveys, which carries out pilot runs for 'statistical' forms. (A sharp distinction is made in government circles between 'administrative' forms going to a claiming public and 'statistical' forms which provide the government with information on what people are doing or possessing. The former tend to be treated as the poor partner in many government departments.)

The Department of Health and Social Security has a small division within its Information Section that is concerned with publicity leaflets and the design of application forms. What advice they have sought on form design has come mainly from the HMSO Form Design Unit. They have had no contact with other workers on form design. Recently they have tried to incorporate application forms into leaflets on benefits. They have been restricted because legal constraints have demanded the inclusion of confusing legal aspects in the leaflets.

For the claimant, the most important consideration in form design is that the form should be designed with his needs, as well as those of the administrators, in mind. Trade-offs between adminstrative and claimants' needs should be based on empirical evaluation of both, rather than on *ad hoc* decisions. Forms should avoid being negative and discouraging to applicants, even if they are not permitted to be encouraging. Boxes labelled 'for official use only' have been found to confuse and upset people, particularly old people. The Batley Welfare Rights Project report emphasised that no practical purpose was served by statements on forms that claimants are 'not obliged to complete' certain sections, nor by frequent warnings on them of the possibility of prosecution for false information; such statements discourage claimants.

If forms were easier to complete there should be administrative saving both in processing costs and in the time spent by social workers, Welfare Rights Officers and others in helping people to fill in application forms; their skills could more profitably be used elsewhere. Forms not only need to be easy for administrators to follow, but must also be capable of completion by someone of a low reading age; nevertheless they should not appear patronising.

A recent move, intended as a step towards simplification, was the introduction of a composite leaflet (M11), dealing with free dental and optical treatment, free milk and vitamins and free prescriptions. This could have been helpful, but unfortunately confusion is introduced because of the varied eligibility criteria for the different benefits, so that applicants for free dental and optical treatment may still need other forms (F1D or F1). Moreover, the cover of the new leaflet states that it replaces three other forms (F11, PC11 and W11), but the penultimate page makes it clear that it replaces only the last two: an impression is given of confusion at the centre as well as at the periphery. Another example of complexity is the existence of a collection of no fewer than nine current leaflets that are all concerned with various aspects of Child Benefit.

Barnard and Wright suggest that probably the best way to prevent problems arising out of form design and wording is to test prototype forms prior to their final issue. The additional cost should be more than compensated for by reduced administrative difficulties after introduction.

Two possible dangers must be avoided when trying to simplify forms. Explanations of entitlements (where those are considered important) must not be omitted or separated in explanatory booklets. Nor must modifications made for computer purposes dominate form design to the detriment of the claimants' needs: it may be better to separate the application document from the input document and then to use an operator to make the transfer.

Complaints both of bad style and of civil service jargon have been around for a long time: 'this is English up with which I will not put,' grumbled Winston Churchill to his civil servants. But considerations of form design go far beyond questions of literary style. Complexity, obscurity, ambiguity and other misuses of language as well as of form design are all matters which affect both the administrative costs and the take-up of the benefit concerned. Considerations of the importance of form design and form wording should, however, be kept in perspective in this context. As Gavin Weightman affirmed in an article in *New Society* (13 November 1975): '*The real need is for fewer forms and a rationalisation of the legislation which has given rise to them*'.

The value of benefits to applicants

In her Rate Rebates study Molly Meacher found that, once full awareness of entitlement had been established, the most frequently cited reason for failure to claim was the low value of the potential gain. She found that 5 per cent of non-take-up was due to a feeling that the benefits were not worth the effort and a further 4 per cent to uncertainty about claim procedures. Amongst people with disabilities the low value of a benefit does not appear in itself to be a major reason for non-take-up, but there seems to be a growing number of instances of non-take-up because of alternatives. The area which has most affected people with disabilities in the past has been the trade-off between Supplementary Benefits and Rate Rebates, and overlap between the Non-Contributory Invalidity Pension and Supplementary Benefit (discussed on page 60) now presents further problems. Unfortunately no statistical information is available on how a trade-off between particular benefits has affected take-up of one and non-take-up of the other.

Difficulties of claim procedure

The Batley study (page 12) concluded that one of the main reasons for non-take-up is that:

'Claimants find trouble in understanding and completing forms, in gathering evidence of income, rent and circumstances to support application, and in making contact with allocating agencies which may be remote and inconvenient. Those who are aware of their entitlement may judge that the obstacles to application outweigh the benefit.'

Difficulties in application procedure, particularly if they involve considerable travelling to and fro, are likely to be especially important reasons for non-take-up by people with physical disabilities, whose mobility and access problems can be severe, and may be substantially increased if the claimant does not have easy access to a telephone. Moreover, people with intellectual handicaps have limited ability to absorb information and to express themselves. Molly Meacher found that articulate families were more likely to have claimed at least one benefit than inarticulate ones, and that unskilled workers and retired unskilled workers tended to claim less than skilled workers.

Pride and fear of stigma

Pride and fear of stigma are often quoted as important reasons for the non-take-up of benefits, particularly of means-tested benefits. The different studies cited here certainly support such an assertion. Sometimes these considerations may be more important than the surveys indicate, particularly where people are reluctant to confess to a fear of stigma, and are more prepared to claim ignorance or to say that they felt they were not entitled to the benefit. This can be especially difficult where a survey is associated with the take-up of specific benefits, and the interviewee may feel that the interviewer approves of take-up, while he himself does not. People with disabilities may not fear stigma, but those who are fairly self-sufficient may have more pride than some other types of claimant – a pride which has often been sharpened by years of being treated as a second-rate citizen. Their difficulty is that, although they may wish to be as independent as possible, their 'needs' are often very 'real', and they are forced to have at least a limited dependence on benefits, services and the support of others.

Molly Meacher's study in Islington (1972) showed that for the means-tested benefits under review stigma and pride were very important reasons for non-take-up, particularly amongst the elderly. As many people with disabilities are among the elderly presumably these factors are important for them, too. The situation to some extent reflects the success, for over a century, at least until the 1940s, of the authorities and of some sections of the general public in inculcating feelings of guilt, shame and stigma.

The 1973 Birmingham study on Rent Rebates looked particularly at problems of stigma. The researchers felt that as long as claimants are publicly regarded as either disadvantaged or in a broad sense at fault, it is unlikely that anyone who considers himself to be an 'ordinary person' will absorb information about benefits, however it is presented. This suggests that stigma is a powerful factor in the non-absorption of information on benefits, and accordingly in the high rates of ignorance cited earlier. They found that the 'stigma factor' was most apparent in the readiness with which the majority of respondents alleged that there were people getting rebates who shouldn't be getting them or who didn't deserve them, even though many of the same respondents were fully prepared to accept that the genuinely vulnerable should get rebates. Presumably this public would include people with disabilities amongst these 'genuinely vulnerable', but one suspects that people with obvious disabilities would be more generally accepted than those whose disabilities are less noticeable.

It is a sad reflection that information about and publicity for benefits has done little to combat these feelings of stigma; much more could probably be done to emphasise that eligibility may depend on a variety of criteria, and may be much more widespread than is generally believed. Such emphasis might not be altogether popular with the policy-makers, as it might show up more clearly the way in which some benefits have been whittled down by making many potential claimants ineligible.

The Birmingham study (like the Islington study) found that 'the elderly were more likely than other tenants to feel that claiming for rebates or allowances incurred a loss of pride, self-respect or independence' (page 97). Certain claimants appeared to fear that the divulging of personal information to the authorities might reduce their independence, and give the authorities a greater influence over them.

Officialdom and officials' attitudes

One category of non-claimants consists of those with a history of mistreatment or discouragement by officials when they have claimed benefits in the past. Such experiences often leave a legacy of bitterness and resentment which inhibits further claims, however great the need.

Some regional representatives of the Department of Health and Social Security unofficially maintain that the successful administration of benefits is commensurate with an ability to slow down take-up. If this is so (and producing evidence of it is naturally difficult) it is highly likely that the officials' treatment of claimants reflects the attitudes of their managers.

Estimating take-up rates

Estimating eligible claimants

A crucial factor affecting efforts to analyse take-up of benefits quantitatively has been the unreliability of the methods used to assess the numbers of people eligible for particular benefits; this applies especially to assessments based on data from the Family Expenditure Survey, which appears to have a bias against the inclusion of some types of lower-income families and consistently has a non-response rate of 30 per cent. After the difficulties resulting from the over-estimating of the numbers entitled to Family Income Supplement, the Department of Health and Social Security appears to have preferred to err on the side of caution and under-estimate. Only where a benefit overlaps with an alternative, as does the Non-Contributory Invalidity Pension, has take-up not come up to the estimates.

Clearly, present estimates of the numbers eligible for benefits still contain wide margins of error. Accordingly, take-up rates based on these estimates are likely to display an equal degree of error. If this leads to a concern about an apparent non-take-up it can result in unnecessary publicity and remedial campaigns; if there is complacency because of seemingly good take-up, however, real need may be ignored. In the one case it leads to waste of resources, and in the other to failure to meet an existing need; both might be avoided by an improved system of estimating the numbers eligible.

It is important, however, to differentiate between those who may be eligible for a benefit, and those who may be eligible *and likely to claim it*. Analyses of the take-up of certain benefits have shown that quite often there is a reluctance on the part of many people to claim benefits even when they are aware that they are eligible. Sometimes this is because they do not consider the benefit worth claiming, or because they believe that the likely administrative hassle is not justified by the reward, or perhaps because another benefit, which overlaps with the one which might be claimed, is better; such overlap problems appear to be growing in importance. In addition, however, there is the recurring problem of stigma, often disguised and often difficult to overcome. Even if the publicity for a specific benefit tries to overcome feelings of stigma, there may still exist a more general stigmatisation of welfare benefits, so that a number of people, who might be both eligible and definitely in need, may forgo claiming. Accordingly there is a need not only for reliable estimates of those eligible for any benefit, but also for reliable estimates of those eligible for that benefit who, given a fair degree of encouragement and information, are likely to claim it. Without such estimates, reasonable assessments of take-up are not possible.

Some local authorities, through surveys conducted under the Chronically Sick and Disabled Persons Act 1970, have tried to make estimates of the numbers in need of various benefits, or likely to be in need in the future. Unfortunately a number of authorities appear to have treated the extent of need as static, and have not tried to prepare accurate estimates of future needs for specific benefits. Nor have their estimates taken adequately into consideration the differences between those in 'need' of certain benefits, and those in 'need' who are likely to claim.

Having drawn attention to the present inadequacies of the systems for estimating the numbers of those eligible, and those eligible who are likely to claim, it would be considered perhaps equally inappropriate if there were a too punctilious attention to establishing estimates of need, thereby drawing on limited resources which might better be deployed in actually relieving need. What is needed is a thorough re-appraisal of the systems of estimating which would take fully into account the degree of accuracy needed, and the use of resources in establishing those estimates.

Further uncertainties

Besides the uncertainty in the numbers considered as eligible for benefits, other factors also affect estimates of take-up rates. Some over-estimates of take-up have occurred where the benefit runs for up to twelve months (for example, free school meals), where people are counted as receiving the benefit who are in fact no longer below the income limits. Thus the numbers claiming become inflated *as a proportion* of the numbers eligible.

Local surveys have tended to return lower estimates of take-up than those made nationally by central government; for instance, local surveys of take-up for Rate Rebates range between 45 and 60 per cent, compared with national estimates of 70 to 75 per cent. Although there are methodological inadequacies (particularly concerning the size of samples) in some local surveys, this does suggest that official estimates tend to be optimistic.

Table 4.9 (page 161) shows that the range in officially estimated take-up rates for different benefits is quite considerable: from free school meals (approximately 80 per cent) to Rent Allowances for unfurnished accommodation (approximately 10 per cent). It has been suggested that there should be minimum acceptable levels of take-up for individual benefits, which if not attained within a certain period should be sufficient justification for reviewing the usefulness of the benefit. When the Family Income Supplement was launched, Sir Keith Joseph suggested an 85 per cent take-up rate as the minimum acceptable level. So far this has rarely been achieved with any benefit. At present it would be difficult to establish such levels with the inadequacies that exist in the present system of measuring take-up.

The take-up levels need to be considered not only in terms of percentages, but also in relation to the number of people involved, and to the reasons for the non-take-up. For example, Supplementary Benefit had a relatively high official take-up rate in November 1974 of about 73 per cent, but because the numbers eligible are high, this means that the non-take-up of 27 per cent represents 990,000 potentially eligible claims, covering 1.5 million people. Put in terms of absolute numbers such take-up is inadequate.

An analysis of the reasons for non-take-up may lead to different courses of action. Where the non-take-up is predominantly due to ignorance of the benefit, its eligibility criteria or its application procedure, there is obviously a need for improved publicity, but where it is due to stigma a *different type* of publicity is needed. If the stigma element is considerable or there is a marked overlap with other benefits, or if the benefit is not claimed either because it is considered to be too small to merit the effort of claiming or because it involves a complex application procedure, then there is perhaps a good case for reviewing the usefulness of the benefit, the nature of its administration, or both.

The Salop study (1976) attempted to discover what prompted people to claim benefits. Where educational benefits were concerned, financial difficulties and the arrival of unrequested claim forms were the main prompters. For Social Security benefits, a change in circumstances and consequent need for support prompted claims. For housing benefits (many of which were reviews) the prompting came from the arrival of a review claim form. The high incidence of reviews in this sample lessens the usefulness of the findings, but the exercise did at least explore the possibilities of examining those factors that prompt potential claimants to claim.

Conclusions and recommendations

Regardless of the inadequacies of the present system for measuring take-up, it is clear that problems of take-up for certain benefits (particularly means-tested ones) are considerable, and that neither increased publicity, however good it may be, or simplifying claiming procedures is likely to improve take-up rates dramatically. This suggests that perhaps more fundamental aspects are being overlooked, and that what is needed is a radical reappraisal of the applicability of different benefits, their eligibility criteria and their administration.

In addition the evidence of several local studies suggests that those most in need of support are those least likely to claim benefits, particularly those that are means-tested or complex. As David Donnison, the Chairman of the Supplementary Benefits Commission, has reminded us: 'complexity is always regressive – because the poorest people find it harder to deal with'.

It must be concluded that tinkering with the present welfare system is of only marginal usefulness in combating its unsatisfactory performance in relieving poverty and hardship, and that the creation of a more appropriate welfare support scheme is a matter of the highest priority. However, some immediate measures could be taken relatively easily to improve take-up rates within the existing system, and accordingly we make the following recommendations:

a. The Department of Health and Social Security should review the system of estimation of eligibility for benefits and publish the findings.

b. Central and local government departments should co-ordinate their efforts to establish more accurate estimates of both the numbers of those eligible for particular benefits for which they are responsible, and the numbers of those eligible who can be expected to claim them, given adequate publicity and bearing in mind changes in future needs. Subsequently, where the take-up rates are found to be low (either in percentage terms or in terms of absolute numbers), they should assess the reasons for non-take-up, in order to determine the most appropriate course of action to adopt regarding each benefit (abolition, modification or different publicity).

c. More attention needs to be given to the publicising of accurate eligibility criteria for particular benefits and the general presentation of benefits to make the public more aware that many benefits are for 'ordinary people', thus reducing the feelings of stigma. Also, more attention should be given to the literary skills and the psychological and sociological constraints of potential claimants when publicity material for those benefits is being designed, in order to encourage eligible claimants to apply and to discourage ineligible claimants. All such material should be pre-tested on representative samples.

d. The distributive outlets for written publicity material (both those used at present and potential new ones) should be reviewed to discover their efficiency, in order to provide clearer guidelines for future publicity.

e. The design, content and wording of application forms for each benefit should be reviewed (preferably in consultation with specialists) to ensure that they meet the potential claimants' needs as well as the administrators'.

f. The constraints on take-up of those benefits which are either specifically for people with disabilities or those for which they are likely to apply should be thoroughly studied and monitored. The following merit particular attention: Supplementary Benefit and additional allowances, Non-Contributory Invalidity Pension, Attendance Allowance, Mobility Allowance, Hospital Pocket Money, Improvement Grants, Rent and Rate Rebates, housing adaptations, rehousing, holidays, day care, aids and appliances, and grants for travel to work.

Chapter Six

A review of combined assessment procedures

Ways to improve and simplify the process of identifying people's eligibility for different benefits have been explored in recent years by a number of agencies. Various schemes for the integration of applications for different benefits into a single, or at least fewer, forms have been considered, as well as the processing of all forms at a single centre to avoid duplication, to increase take-up and to reduce administrative costs. Some of these schemes have involved the use of computers. The principal aim has been to show that centralised procedures could not only speed up the administration of benefits – itself of great value to claimants – but could also actually reduce administrative costs sufficiently to counterbalance the additional costs of a higher take-up. Only one study has been concerned specifically with people with disabilities, but most of them have been concerned with benefits for which such people are likely to be applying.

These studies are a logical response to the growing number of benefits and the resulting complexities and overlaps of their administration (discussed elsewhere in this book); for example, a low-income family may each year need to make at least five applications to three or more departments, and each application must be supported by, at least, evidence of rates, rent and income over a five-week period (P Taylor-Gooby's 'Providing more for less').

The more automatic the assessment of benefit eligibility, the less the stigma for the client, the less the administrative costs, including those of expensive publicity, and the higher the take-up rate. The exorbitant cost of the present system was demonstrated in a study of the cost of administering Rent Allowances. The average value of a six-month Rent Allowance was found to be about £60; the cost of administering the benefit averaged £18.10 in a London borough and £7.10 for an authority in the North-east. In addition in 1972 the central government had spent £612,000 on publicity (the equivalent of £10 claimed for every allowance). Even so, it was estimated that the benefit reached only 10 per cent of those who were entitled to it.

The DHSS Shropshire (Salop) study

The M1 form

The Department of Health and Social Services began to discuss the possibilities of testing 'combined assessment' in 1969 when Richard Crossman, then Secretary of State for the Department, set up an interdepartmental working party to design a multi-purpose means test and an appropriate machinery for its operation. Discussions were protracted. Out of them came only one scheme, the multi-purpose claim form known as the M1, which was introduced for trial in Shropshire (Salop) in August 1975.

The M1 form was introduced in order to study the value of a single, self-completion form in which twelve means-tested benefits could be claimed simultaneously (see Table 6.1), thus replacing a variety of separate forms in use by local authorities and the DHSS. Seven categories of claimant were analysed: full-time workers, part-time workers, unemployed people, sick people, retired people, housewives and students. People receiving FIS or Supplementary Benefit were excluded (and with them many disabled people) as they were considered to have 'passport rights' to benefits already. An interim report appeared in 1976.

The new form is rather cumbersome, consisting of three pages of A4 paper and containing some fifty questions; in addition, there is a ten-page instruction manual. Clearly it presented some problems to the respondents, about a quarter of whom asked for help in filling in the form. Non-form-fillers were significantly older than form-fillers; almost half of them had no dependants. Widows tended to be non-form-fillers. Some people who did not fill in the form themselves were physically unable to do so; others habitually did not fill in claim forms. (Some of these responses may disguise adult literacy difficulties.) Terms such as 'ground rent', 'gross rent and rates' and 'pension or superannuation from employer' presented difficulties. Some invalidity pensioners and retirement pensioners said they did not know where on the form to declare their income. Claimants for educational benefits found there was insufficient space for the information sought.

The report commented that

'some of the difficulty seems to derive from claimants' ignorance of the means-testing machinery. Because they are not told exactly what information is needed to make a decision about their claim and how it is assessed, they find it difficult to judge the importance or relevance of particular details of their circumstances'.

This is surely in itself an admission of failure, as is another comment that

'Many of the difficulties stemmed not so much from lack of clarity in the questions themselves as from complexity in the form-filler's circumstances, for which no provision was made in a form designed for the 'average' claimant'.

Indeed, the concept of the 'average claimant' may well be a figment of the administrator's imagination, which it is time he recognised as such.

The interim report concluded that for many people the M1 form was more difficult to complete than conventional forms. (Though it may well have been easier than the alternative task of successive completion of twelve different conventional forms with their often arbitrary diversities of format, of wording, of definitions of 'purpose' and of eligibility criteria.)

Table 6.1 Benefits claimed on M1 combined claim form

	Group claiming primarily education benefits	Group claiming primarily DHSS benefits	Group claiming primarily housing benefits
	(% claiming each benefit)	(% claiming each benefit)	(% claiming each benefit)
Free school meals	89	8	2
School clothing grant	23	5	(1)
Educational maintenance allowance	1	—	—
Free milk and vitamins	6	16	(1)
Free dental treatment	3	27	—
Free optical treatment	3	47	(1)
Free prescriptions	6	20	(1)
Fares to hospital	(1)	8	8
Wigs and fabric supports	—	—	—
Rent Rebate	39	24	55
Rent Allowance	2	—	4
Rate Rebate	44	34	99
Base for percentages	158	158	170

Because of multi-claiming, percentages do not add to 100. Brackets denote number not percentage.
Source: Salop Interim Report (1976)

A sobering finding was that, although claims were increased by the use of the M1 form, awards actually decreased (although 10 per cent of M1 claimants were awaiting decisions on their claims at the time of the survey). This suggests either serious inadequacies in the M1 form, or greater stringency of the DHSS and local authorities in awarding benefits claimed on the M1 – perhaps both.

The difference between the number of claims and the number of awards was largest for housing benefits, and the unsuccessful claimants for these benefits were often people who had been primarily claiming for educational and DHSS benefits.

The trial was unable to estimate non-take-up as such, because respondents had not been asked about their financial circumstances, but the data did show that some people had not claimed benefits which appeared on the basis of non-financial circumstances to be relevant to them.

The M1 project is disappointing in both its planning and its results. The form itself contains obvious errors and presents a number of difficulties which could have been avoided had it been better designed and given a preliminary testing. It still bears the negative traits of many DHSS application forms, discouraging applications and enhancing stigma. Automatic assessment to check entitlements was not incorporated, and the initiative was still left with the claimant to list benefits he wished to claim. Two-thirds of the information contained in the instruction manual is devoted to circumstances of non-eligibility rather than eligibility.

The DHSS' negative approach to the problem is perhaps the most important finding: the failure to consider administrative restructuring (claims still being distributed as before to multiple agencies) or to try 'automatic' assessment or a check-list approach, and the clear reluctance to give any encouragement to take-up. Some of the most important and problem-ridden benefits (Supplementary Benefits and FIS) were excluded from the form, though relatively minor benefits such as Rent and Rate Rebates, already being assessed together successfully by local authorities, were included.

From the point of view of people with disabilities the scheme is of limited importance. It does not assess very deeply the problems of elderly and handicapped people in completing forms or even in having access to them. Unfortunately, the data so far available do not analyse the differences between claims and awards of different benefits by age group or handicap, which might help to clarify this if the resulting sample were large enough.

City of Liverpool

Multi-purpose benefits form

One other large scheme has had central government sponsorship: the multi-purpose benefits form scheme introduced by the City of Liverpool with the support of the Department of the Environment. The application form was researched by the Impact Foundation in conjunction with the City of Liverpool Area Management Unit District D. It is an improvement on the Salop form, in that its wording caters for people with a reading age of seven years (about 60,000 adults on Merseyside have poor reading ability). It covers five local authority benefits: Rent and Rate Rebates, free school meals, school uniform allowance, and cash to keep a child at school beyond the age of 16 years.

The form was distributed door-to-door in selected 'deprived' areas of the City of Liverpool, accompanied by reply-paid envelopes. All returned forms were processed through a central point. Attention was directed to children at school and recipients of Supplementary Benefit. There was no provision for automatic assessment and copies of the form were sent to the Treasurer's Department (for housing benefits) and/or to the Education Department (for benefits related to children at school), and then relayed to the central unit.

The scheme's organisers are at present considering what modifications would be necessary if the form were used throughout the city, including changes to facilitate computer processing, although such processing may not be applicable to the present task. Preliminary assessment indicates that the response to the scheme was disappointing, though there was some improvement with supplementary visiting. A high proportion of non-take-up had persisted, and people had still been reluctant to claim educational benefits. One worker felt that the main advantages had been that the forms overcame some of the worst elements of application procedures by reducing their number and making application more automatic, and also that they helped, by reducing discretion and stigma and treating benefits as more a right than a charity, to improve the relationship between claimants and administrators.

Batley

Rate and Rent Rebates scheme

In early 1973, Batley local authority invited applicants for either Rent or Rate Rebates to tick a box on their application form asking for information on the complementary benefit. This scheme resulted in a 130 per cent increase in Rate Rebate claiming in Batley.

Manchester

Rate and Rent Rebates scheme

In 1974 and 1975 the Manchester local authority tried a single-form application scheme for both Rent and Rate Rebates. A study throughout the city of Birmingham had shown that 50 per cent of council tenants and a far greater proportion of private tenants entitled to rent benefits were failing to claim in 1973. Also official figures showed that at least 1.5 million entitled households in England and Wales did not get their Rate Rebates in 1974/75.

Because of this lack of take-up, because of publicity costs, and because eligibility for rent benefits often corresponds with eligibility for rate benefits, and also because it was found that compound-rated tenants were often unaware (despite publicity) that their rent included a rates element, Manchester local authority decided to combine applications for both benefits on the same form. The use of the new form led to a 277 per cent increase in Rate Rebate take-up among council tenants in Manchester in 1974/75.

The combining of applications for Rent and Rate Rebates is a fairly logical idea, considering the similarities in eligibility, and has since been followed by other local authorities. It has the added advantage that Rate Rebates and Rent Allowances qualify for a 100 per cent central subsidy, and Rent Rebates qualify for nearly 100 per cent in most authorities. Thus increasing the take-up of these benefits through more automatic assessment offers local government a way of cutting down its administrative costs, which fall on the rates, while increasing the flow of Exchequer aid to those in need in their area. In addition, it has been possible to amalgamate application processes for Rent Rebates and Allowances with the process for Rate Rebates in this way since the Local Government Act 1974.

At present the onus of deciding whether to integrate applications still rests with local authorities, and many still have not done so. The reasons for their not doing so seem often to be linked more to interdepartmental rivalries or to administrative inertia than to the needs of potential recipients.

Merthyr Tydfil

Housing and educational benefits scheme

In 1976, the Welsh Consumer Council (Cyngor Defnyddwyr Cymru) conducted a project in Merthyr Tydfil distributing both a new simplified form and the existing forms for housing benefits and education benefits to council tenants and private householders.

The housing benefits included Rent Rebates and Allowances and Rate Rebates. The follow-up survey is still in progress at the time of writing. The initial analysis has shown a marginally greater increase in take-up by people claiming with the WCC form, but it was still comparatively low. The major problems were administrative. The staggering of claim times resulting from the difference between financial and school years led to a need for the successive completion of the form at least six times in the year, and difficulties were encountered as to the order in which different departments received the form. The Welsh Consumer Council concluded that:

'It seems clear that these problems could be effectively overcome if multi-purpose forms were administered in a central office. However other problems would remain, not least the question of whether it is worth the cost and effort of establishing Central Assessment Offices just to shore up a system of means-testing which will inevitably have to be replaced'.

They also concluded that:

'The framework of values and norms defining the roles and "controlling" the relations between consumers and administrators of means-tested benefits (i.e. the structure of the system) is such that no attempt at shoring it up could have more than a marginal effect. What is needed is radical change striking at the root of the system – its values. This, due to the inertia of social systems, inevitably requires the replacement of the present system of means-testing and not its perpetuation via Central Assessment Offices'.

Calderdale

Centralised Benefits Assessment Unit

Following the local government reorganisation of April 1974, Calderdale Metropolitan Borough decided to create a Centralised Benefits Assessment Unit which would combine assessments for the benefits provided from different local authority departments and so extend the public's awareness of the various benefits by linking assessment with publicity. The prime intention was to achieve greater take-up; but it was also hoped that the unit would be of greater convenience to the public, would increase the efficiency of the administration's notification arrangements and assessment for benefits, would help in the control and reduction of false claims, and would encourage progress towards a rationalisation of the various assessment scales.

The unit administered Rate and Rent Rebates, Rent Allowances, free school meals, school clothing grants, school maintenance grants, school camp grants, places at day nurseries, places at homes for the aged or mentally disordered and parental contributions to children in care. Domestic help was to be included, but was withdrawn following changes in policy. Repair grants under the 1974 Housing Act were also proposed for inclusion, but they have not yet been brought in.

One standard application form is used for all benefits. Indications of entitlement to other benefits are given at the time of assessment. Non-statutory assessment scales are subject to regular review to ensure a balance between the interests of ratepayers and benefit recipients and that benefits supplied do not overlap with DHSS benefits. Home contact relating to the completion of the application form rests with the respective service departments, and all office contact is through the unit.

The Principal Assistant (Revenue) in the Finance Department is responsible for the unit, which consists of twenty-one people in three teams of seven. Each team is headed by a team leader who is responsible for the whole range of benefits, while being himself a specialist in one major benefit. Each team deals with the whole range of benefits. It had been intended that no additional posts would be created for the unit; staffing would come from the pooling of staff from various departments and from the merging of authorities, to provide a reserve of specialist knowledge for all benefits administered. This was not wholly possible, and some posts had to be filled by untrained clerical staff.

After one year's operation some advantages and disadvantages had come to light. There had been an increase in take-up, particularly in educational benefits (school clothing grants and free meals) and in rent and rate benefits, particularly in the private housing sector, though here the increase was less than expected. The scheme helped the public in that the unit was located in the same building as the office for Rent and Rate Rebate payments, and provided a single focus for inquiries relating to benefits. Other advantages were an improved working relationship with the DHSS and the readier availability of statistical information, providing greater opportunities for introducing computerised systems and enabling continued assessment through holiday periods.

Difficulties included a lack of adequate specialist knowledge, failure to obtain early responses on income details where circumstances changed (particularly for social service benefits), dependence on service departments for home visiting and information, a lack of inspectors to investigate possible false claims and omissions, and excessive volumes of work at peak periods where a review of a benefit did not coincide with other benefits.

This scheme is one of the most imaginative and practical so far introduced, and is one of the few that has been accepted from the beginning as an on-going scheme. Detailed analyses of changes in take-up and administrative costs have not so far been forthcoming, but the scheme has shown a feasibility and commendable preparedness to re-assess administrative structures. It is concerned with both clients' and administrators' needs. It is hoped that, as the unit establishes itself, other benefits may be included within its scope.

London Borough of Hammersmith

Central Assessment Unit

Following a report by the Borough Treasurer and Director of Financial Services on assessment scales (7 March 1972), the London Borough of Hammersmith set up a working party on assessment charges to determine the extent of need for assessment scales and what information would be required for them, what possibilities existed for the standardisation of scales and the establishment of a centralised index and what publicity was necessary for changes.

The seventeen different assessment scales in use in Hammersmith at that time showed differences and inconsistencies in the treatment of capital, in the use of gross or net income, in allowable deductions in arriving at available income and in the treatment of income from lodgers. Review of the assessment procedures had shown that in some cases the estimated cost of administration exceeded the income obtained from clients. Financial assessments for provision of portable home aids and gadgets, holidays for the elderly, handicapped and blind, and recuperative holidays were considered inappropriate. Fixed home aids, works of adaptation, tuberculosis care and after-care, creches, welfare homes, tuberculosis hostels and mental after-care were considered unsuitable, and day nurseries, children in care and home helps suitable, for comprehensive assessment. A new comprehensive procedure for the last three was recommended, using data on net available income as calculated for Rent Allowance purposes. People on Supplementary Benefit or Family Income Supplement were assessed as nil. For home helps it was felt that the applicant should be assessed according to his ability to pay rather than to the degree of service required, subject to the maximum charge not being exceeded. A computerised central index system was also recommended, bearing strongly in mind questions of confidentiality.

The new comprehensive system of assessment was established on 1 April 1974, with a central computer index for Rent Rebates, Rent Allowances, Rate Rebates, home help, children in care and day nurseries. The central assessment section for housing benefits is located in the Finance Directorate, whilst the section for Social Service benefits is under the Social Services Department.

By 16 December 1975, the number of people on the central index was 4,781 for Rent Rebate and Rent Allowance cases, 6,154 for Rate Rebate cases and 1,343 for home help cases (of whom 127 were receiving Rate Rebates and 80 Rent Rebates). The take-up of benefits was increased (for instance, the number of Rate

Rebates paid at 30 October 1975 was 6,200, compared with 2,100 at 31 March 1974), although the scheme had been dramatically affected by the transfer in 1974 of the responsibility for paying housing benefits for Supplementary Benefit recipients from the local authority to the Department of Health and Social Security. The index has proved useful as a basis for provisional assessments for children in care and in day nurseries, particularly when the need for services is temporary, but is of little value in home help assessments, since these are made when the need is investigated by this service's organisers. The index also indicates potential rebate cases and alerts staff to obtain up-to-date information for re-assessment.

Coventry

Review of combined assessment

The City of Coventry's departments reviewed existing combined assessment schemes during the summer and autumn of 1976, and looked at the feasibility of introducing such a scheme in Coventry, but at the time of writing no decision had been taken.

The Inverclyde project

Computerised assessment

In July 1973, a feasibility study was undertaken in Dalkeith, Midlothian, Scotland, to test a computer program to determine eligibility for and the extent of entitlement of individuals to twenty-five means-tested welfare benefits, using a single assessment form and assessing entitlement on both non-means-tested and means-tested criteria. A total of 45 families was assessed. It was concluded that the computerised assessment of entitlement to means-tested and other welfare benefits was both viable and practicable, provided that help was available from a support agency to explain the scheme to the public and to assist in completing the assessment form. Where such help was not provided response rates were very low and the frequency of errors in the information collected was 'uncomfortably high'. The costs, excluding overheads and current costs, were only 20p per household. On that basis it was estimated that for £750,000, which was the sum spent on advertising the Family Income Supplement between 1971 and 1973, about 4 million families could have been assessed for their entitlement to twenty-seven benefits.

Following this study, Edinburgh University, Greenock Corporation (now Inverclyde District) and IBM agreed to develop a computer system for determining eligibility for means-tested and other benefits in what is now the Inverclyde District; this system started operating in May 1975.

The benefits included in the scheme were as follows:
Schemes applicable throughout the country:
M   Family Income Supplement

M	Rate Rebate (local authorities may vary the standard scheme slightly)
M	Rent Rebate/Allowance (local authorities may vary the standard schemes slightly)
M	Supplementary Benefit
P	Exceptional Needs Payment
PMN	Free prescriptions
PMN	Dental treatment
PMN	Glasses, frames, lenses
PMN	Wigs and fabric supports
PMN	Hospital fares
PMN	Milk and vitamins
PM	Legal advice and assistance
PM	Legal aid (civil cases)
PM	Free school meals
M	Higher school bursaries (this scheme nationally applicable within Scotland only)
N	Attendance Allowance
MN	Old Person's Pension

Local authority schemes applicable in Inverclyde:

PM	Home help
N	School clothing grants
N	School travel permit
N	Meals-on-wheels
N	Meals in day centres
N	Chiropody
N	Bus concessions schemes
N	TV licence or fuel vouchers
N	Benefits for blind people
N	Benefits for disabled people

The meanings of the code letters are as follows:

M available (in Inverclyde) through a means test
P available on a 'passport' (i.e. as a consequence of being in receipt of Supplementary Benefit or Family Income Supplement)
N available on non-means-tested grounds, such as 'under 16', 'registered as disabled' or 'a housebound pensioner'

Benefits available through a means test or a passport also normally require certain non-financial conditions to be fulfilled, for example, to receive Family Income Supplement the head of the household must be in work for at least 30 hours per week.

The assessment form was designed for direct punching and issued with an instruction booklet. Different forms were devised for private tenants, council tenants, owner-occupiers, commercial lodgers and non-commercial lodgers respectively. Because self-completion had been found to be inadequate in

Midlothian, and even social worker-assisted completion proved unsatisfactory here, a system of completion by trained clerks was successfully introduced.

In the computerised assessment procedure a validation program initially checks for errors, and then a calculation program calculates entitlements. Because of the complexity of the benefits the calculation program errs on the side of caution, usually making the most pessimistic assumption from the claimant's point of view.

The output print-out is returned to each family as part of the output report. This includes a letter telling the recipient the addresses at which to claim benefits, a statement of probable entitlement to benefits either of the household as a whole or of at least one of its members, and a statement of declarations containing all the information which has been given by the family on the assessment form. A guidance booklet on application for benefits is now also provided to potential claimants.

The people to whom the forms were particularly directed were:
families with chronic debt problems or other financial difficulties who were known to the Social Work Department;
those who had already requested help under section 12 of the Social Work (Scotland) Act;
people coming to the Greenock Information Centre;
applicants for rebates from the Chamberlain's Department;
applicants at the National Insurance Office and Employment Exchange;
interested people referred by home helps;
referrals from community and voluntary groups;
people on the local authority register of disabled;
people at lunch clubs;
all residents in one low-income-group neighbourhood.

Usually only a day or two elapsed between the form being completed, and the household receiving the output report.

Over the period February to August 1975, 481 forms were submitted for assessment; after the Greenock Information Centre started assessing in May 1975, 400 forms were submitted. Only 341 of the forms were included in the sample used for analysis of data in December 1975 because some of the 400 forms had had warnings of errors in them or had been reviews of earlier applications. Out of the 341 families covered, it was found that 126 would have been better off claiming alternative or additional benefits. In particular, 83 households (24 per cent of the sample of forms assessed) who were not claiming either Supplementary Benefit or rebates appeared to be likely to be better off claiming rebates. Also, 5 per cent of the households claiming Supplementary Benefit at the time would have been better off claiming rebates, while 3 per cent of the people claiming rebates would have been better off claiming Supplementary Benefit. The forms completed in August contained a high percentage of pensioners attending old people's lunch clubs, so a comparison was made with earlier claimants. It was found that of the May-to-July respondents 37 per cent were entitled to, but not claiming, any of four benefits (Supplementary Benefits, FIS and rebates), compared with only 15 per cent in August. Also in May to July, 12 per cent were claiming, but would have been better off with alternative or additional claims, compared with only 5 per cent for August.

Preliminary evaluation of the system

An independent evaluation of the project is being prepared by John MacDonald of the Department of Social Administration of the University of Edinburgh. His report, *Information and welfare benefits in Inverclyde – an evaluation*, was unfortunately not available at the time of writing. Michael Adler, who worked on the project, is assessing the extent of take-up using the scheme, and assessing more fully its costs. Accordingly a more complete evaluation must await the conclusions of these analyses.

The scheme has succeeded in devising a useful computerised system for assessing entitlement to welfare benefits and has shown that it is also important to include individual analyses both of individual benefits and of particular client categories. It has also explored very fully some of the difficulties of the completion of assessment forms and has tried different strategies to overcome them. It has recognised considerable inadequacies in the publicity of the scheme, in the numbers of the sample that responded, and in the suitability of the assessment forms for easy completion. These findings have been acknowledged and the appointment of a Welfare Benefits Officer or local co-ordinator has been recommended. Part of his function would be to aid publicity and to stimulate completion of more forms, and part to assess take-up and the effectiveness and value of the computer system.

At present the system still has the failing that claimants must, as before, claim for individual benefits once assessment has been made. A system providing automatic assessment and application using computer print-outs might ensure a higher take-up. Only 126 respondents appeared to be entitled to more or alternative benefits, and larger numbers are needed for true assessment of the effect on take-up, and of the computer print-out as an adequate guide to successful applications for benefits.

From the point of view of people with disabilities, this scheme has more to offer than some of the others reviewed, because of the range of benefits it could assess. Presumably some of the 400 respondents were people with disabilities, but their particular entitlements were not isolated, and information on individual cases is no longer available within the computer storage to facilitate a print-out on their circumstances and entitlements.

The costs of this scheme are an important consideration that has only been covered very marginally so far in its analysis. A comprehensive assessment of the different administrative costs involved, and of its running costs, would be of great interest.

A second important consideration is whether the existing administrative structure could be modified even further to secure a still swifter, more automatic increase in take-up, and a smoother administration at less cost. The people working on the project concluded that

'the two goals of improved take-up and of structural reform do not necessarily work against each other. Obviously structural reform could have major effects on take-up (and might render the term 'take-up' redundant); but conversely, the pursuit of increased take-up may well help create the conditions for, and point the way towards, structural reforms. Indeed, the present project can be seen as a step in that direction' (Adler and Du Feu, 1975, page 37).

Perhaps the most significant aspects of this scheme, however, are that it reflects the unwieldy system of welfare benefits that exists, and also how the consideration of computer use indicates an essential response to this complexity. As Adler and Du Feu concluded:

'The very fact that a computer is required, not to improve efficiency or accuracy of calculations, but just to attempt for each household to cut a relatively clear path through the tangle of benefit provision, is an indication of the degree of complexity that has been reached in the current system of means-testing. However, it could well be argued that a radical simplification of the welfare benefits system would be more beneficial than bringing in a computer to overcome (and perhaps perpetuate) the shortcomings of the present system'.

Ayrshire: Cunninghame District

Welfare benefits project

Following on from the work in the Inverclyde Project, the Ayrshire Division of the Strathclyde Regional Council has been preparing to adopt a similar but on-going project in the Cunninghame District, using an Integrated Advice Centre and trained staff to help individuals with the assessment forms. Unhappily they lack the funds to proceed further at the time of writing.

The scheme follows closely the revised approaches used in the Inverclyde project; while awaiting the necessary funds, the organisers have sharpened up the format of their assessment forms and the instructions and notes on completing the application forms. A new version of the forms appeared in May 1976. They have also been training the staff who will help with the completion of the assessment forms, to a high degree of proficiency.

Berkshire

Review of computerised assessment

In 1976, the Berkshire Social Services Department, in association with the Operational Research (Health and Social Services) Unit of Reading University, was preparing to review the possibilities of computerised assessment of apparent entitlement to welfare benefits. At the time of writing, however, the scheme was only at a formative stage.

London Borough of Lambeth

Combined assessment form

The only combined assessment scheme specifically oriented towards people with disabilities was the one initiated in 1976 by the Directorate of Social Services of the London Borough of Lambeth, which was testing the utility of using a single assessment form for three benefits – Attendance Allowance, Mobility Allowance and Invalid Care Allowance. As the Invalid Care Allowance was not then fully operational, testing had focussed on the Attendance Allowance and Mobility Allowance.

Up to the time of writing the project had attempted to test the acceptability of its draft integrated form NI 220 on a sample of 50 people with disabilities, drawn from Lambeth Social Services Department records, who received either Attendance Allowance or Mobility Allowance. This sample was intended to cover both sexes and a wide range of ages and disabilities, but claimants of very low general ability or who had acute personality difficulties were excluded, as it was considered that they would not help evaluation, and would need help with any type of form. The respondents were asked:

a. to complete a short questionnaire concerning:
i. the way in which they first came to hear of the cash benefit received (Attendance Allowance and/or Mobility Allowance),
ii. the way in which the leaflet (including application form) was obtained,
iii. the places where they would like leaflets to be available in the future;

b. to look at the DHSS leaflet concerning the benefit now received and to grade the various sections in degree of importance to themselves and to identify any difficulties in comprehension;

c. to consider NI 220 and to comment upon it generally (the organisers avoided asking highly specific leading questions).

Only 20 of the 50 people were interviewed. Responses to the questionnaire indicated that the national press was by far the most important source of initial information, much more significant than sources related directly to the health/handicap 'network', such as the Invalid Children's Aid Association, the Church of England Children's Society, clinics, doctors, or hospitals, or even radio, television, local press or Social Services Departments.

People did not respond very willingly to questioning on the subject of the existing DHSS forms, so the interviewers concentrated on the draft NI 220 form. Responses showed that people appreciated the first section of the form, which described for whom the benefits were intended, and also the larger size of the form compared with DHSS leaflets. Most respondents did not understand the terms Constant Attendance Allowance and Private Car Allowance. Several people also had difficulty in indicating, at the end of the application form, which benefits they wanted. The responses were all so similar that it was decided to stop after 20 interviews had been conducted, as it seemed that little more was likely to be gained.

This experiment seemed to suffer from an association of the new form with the interviewer (who was known to some of the respondents), giving an associated 'halo effect', and also from the hypothetical nature of the interviews. It was felt that what was really needed was pre-testing of the form by the DHSS in 'real' circumstances, over a set period of time and in a designated geographical area. The DHSS had shown some interest in the scheme, but had not at the time taken it any further.

As it stands, this experiment is little more than a slight test amongst claimants of the particular benefits concerned to see how the design and combination of application forms might be improved. As such it is of marginal usefulness, but it is worthy of recognition as the first attempt directed specifically towards the needs of people with disabilities.

The Finnish computerised pensions system

Although this study is mainly confined to developments in Britain, it has been considered worth including some general details about the administration of social security benefits in Finland, a country with many features in common with Britain. There, the Finnish Social Insurance Institute administers a range of benefits similar to those provided by the DHSS, but tends to avoid the 'poverty trap' and the overlapping of benefits by the efficient use of a computer. The system has the added complexity of automatic index-linking.

In the late 1960s and early 1970s the Finnish system was experiencing similar complexities and problems to those the British system is currently facing. The introduction of a computer in 1972, with instant checking systems, increased head office staff productivity and helped the speed of service to the public. The provision of visual display terminals in the principal local offices has reduced the checking time to a few seconds. The index-linking of the system meant that in 1974 (when there were four adjustments) recipients received their benefits in the normal way without delay, and the cost of readjustment was only £500, compared with £500,000 if it had been conducted manually. The savings on this part of the operation alone covered about a third of the cost of the annual rental of all the data processing equipment.

Conclusions and recommendations

Considering the possibilities that combined assessment schemes offer for increasing the take-up of welfare benefits while at the same time reducing administrative complexity and costs, it is surprising that they have hitherto been used so little. The schemes reviewed here show some tentative efforts in these directions and their review could stimulate further initiatives.

Some people have seen this slow development as a reflection of filibustering or procrastination on the part of vested organisational interests in the various departments administering these benefits. Others see an opposition because of the challenge of combined assessment to the social control function of welfare benefits. Peter Taylor-Gooby, reviewing combined assessment schemes, wrote:

'Selective benefits share the value-accretions of charity; charity operates within a tradition that stretches back to the days when systematised giving from the powerful to the powerless confirmed both the authority of the former and the client-status of the latter. Welfare benefits still fulfil a social control function. The full advantages of combined assessment can only be realised if the system is extended to include benefit administration. This means the rational-bureaucratic, impersonal application of rules – in short an extension of rights for the claimant. The advocate of Combined Assessment is asking the Education Welfare Officer to surrender the sanction of discretion in regard to education welfare benefits. The Housing Manager must give up the possibility of diverting rent benefits to pay off rent arrears. The Finance Department may lose the right to insist that compound-rated tenants produce a paid-up book before a rate rebate is doled out. Combined Assessment means more control for the poor over their own incomes. Opposition is hardly surprising' (*Poverty*, no. 34, summer 1976, pages 19–20).

These comments might be dismissed as malevolent interpretations of administrative inactivity, but they do appear to have some justification, though not constituting the whole picture. Considering the publicity given to some of these schemes, continued indifference and procrastination by local and central government may be seen as culpable. In a time of drastic cuts in government spending and welfare administration, it is important that combined assessment schemes should be given high priority, with the hope that, as so many people believe, the economy in administrative costs would pay for the increased take-up.

This study is primarily concerned with the needs of people with disabilities. Until recently combined assessment schemes have scarcely dealt with those benefits and services most relevant to these people. But any well-planned combined assessment scheme must reduce the difficulties of disabled people, currently failing to retrieve from the system the benefits to which they are entitled but which so often they do not secure. At least as long as the present immensely complex system of benefits and services is retained, some sort of computer-based information, application and eligibility assessment system, such as the Inverclyde project (page 195), may offer hope to government for cheaper, more effective administration as well as fairer, speedier and less supplicatory access for the beneficiaries.

It is therefore recommended that all local authorities which have not as yet reviewed the applicability of combined assessment schemes to their areas should take the initiative and, learning from the experiences of local authorities which have already explored these possibilities, should **introduce such schemes where appropriate, especially in the fields of education, Social Security**

and housing benefits. Particular attention should be paid to minimising the number of times that an assessment of a claimant's income and family circumstances is made.

Although there is scope for local authority initiative in these directions, the onus of responsibility rests with the Department of Health and Social Security. The Department has shown some support for such schemes in the past, particularly regarding the Salop project, but the time taken to introduce and conduct this scheme is too long. Future schemes will need to be introduced far less dilatorily.

Although we do not advocate the extension of a cumbersome bureaucracy, it would seem appropriate that **the Department of Health and Social Security should create within itself a division responsible for reviewing the application procedures for all central and local authority benefits**, for reviewing more fully past and present combined assessment schemes, and preparing more thorough schemes for the introduction of combined assessment in the future. It is important that this division should be at least partially responsible to an outside authority – maybe a parliamentary one – to ensure that its activities proceed with the necessary swiftness.

The proposed DHSS division should also:
a. be responsible for giving advice to local authorities in matters of combined assessment, and where possible integrating assessments for central government benefits with those of local authorities;
b. review very thoroughly past and present combined assessment schemes, and develop much more comprehensive ones which would pay particular attention to assessing changes in take-up of individual benefits and changes in administrative costs (the reviewing of administrative costs should take into full consideration miscellaneous costs such as publicity and the support of back-up staff, which are sometimes neglected);
c. review payment methods for cash benefits;
d. be prepared to assess the applicability of the existing administrative structure in regard to combined assessment, and where that structure is found to be inappropriate, to advise and test new ones.

Chapter Seven

The effect on the client

Underlying the complex structure we have discussed in the preceding chapters – underlying even the name of the system – is the idea that all this is for the *benefit* of disadvantaged people. It is the whole object of this study to examine that assumption in some detail, and throughout this book the experiences of individuals are used to illustrate the real meaning, in human terms, of the complexities and shortcomings of the system. In this chapter, by reference to the circumstances of particular individuals and families, we shall look specifically at the effect of the system upon its 'customers' among people with intrinsic handicaps. In the analysis of the Disablement Income Group's files in Appendix 1, further illustrations are given of the way in which the system fails its intended beneficiaries.

The cases we have used throughout the book are actual cases, modified as regards names and places and thinly disguised in order that they should not identify individual households. This has become particularly important in recent months as many recipients, particularly of Supplementary Benefit, are now finding themselves the victims of hostility, fuelled by people of whom more responsible behaviour might have been expected, whose witch hunt against so-called 'scroungers' is causing great distress to many.

Our experience, and that of other people throughout the country who are involved in casework, has led us to exclude some cases where we felt that human error was the critical factor. (Whatever the system, there will always be an irreducible minimum of such disasters.) We have left out others where we felt that the whole story had not been given. But our object was to document our conclusions from actual cases: let no-one say 'it couldn't happen like that because the regulations say . . .' because in every case, it *did* happen like that.

Some of the problems have since been put right by changes in the regulations or (where ignorance was involved) by expert advice. But the very frequency of such changes, and their arbitrariness, is adding to the difficulties of administrators, advisers and clients at the present time.

Some clients have had to take a course of action which does not represent a 'choice' at all – as when they are forced to take accommodation they do not want, or give up working when they would prefer to carry on. Some are in the same or worse plight today as when they first asked for help.

Nor are these isolated instances: for every story we have included there are hundreds of others, and innumerable other permutations of problems arising from the way 'help' to handicapped people is dispensed. We have attempted to discover and illustrate the most common problem areas by using the DIG files, the experience of the Mirror Group Readers' Service and letters from case workers up and down the country.

Thus the undue reliance now placed upon the intended 'last resort' of Supplementary Benefit has been illustrated earlier in this book in relation to the total structure of Social Security provision, but among the 1,300 families whose cases are in DIG's files its significance is even greater, almost half being dependent for all or part of their income upon this source. It is not surprising, therefore, that the various elements of Supplementary Benefit (pension, allowance, Exceptional Circumstances Additions and Exceptional Needs Payments) constituted the largest source of identified problems. Nor, in view of all that has been written elsewhere on the problems of means-tested benefits, of which local authorities now administer *over forty different types* (quite apart from variations in methods of application between local authorities), will it be surprising that local authority benefits as a group provided the next largest area of difficulty.

The most disturbing thing about these 'horror stories' of individuals' difficulties with the system is that they are not confined to the files of DIG, which, as a pressure group, might be expected to attract them. On the contrary, they are common throughout the country – from Scotland to the South-west, from East Anglia to Wales – and they centre on the same benefits.

It should be noted that in dealing with particular cases we have quoted wherever possible the benefit levels, wage levels and prices ruling at the time. If, despite repeated checking, errors have arisen, they are our own and only offer further proof of the difficulties which face handicapped people all the time in their efforts to discover to what they are entitled.

Supplementary Benefits

Supplementary Benefit problems identified among the DIG cases fell into three broad categories:
a. refusal of benefits and wrong information given by officials;
b. unmet need even when a benefit was granted, due to the inadequacy of the payments made; and
c. the manner in which clients had been treated.

This experience was paralleled in the Holyhead Information Project in October 1975; the researchers commented as regards their own findings:

'the dominance of Supplementary Benefit problems in the non-contributory benefits category reflects the nationally documented failure of means-tested benefits to meet need effectively, and, in particular, the rigidity of the Supplementary Benefit internal regulations governing the exercise of discretion. This field showed the highest level of dissatisfaction ... much of the dissatisfaction was generated by the way in which claims were initially dealt with. Callers complained of the unhelpful and sometimes disapproving attitude of the interviewing clerk. There were cases in which claimants were told that they were not entitled to benefit (such as an Exceptional Needs Payment for house repairs), returned to the Supplementary Benefits Office on our advice, and, after insisting with some vigour, were eventually able to make a proper formal claim – *which was then approved.*'

After explaining that this brought the project's workers into conflict with the staff of the Supplementary Benefit office, they added:

'our social work orientation may well have contributed to the divergence of approaches between ourselves and the Supplementary Benefits Commission.'

What they describe as 'social work orientation' is another way of putting what is meant in the context of the present study by 'client orientation'. People administering DHSS benefits often give the impression of being *benefit* oriented, and of concentrating on meeting the complicated letter of their administrative code, without appearing to understand the frustration and despair created by their decisions and their method of approach.

In an article for *Social Work Today*, David Bull, of the Department of Social Administration at Bristol University, told the story of applications for a diet allowance for one client, consistently refused even when supported by certificates from his doctor diagnosing hiatus hernia and prescribing a 'gastric diet', because this condition was not among the five for which the Commission awards this allowance. Nevertheless the allowance was granted, after the doctor had mentioned that the diet was the same as that for an ulcer and was asked, by the social workers to whom this had been related by the client, to send in a letter to this effect. If, however, the doctor had not happened to make that remark to a client who was alert enough to note and repeat it, and if the client's contacts had not in turn been alert enough to see its potential usefulness, one more person would still be struggling to pay for his diet without the extra allowance to which he is 'entitled'. An indication that this kind of problem may not be uncommon was given by a 1972 study of two-parent families poor enough to qualify for Family Income Supplement, in which special dietary need was found to be the most common cause of extra expense arising from disability.

Inadequate benefits

The inadequacy of benefits is a recurring theme. We have referred elsewhere to Exceptional Needs Payments for clothing which are inadequate for the articles which it has been agreed are necessary (page 230) and to unrealistic heating, diet and laundry allowances (page 57). The authors of the Grassmarket (Edinburgh) study wrote that:

'insufficient clothing was allowed for and the guide to required clothing stocks ... is no way followed. When grants were given the clothing specified could not be obtained locally for the money allocated and often the levels given in the DHSS national price list (itself outdated) were not met. [Those in receipt of Invalidity Benefit] whose clothing needs were a constant problem due to specific types of disability, were given the impression at local offices that they were ineligible for a discretionary payment.'

This was so even though the clients' benefit rate was often little more than £1.00 above the Supplementary Benefit entitlement and there is nothing to restrict such a payment solely to those already receiving Supplementary Benefit in section 7 of the Social Security Act 1966, which says:

'where it appears to the Commission reasonable in all the circumstances they may determine that benefit shall be paid to a person by way of a single payment to meet an exceptional need.'

Nevertheless the belief is widespread among case workers as well as potential clients that unless a person is receiving regular Supplementary Benefit they have little chance of getting an Exceptional Needs Payment.

In recent months Supplementary Benefit allowances have been increasingly unrealistic in the realm of heating allowances: one recent example from the DIG files is mentioned on page 57.

The cost of incontinence has long been one which is treated unrealistically in terms of Supplementary Benefit allowances. It is usually acknowledged by a payment of some pence per week for additional laundry costs – often worth little more than one trip to a launderette, and sometimes less than the cost of a packet of detergent. Yet it represents not only extra costs in detergents and in heating for the water to do the extra washing (and perhaps also to dry it) but other costs as well, less obvious at first sight to the inexperienced: additional stocks of clothing and bedlinen are required when articles are often in the laundry basket, and there is extra wear and tear on these items as well. Some people need to use disposables – which may or may not, in practical terms, be available on prescription or through the Community Nursing Service – and other chemists' goods such as toilet soap, talc, sprays and, in some cases, pads and adhesives.

The question of 'availability on prescription' is a vexed one. Handicapped people find they are refused any kind of financial help for items, including those mentioned above, which are technically 'available on prescription'. In practical terms, however, the prescription may be of relatively little help: DIG members report instances where special foods (such as gluten-free bread) are simply not available at local shops, and have to be obtained *by post* from manufacturers who may have no facility for accepting NHS prescriptions in lieu of cash. Some individuals whose problems include incontinence have difficulties with items like padding and adhesives; some doctors either will not prescribe the item, or will not prescribe it in sufficient quantity, so that use of prescriptions would mean visits to the surgery every few days for no other reason – a procedure that can be more difficult, time consuming and expensive than struggling to pay for some, at least, of the goods that are theoretically available free.

Inadequacy of benefit applies also to incapacity benefits such as Attendance Allowance. One of the most topical areas of complaint on this score is mobility, and in particular the Mobility Allowance. This allowance is intended to *add to* that portion of the recipient's income normally used for mobility – thereby showing a complete failure to understand either that many handicapped people have little or nothing left of their income to allocate to mobility, or that the sum total of the allowance and what they can so allocate is all too likely to remain insufficient. A young wheelchair-user had the misfortune to become the mother of twins just days after the ending of the old Vehicle Scheme (under which she would then have qualified for a car in place of her three-wheeler – in which no passengers can be carried); she was told instead to claim the £5.00 Mobility Allowance. She lives on an estate in the north of England at a distance from most facilities and her letter shows the real effect of such a 'provision':

'This, I am afraid, would not even cover the cost of one weekly trip to the baby clinic, let alone to the hospital, or for a taxi to wait outside a chemist while I obtain the babies' food. It is for the babies that I worry, because their way of life is going to be too restricted. Just one example is the fact that they have never yet been to their grandmother's house, for whom I'm sure it would be the proudest day of her life. You will realise that, at the moment, the problems are endless, and the situation of getting them to and from school later on is unthinkable.'

This young woman used every avenue of protest known to her to no avail, even though her MP took the matter to Alf Morris, the head of the appropriate DHSS department. Happily for her, she also went to the Mirror Group Readers' Service, which took up the fight, and she has now been told – after almost a year of coping with twin babies, a wheelchair and no adequate mobility provision – that she will be supplied with a car.

There are two alarming things about this case. One is the fact that there is no provision in the regulations for this particular piece of 'discretion' and one cannot but question whether it would ever have been exercised had not a powerful national newspaper been involved. The other is the unwise advice to take the Mobility Allowance in preference to retaining her existing Invacar; had she accepted it, she would actually have been left *worse off*, both in terms of the total value of the two contributions to her budget and in terms of usefulness. At least, with the Invacar, she could be mobile if her husband or a neighbour was able to mind the twin babies and later when they become toddlers, someone else might have been able to take them on a bus while she followed – in the unsocial way Invacar families have long had to adopt – in her three-wheeler. If she had opted for a payment of a few pounds a week which she herself could not use on public transport because of the wheelchair, even that would not have been possible.

Misinformation

Wrong advice like that just mentioned is becoming increasingly common. Often it comes from the most 'authoritative' levels, and usually with no explanation of the reasoning behind it (which might enable the client to see that it was inappropriate). Part of the reason is exactly the complexity and frequency of changes in the regulations – as many as 10,000 changes in benefit regulations in a year have been claimed. *There is no come-back for the client in this situation.*

Wrong information and poor advice given to one claimant had a direct effect on his pension rights. To quote from the correspondence:

'From 1952 until 1968 I and my family were virtually living on Social Security and, being considered by the Ministry of Employment to be unable to be gainfully employed because of my physical disability (spina bifida), I was advised to seek exemption from paying weekly health contributions. This I succeeded in doing but was told that, in my case, there might be some loss of pension from the age of 65, but the reduction would be small. I succeeded to my parents' estate in 1968 and offered to resume contributions, but was told that the reduction in the pension would be little affected and it was not worth my while to resume payments for the few years remaining (to 1973).

However, last winter, the manager of my local branch of the ministry suddenly called on me, without previous notification, to say that I was coming up to pension age but I owed several hundred pounds and I should not have been told that I need not resume payments from 1968.

I asked my solicitor to take up my case with the ministry and he succeeded in getting a reduction for me of back payments. This, with an instalments payment, I was forced to accept. I am aggrieved that I was made to suffer because of an official's mistake in 1968.'

The client's helplessness in this situation is almost absolute. Not only must he pay for an official's error made years earlier, but he was given no warning of the visit to tell him of his unsuspected debt. He might have been alone; the shock of such a shattering and unexpected announcement could have seriously affected his physical condition (asthma and multiple sclerosis sufferers are especially liable to experience aggravation of their symptoms by shock); some clients might even have been driven to suicide. Fortunately, this client was driven to a solicitor – but the responsibility ought never to have fallen upon him.

Not only does the system at present place all the onus of effort and expenditure of time and of mental and physical resources upon the very people whose resources are reduced by their handicaps, but it provides no real means by which administrators can be made answerable for their wrong or misleading advice.

Often the client has no means of knowing that his or her benefit is being reduced by some false assumption or decision. A Supplementary Benefit recipient may ask for an analysis of the way in which his benefit is made up (the form A124) and from bitter experience some clients have learned to apply automatically for one of these every time their rate of benefit changes. Significantly, however, failure has so far attended all the efforts of Welfare Rights Officers and social workers to make *automatic* the provision of such a statement to the client. Yet the present situation creates administrative waste: almost every case worker can give instances where clients have made applications for extra payments (for extra costs of diet or laundry, for example) only to be told that their existing payment *includes* an element intended to cover this.

The closing trap

For most clients, problems do not come in neat parcels under the heading of any one benefit: the interaction of inadequate provisions only escalates to clothing/dietary/mobility allowances after it has already affected basic income maintenance. An all-too-typical complex is that of Mrs W, a lady living in the west country, paralysed from the waist down and doubly incontinent. Mrs W received Invalidity Pension and lower-rate Invalidity Allowance and was granted an Invacar and a petrol allowance. The Ws sometimes found it necessary to use this money to get the husband to and from his work. Mr W, in order to avoid redundancy, had had to accept a lower-paid job, which also involved shift work, including night-time working. At the same time as their income was thus reduced, the telephone therefore became a vital lifeline for his wife. The local authority paid for its installation but the Ws paid the rental.

Meanwhile the local authority assessed the Ws' eligibility for a Rent Rebate using a 'needs allowance' which was 'hardly equal' to Mrs W's outlay on talcum powder, sprays and other chemists' goods essential for her hygiene and comfort (but not strictly 'medicines'). As a result, since her invalidity benefits were counted in with her husband's wage as 'resources' but the substantial expenses of her incontinence were not taken into account in assessing their 'needs', the Ws were not allowed any Rent Rebate at all. Yet, in effect, virtually the whole of Mrs W's benefits were spent on her needs for extra laundry, fuel and chemists' goods, so that this money in no way formed a part of their basic income. The Ws were thus paying exactly the same rent that they would have paid had she been an able-bodied person going to work and *contributing* to the household resources. This happened even though the local authority Housing Department technically had discretion to increase needs allowances in special circumstances.

The rent of the Ws' council flat doubled between 1970 and 1974, during which time Mr W's income had deteriorated because of his enforced change of job, and their essential expenses were increased by the need for the telephone.

In 1974 they were among the people who found themselves involuntarily shifted from one local authority to another by boundary changes, and they found that an application for bath rails and a concrete parking area for the Invacar met with little response, probably because of reorganisation problems.

At that date Mr W's net weekly income was	£21.50
Mrs W's Invalidity benefits were	£10.65
giving them an income of	£32.15 plus the petrol allowance, nominally for the Invacar

Their outgoings were:

Rent and rates	£4.70
Average costs of heating	£5.80
Medicinal supplies *other* than those on prescription	£3.50
Special clothing, underwear and sheets	£4.50
Telephone (per week)	£0.90
	£19.40

leaving £12.75 for food and all other expenditure for two people; soap and detergents were costing £1.25 a week *extra* to normal usage.

In 1975 Mrs W successfully applied for Attendance Allowance, being awarded the lower rate (then £6.20) – but by then the rent had gone up a further £1.52 a week and telephone charges had risen so much that they were at the point of having to choose either to give up their telephone lifeline or to send back the Invacar because there was no money for petrol. The Attendance Allowance was immediately absorbed into their general budget, and with it they decided thankfully that 'with care' they would now be able to 'rub along' for a little longer. Even at that date (mid-1975), however, electricity bills had become 'a nightmare' because of the high cost of running the immersion heater for the extra washing. They had not had a holiday since before Mrs W's original illness *fifteen years* earlier. She bought her first coat for ten years after receiving the Attendance Allowance, and a charity gift of £10 was used to replace a ten-year-old pair of shoes and to put by £3 for petrol. Mr W wrote:

'I have got used to writing out my grocery list and then having to cross out many items. We rarely buy fruit, or eggs, and saddest of all . . . have not been able to send Christmas cards.'

Yet this lady's dignity and her appreciation that she and her husband were 'better off than many' remained unassailable. Nevertheless, while the publicity surrounding the 'provisions' for handicapped people creates an impression of dignity and independence, this is hardly borne out by this instance of someone already suffering the miseries of paralysis and incontinence and dependent on the telephone for help while her husband was out working at night, unable to use the Invacar she had been supplied with because her basic income was too low to allow for petrol, and cut off from communication in the form of Christmas greetings.

Moreover, since 1975 the price of food has risen still further; so has the cost of the telephone and, above all, the cost of fuel, so that increases in benefits have not improved the situation of people like the Ws.

In 1977 Mrs W reaches retirement age. For anyone in her situation, a fresh shock is in store at that point because while Invalidity Benefits are not taxable, Retirement Pensions *are*, if the combined income exceeds the tax threshold (allowing for age relief). Along with the loss of Mobility Allowance, this forms another of the further deprivations which come with retirement.

It is also one of the many ways in which handicapped people find *dates* of greater significance in determining their income than the facts of their disabilities. Indeed it is very striking how large a proportion of the problems brought to the Mirror Group Readers' Service by handicapped people would cease to exist if these clients qualified for help on the basis of handicap rather than the calendar.

Long term or short term?

Reference has already been made (pages 54–55) to the way in which the framing of the system for more generous provisions for *long-term* incapacity actually operates against people with intermittently disabling disorders. Another trap, and a related one, is built into the benefits system by the relationship between Invalidity Benefit and Supplementary Benefit. The latter is payable at a more generous long-term rate, which can only be reached after two years on the short-term rate. But Invalidity Benefit works out at slightly more than the Supplementary Benefit short-term rate. Because the higher of these two benefits is paid, many disabled clients find that they can never qualify for the long-term Supplementary Benefit which would increase their incomes by some £3 per week. Advisory service workers at DIG have battled against this trap in vain. It is well known to the Mirror Group advisors, who include this among a number of technical ways of preventing the client from reaching higher benefits which they refer to collectively as 'shunting'.

Two classic examples of this kind of long-term/short-term shunting and its consequences were recently quoted by the Batley Advice Centre (in *Social Services*, 15 November 1976):

'a family with children, whose head was medically disabled and dependent on the National Insurance Invalidity Benefit [and] had been unwell for three years, was 80p better off than if they had been on [Supplementary Benefit at the short-term rate]. However, if they *had* been on SB from the outset they would now be on the long-term rate and would therefore be £3 better off than they are now'

and

'the DHSS have stated that for a very small number of "severely disabled" claimants (they used to just say "disabled") they will operate their discretion after two years and allow such claimants the long-term rate. Now that the government has chosen to increase the differential between long and short-term rates, the plight of this group of claimants is becoming more and more desperate'.

The Advice Centre had represented at a tribunal a worker who

'was forced to leave his job as a coal miner because of a chest condition, and who is now seriously hampered in his search for work by his continuing disability but who has been refused the long-term rate. *The result of living for four years on an income which was never designed for long-term support has meant that his family is now seen as a 'problem family' which attracts a battery of welfare officers.*' (The italics are ours.)

The examination of Non-Contributory Invalidity Pension in Chapter 2 (page 60) demonstrates another instance of how easily clients may be 'shunted' – even in good faith – to a benefit which is not ultimately to their advantage, and the similar dilemma as to whether they would be better off receiving Supplementary Benefits or local authority rent and rate benefits has also been discussed elsewhere in this book (page 36).

Struggling to stay in work

Perhaps because the majority of the Mirror Group readers are younger and working people, many of the problems reaching their Readers' Service concern employment and handicapped people. Those who are currently branding as 'scroungers' anyone on Unemployment and Supplementary Benefits might be surprised to know how unwillingly many of the recipients are there, and to read the desperation of the letters in which they recount their struggles to work, only to be penalised financially.

Since the introduction of long- and short-term benefits, case workers have noticed an increasing tendency for sick or handicapped people who have little or no chance of obtaining employment to be put on the register of *employable* disabled, so that after 312 days they are left without benefit or entitlement to a contributory benefit. Even where such people attend Medical Appeal Tribunals, consultants' reports and long-established records are not always consulted, or the person concerned may be classified as fit for 'light work' even if the local employment situation and the client's age make it extremely unlikely that any employer will consider him.

One such case is that of a man, disabled from childhood by a progressive disease, who had struggled through to his middle fifties, always self-supporting, and bringing up a family, paying his full insurance and taxes. In addition to disabilities of arm muscles and one foot, he had by then a duodenal ulcer and had had one heart attack. After a road accident which left his arms almost useless, even the man who had employed him over all these years was forced to admit that it was impossible to find him work. According to his doctor, he had not been capable of following employment at any time during the previous three years. Although officers of the Department of Employment and DHSS (both National Insurance and Supplementary Benefit sections) all saw this man, he was not considered eligible for invalidity benefits, but put on the Disabled Employable register and subsequently denied Unemployment Benefit on the grounds that he was briefly self-employed before his accident. He was put on to Supplementary Benefit, without being credited with National Insurance contributions, so that he lost entitlement to contributory benefits. His wife then began a full-time job, whereupon his Supplementary Benefit was stopped and he was left completely dependent on his wife's earnings. Like many others, he was not aware – and was not told – that he could appeal to be re-classified, nor that being 'on the Disabled Register' offered no protection of his entitlement to benefit.

A comparable 'reward for effort' was meted out to a 36-year-old mentally handicapped man who had lived on Supplementary Benefit since he was 16. A job as a kitchen porter was found for him by the instructor at a day centre he had attended, in the belief that the work would be therapeutic. For fifteen weeks the man managed to cope with the job, but he then became ill. When he gave in and re-applied for his Supplementary Benefit he was given the lower, short-term rate, because the period of employment had exceeded thirteen weeks! When the case was taken up on his behalf, the Supplementary Benefit Commission chairman agreed that such cases would be looked at more generously, but no evidence has yet come in to show that this is in fact being done.

Other disabled people have been persuaded to take work which has proved too much for them, and their comments illustrate their helplessness in the situation:

'I was green in these goings on and thought that if I refused the employment, my benefit would stop ... *they knew the rules, I didn't.*'

Compared with some other benefits, the Industrial Injury scheme appears to be relatively trouble-free. There is, however, one savage aspect of its rules which has concerned Mirror Group advisers: this involves people with hearing impairment resulting from industrial conditions. Problems arise because claims must be made within *one year* of the date of the last employment in the process in question. As industrial deafness is made worse by every year spent in these conditions, this clause implies that people should work until the last possible moment in an environment which is actively injuring their hearing, instead of taking work in less damaging conditions as soon as medical opinion recommends that they do so. Otherwise they lose their claim to benefit, or receive only partial recognition for any subsequent progression of the damage.

Care and attendance

Another major – and frequently, in the long term, *expensive* – shortcoming of the system is its built-in attitude to 'care' and 'attendance'. Although some improvement has been achieved in recent years in respect of the treatment of people living together as man and wife but not legally married, the system makes no allowance for the supportive function of relationships other than close blood ties – and not always those. The non-eligibility of wives for Invalid Care Allowance has been mentioned earlier, as has the failure of this benefit to recognise life-long care between friends. Single handicapped people wishing to maintain their independence by sharing their home in return for 'attendance' find the system most unhelpful. One case, won recently after a hard-fought appeal, concerned a young man, severely handicapped by cerebral palsy, who found another young man who, in return for a roof over his head, was willing to provide the virtually round-the-clock presence and occasional assistance which he needed. The 'attendant' could not present himself as 'available for employment' without destroying the whole point of his being there – the handicapped man falls frequently and then cannot get up unaided, and he cannot reach the toilet without help. Nevertheless the housing authority and DHSS, under a direct payment arrangement (see page 61), were stopping a rent share from the handicapped householder's Supplementary Benefit. Since he was in fact paying his attendant nothing at all, the DHSS were thus requiring the attendant to *pay* for the privilege of a twenty-four-hour-a-day attendance commitment! Yet without some such arrangement, this man would have required institutional care costing at least £70 a week.

Where a relative is providing accommodation for someone living on Supplementary Benefit, the benefit will be paid at the non-householder rate, so low that it is virtually impossible for the recipient to make an economic contribution to the household budget. Thus on top of the obligation already felt to those who make it possible for such a person to remain in the community, relationships are strained by the enforced pressure on the resources of the caring household. This is in sharp contrast to the practice in some other countries where it is possible to *pay* relatives as the caring agents.

A few local authorities have in fact shown flexibility in their treatment of this problem, paying for home help even if provided by a relative.

The Crossroads scheme The most economic and flexible form of care in use in 1976 (average costs in 1975/76, £5 per household served per week) is the 'Crossroads' scheme, operating in Rugby. This uses specially trained staff to provide whatever care and assistance an individual household requires, with a flexibility as regards hours and services provided which is unknown in either traditional home nursing or Home Help Services. Client satisfaction is high because the service provides what *they* want at the times they need it. In one characteristic case, help was provided on several nights of each week, from the time the handicapped (working) member of the household went to bed, to help with the process of going to bed, to provide attendance through the night (to allow the able-bodied member of the household some uninterrupted sleep), and to help with getting up. With this relief for part of the week, the household was enabled to cope for the rest of the time. Without such help it would almost certainly have broken up, with the working member becoming a non-working inmate of some form of residential institution.

Local authority benefits

Among local authority benefits the chief problems, which have been outlined elsewhere, arise firstly from top-heavy administration and, secondly, from the application of highly variable and increasingly rigid eligibility rules. The latter presents particularly acute problems at present because of the financial restrictions imposed by the economic situation. The main impact of the former upon the client is through the consequent inordinate delays, particularly in respect of the supply of small aids and appliances and of adaptations: the case of the reaching aid quoted on page 128 is typical of many. A client who only wanted four special handles on doors wrote wistfully that if he had had the money he would have bought them – but that requires resources either to get to shops or to telephone suppliers, as well as to pay for the handles. They are 'available' from the local authority – but at a cost in delay and administration which is often out of proportion with the items needed.

Moreover, since the latest cuts in local authority social services budgets, letters like the following are being received:

'Dear –,
Sister X of Dr Y's practice has been in touch with us by telephone to say that you were requiring bath aids.

I regret to have to inform you that because of staff shortages the Social Workers are not assessing for aids at the moment. If, however, you attend an out-patients department of a hospital it may be possible to get them through the Occupational Therapy Department.

The other alternative I can suggest is that you watch the Sunday papers for advertisements and obtain a bath mat at a chemist such as Boots.'

So leisurely, so unrealistic – about the urgency of the need for the aid, the ability to trot out to Boots, to wait till the next hospital appointment, to find the money to buy not only the aids but Sunday papers! A case 'administered' already, both by the nursing service and by a senior social worker. The net gain to the client (an elderly man with a heart condition)? – some advice which there were no resources to enable him to take. And if, in the meantime, without rails or other aids, he falls – perhaps a hospital case costing over £100 a week.

Bath aids, referred to here, in fact represented the numerically largest need for aids discovered in the Outset study of the City of London. These are inexpensive items and their supply is time consuming to administer; moreover, many clients would willingly pay for them if they had the money and access to advice. The letter quoted above also illustrates very clearly the buck-passing which sometimes goes on between health service outlets and local authority Social Services Departments. In some areas the working relationship is good and efficient. In most, it is less so now that budgets are tighter.

Similar problems seem to occur with telephones – now almost unobtainable in many areas. Only a few years ago, some Social Services Departments were building into their services to clients a greater use of the telephone, because it made more economic use of staff time (to go *when* they were needed, rather than in order to find out *if* they were needed, provided that telephone contact was real and well maintained). As telephone costs have escalated, however, handicapped people who sorely need the contact are having to give up even telephones already installed – but there is no way, in the present state of the budget, that the Social Services staff can be increased to replace them.

Home Help Services, too, are a source of problems, not least because they are too limited – both in the total number of hours of help they can provide, and in the degree of flexibility they offer as regards the help that can be given.

The situation with regard to adaptations and Improvement Grants has been discussed already (pages 37 and 122), as has that relating to the whole confused issue of Rent and Rate Rebates (page 36).

One point at which the system of cash benefits interacts with local authority provisions to the detriment of at least some handicapped people is in respect of residents in local authority residential accommodation. Here, most of the central government benefit is transferred to the authority providing the accommodation, thus leaving the client with virtually no income. This is particularly inappropriate to those people encouraged to try to maintain their personal activity (such as the use of an Invacar) on sums determined long ago on the basis that all clients so accommodated would sit in their slippers in armchairs all day.

Conclusions

a. The main impact upon the client of the present system is *confusion*. His reaction may be to give up (see Chapters 4 and 5 on take-up), he may make the wrong decisions (in which case he does not receive that help to which he is 'entitled' and for which he may well have contributed for many years) or he may become aggressive – in which case also he probably gets less than his entitlement, unless he is fortunate enough to find champions with more resources.
b. One way or the other, the client is often not getting his entitlement, and some clients are simply excluded by the rigidity of the rules.
c. The waste involved is enormous – see also Chapter 3 on administrative costs.
d. The onus of effort, knowledge and demand upon resources is thrust upon the participant least able to meet this demand – the client.
e. It is not possible to make the system, *as it is*, work efficiently, even for the administrators.

Whose benefit indeed?

Chapter Eight

Implications and recommendations

1. Chapter 1 on the legislative background and Chapter 2 on **the benefit system** which has evolved therefrom make it clear that this **is a ragbag of provisions** based on a variety of principles, some of them relating to a bygone social order. 'Tinkering' will not put this right.

2. **The clear message is that a 'new Beveridge' is needed** – a wide-ranging, independent re-structuring of the system. The body responsible for this would need to have official status and full access to all the data it required, but to be detached from current DHSS operation, as Beveridge's inquiry was detached.

3. Our point is not merely the judgement that handicapped people should not be the ones called upon to 'pay' for their own unavoidable extra needs, but an economic one: if they are not given the resources to pay, the cost will nevertheless be extracted from the community in some other way. Chapter 3 on administrative costs suggests that **we cannot afford *not* to change the present system**. Available figures, with all their limitations, indicate that there is upwards of £3.5 million per year of totally unproductive spending on false alternatives alone, and to this must be added an unknown proportion of the total administrative costs detailed in that chapter. The cost of overlapping benefits must include the cost of the four-year DHSS study of thousands of records leading to a shift of nearly 90,000 people across from Supplementary Benefits to local authority housing benefits, for gains in individual incomes which for the most part were comparatively small. Another example is the administrative cost of using Improvement Grants to assist handicapped people with house adaptations, which is becoming prohibitive (see page 122).

4. **If payment is not made in the form of benefits, it is often made in other and ultimately more expensive ways**, such as hospital or institutional care or, for younger people, in the loss of their potential contribution to the national product. At present the system ensures that handicapped people often have too little cash to buy themselves small items (for instance, of equipment) and these are then provided in kind, at greater expense and often with wasteful administrative on-costs.

5. The whole system of benefits for people with disabilities, however, has become so complex that **nobody can work out just how much it is costing**. Government departments, local authorities, academic studies and pressure groups, as

well as the press, are all trying to determine the cost – and all failing. In an article in the *Financial Times* (27 July 1976) Joe Rogaly spotlighted this inability of even those in government to disentangle what is being spent on help for handicapped people, and argued that a 'budget for the disabled' is needed. Other writers have pointed to the waste represented by the whole transfer payment cycle, occupying many civil servants in the paying of benefits subsequently clawed back because of the tax threshold situation outlined in Chapter 2. A re-examination of this issue ought to form part of any long-term revision of the benefits system.

These macro-economic arguments point forcefully to the need to stop groping in the dark and tacking bits here and there on to our creaking assemblage of benefits as and when circumstances force us to do so.

6. The evidence from individual cases argues from the other end that **it is time to stop making additions to services, regulations and qualifications on an *ad hoc* basis**, in ways unrelated to each other or, very often, to their effect upon the recipient.

7. Our principal recommendation therefore must be that, in the immediate future, while the state of the economy makes it certain that additional resources are unlikely to be available, **development time should be devoted to a wider-ranging examination of the benefit structure *as it affects handicapped people* than has been undertaken since 1942**. This inquiry must have power to question the appropriateness in today's – or, better still, tomorrow's – conditions of the system of benefits and related provisions available to people with intrinsic handicaps, and the way in which these are administered. Among the foreseeable changes in the near future which need to be taken into consideration *now* are the implications of devolution for the locally administered provisions upon which handicapped people have been made increasingly dependent, as well as the outcome of current discussions regarding the age of retirement: if the latter issue is resolved in a way which changes the existing fixed five-year gap between provision for men and that for women, there must be considerable changes in tax and benefit regulations.

8. **Inefficiency in any service is wasteful.** In an area of such delicacy as the incomes of handicapped people and their families, the repeated need to go to the same or different places, answer the same questions, or write out the same data in letters several times over for a small total sum is not merely wasteful, but itself creates stress in circumstances which may already be imposing something near the limit of tolerable strain.

9. Perhaps **the most urgent priority** in terms of economy and dignity **is to tackle the problems at the fringes of employment**. The emphases within the present system on incapacity for work and 'periods of interruption of employment' are inappropriate to many handicapped people. Too much depends upon the calendar rather than their condition. Contrary to often-expressed views, it

is not the benefits which are a disincentive to working, for handicapped people – it is the abrupt *loss* of benefits if these people try to work within their limitations.

10. It is, moreover, no use pretending that changes in respect of employment will help many handicapped people unless the system is also to be made **realistic about mobility and its cost**.

11. In term of the largest *numbers* to be helped, **the need is to raise the level of basic benefit**. It has been argued that a choice has to be made between a 'universal' solution (standard benefits paid as of right, but irrespective of the wide variety of individual needs) and a 'selective' system. The present system leans heavily towards selectivity for identifiable sub-groups and 'discretion' of the most arbitrary type. One result is that it is so complex as to be near impossible to administer. The 'universal' and 'selective' approaches to a solution are not necessarily mutually exclusive. By lifting the level of 'universal' provision for those who have an intrinsic handicap, and introducing greater freedom in respect of part-time or intermittent working for those whose handicaps were medically established, it would be possible to reduce the demand upon the necessary *discretionary* element to a level at which it could operate as it was intended to do. The optimum balance between the two elements would have to be worked out in relation to the resources that could be released in this way, added to any additional resources which might be able to be made available at the date when the system was to be introduced.

12. As an ultimate design, a two-part structure could be devised which would pay **a benefit (*A*) as of right to handicapped people which would provide a reasonable income**. This benefit should be taxable, but should not cease abruptly for those who were able to secure a limited or intermittent income from work, being so designed as to taper away, leaving them slightly better off as a result of their efforts, while at the same time providing them with underlying and *immediately* available security when working was impossible (i.e. without going back to periods of waiting, lower short-term rates and so on). **The second element (*B*) would be an allowance for the additional expenses of disabled living**, related to the handicap of the individual, and *not* subject to tax or means test. Its function would be to help redress the balance between handicapped and non-handicapped people in coping with unavoidable outlay. (This structure would correspond in many respects to the National Disability Income proposals of the Disablement Income Group.)

A would be used to live on, or to supplement earnings as and when necessary, the recipient paying tax on the same basis as everyone else whenever his income crossed the tax threshold. *B* would act as a recognition that ordinary tax thresholds take no account of the extra cost of disabled living.

13. **Introduction of the second of these elements ought perhaps to have priority**, as it would help most those with the most acute problems and, in so doing, take a considerable load off the Supplementary Benefits mechanism.

14. In terms of the *most acute* need, where the least help has been given under the existing system, **disabled housewives must receive the highest priority**. Help for them is scheduled, and it ought not to be postponed again. (For some, at least, this recommendation will be implemented in 1977/78.)

15. The possibility should also be explored of **paying benefits on a basis which eliminated the male/female distinction**, treating either as a handicapped individual, the presence or otherwise of dependants being a matter of *fact* not a matter of sex.

16. **The introduction of benefits paid *as of right* would largely dispose of the problem of non-take-up in relation to cash benefits.** The studies discussed in Chapters 4 and 5 clearly indicate that the present structure does not work. Combined assessment (see Chapter 6) is not enough to solve the problem, though it may be of some help while the system remains unchanged.

17. Even before any change is effected in the present structure, **central government ought actively to take responsibility for mistakes made and wrong advice given in its name** – even if only in cases where evidence could be provided. This, after all, is the principle underlying the 'seek and serve' aspect of the Chronically Sick and Disabled Persons Act. It would be part of this responsibility to record visits and telephone calls by clients to benefit offices, as well as letters, and to provide recipients automatically with details of the basis upon which their benefits have been calculated.

18. While the system remains as it is, the possibility ought to be examined of some **inversion of the present hierarchy of administration within the DHSS** at the end which is in contact with the consumer, so that initial contact is with a more senior officer, who will pass a case to less experienced staff only when it has been established that it is clear cut.

Together, points 17 and 18 above should help to reduce the impact of wrong information or failure to pass on relevant additional information to the claimant.

19. The issues raised concerning **payment through post offices** (see page 51) also suggest that some consideration should be given to possible modifications of this aspect of the benefits system.

20. In view of the importance, and the financial difficulties of home care and domestic help facilities as at present provided by local authorities, attention might usefully be given to the possibility of **extending to other areas the 'Crossroads' care scheme** (page 215), operated in the Rugby area on a very high level of consumer satisfaction and economic efficiency.

21. Finally – and with distressing topicality – whatever system is devised, **the possibility of abuses should not be allowed to interfere with payment as of right to those genuinely eligible**. It is a matter of historical fact that at

times of economic difficulty the community tends to turn on its most vulnerable members, and disabled people today are acutely aware of this. In the past the need for 'safeguards' has often been the occasion of difficulties for the very people who are genuinely eligible for help from the system. A clear distinction must be made between (*a*) cheating the *system* in order to get what, in theory, its inventors wanted to give, and (*b*) trying to obtain by fraud something for which there is neither entitlement nor need (as in the case of organised multiple fraud). 'Playing the system' in the first of these senses has become fairly common precisely because the system is so extraordinary. Examples include:

doctors' 'perjury', where to have filled in forms with literal accuracy would have negated the intention of the system (as, for instance, in the early days of Attendance Allowance, or in the statements on medical certificates as to when chronically sick or handicapped people were last seen);

the use of 'sick' statements to save handicapped people the effort of regular reporting as available for work;

switching between housing benefits and Supplementary Benefits to gain the best advantage;

getting a husband to stay at home to care for grandma and his wife to work because Invalid Care Allowance cannot be paid to a married woman living with her husband;

the many instances of 'misappropriation' of benefits when more appropriate ones cannot be obtained (see pages 91–92).

It is an indictment of the system that this form of 'cheating' happens precisely when its administrators are making the most determined efforts to operate it in a manner which will be both *humane* and *effective*. We may indeed ask for *whose benefit* the system is being kept in its present form?

Appendix One

Problems identified in the Disablement Income Group's case files

Introduction

Since its inception in 1965, the Disablement Income Group has accumulated a considerable quantity of detailed information about the problems of some 1,300 disabled individuals and families with disabled members. This information exists in the form of completed questionnaires – questionnaires which were designed to provide DIG with a clearer picture of the particular circumstances of the individual or family – and the accompanying correspondence, some very extensive indeed.

Although the questionnaire was not designed for the purposes of the present study, it has (supplemented by correspondence wherever possible) provided sufficient information about cash and related benefit problems to allow a tabulation to be made, showing general types of problem, particular problem benefits, and the frequency with which they occur.

From the beginning it was clear that it would not be feasible to include in this analysis every benefit which might be claimed by a handicapped person, and we decided to consider principally cash and cash-substitute benefits (such as Rent and Rate Rebates, prescription waivers and so forth) and provisions in kind which, if not made available by statutory bodies, would require to be paid for in full by the individuals or families concerned.

Not all the 1,300 case histories were usable. Some problems were inadequately or unclearly documented, often because of recipients' inability to see through the complexities of the Social Security system to precisely how their income was made up. Other cases were excluded because the problems lay outside the scope of this study, and yet others because no reference to specific problems was made. Altogether 359 cases proved to be usable, from which a total of 420 specific problems could be tabulated. (This does not mean that they did not have other problems as well; many did.)

These cases could in no way be considered as belonging to a valid statistical sample. Apart from the fact that their knowledge of DIG's existence places these people among a relatively informed minority, many of the cases used, through membership of local DIG groups, would exert some degree of influence over other cases, particularly where the successful outcome of one person's efforts might lead other members of the group to take similar action. Moreover, the regional distribution of the cases is far from even, with some large areas of the country being represented by a very few cases, and it corresponds as much to the relative strength of local DIG activity as to the distribution of problems among people with disabilities.

Recognising the limitations of this information, we decided that it could be most effectively used in a general qualitative view of problems occurring in the case histories from 1970 onwards, partly because information from this date still has great relevance to the present day, and partly because this would allow local authority provisions to be seen in the light of the Chronically Disabled Persons Act 1970.

The clients

The age and sex of the 359 clients included in the tabulation were as follows:

Male:	166	0–20 years:	7
Female:	193	21–40 years:	48
		41–60/65 years:	191
		Over pensionable age:	113

The problem areas

The benefits reviewed in this study are listed in Table A.1.1.

Problems relating to these benefits were classified as follows:

a. refusal or reduction due to ineligibility (mainly Attendance Allowance, Supplementary Benefits and telephones): *94 problems*

b. refusal due to local non-availability of benefit, owing to the local authority's inability to provide it (mainly telephones and adaptations to private housing): *23 problems*

c. refusal or reduction of benefit due to interaction with another benefit, where these are intended to cover separate needs (mostly reductions in Supplementary Benefits): *11 problems*

d. refusal or reduction of benefit through error on the part of the issuing authority (almost exclusively Supplementary Benefits): *8 problems*

e. benefit inadequate to cover the claimant's needs (mostly Supplementary Benefits): *90 problems*

Table A.1.1 Benefits tabulated for study of problem areas in analysis of DIG case files (from 1970 onwards)

Social Security benefits

a. Cash 'as of right'
Sickness Benefit
Earnings-related Supplement
Invalidity Pension
Non-Contributory Invalidity Pension
Retirement Pension
Old Person's Pension
Invalid Care Allowance
Attendance Allowance
Mobility Allowance
Hospital Pocket Money

b. Means-tested cash
Family Income Supplement
Rent Rebate
Rate Rebate
Supplementary Benefit
   Heating Allowance
   Diet Supplement
   Laundry Allowance
   Clothing grants
   Other extra-needs payments

War and Industrial Injury benefits

War Injury Pension
Industrial Injury Pension
   Unemployability Supplement
   Invalidity Allowance
   Special Hardship Allowance
   Hospital Treatment Allowance
   Constant Attendance Allowance
   Exceptionally Severe Disablement Allowance

National Health Service provisions

Artificial limbs
Wheelchairs
Personal vehicles (cars and invalid tricycles)
Private Car Allowance
'Own car' adaptation grant
Vehicle Excise Duty exemption
Appliances and special footwear
Incontinence equipment
Free prescriptions
Free dental and optical treatment (or reduced charges)

Local authority provisions

Improvement grants for housing
Local authority house adaptation
Private home adaptation
Aids and appliances
'Disposables'
Telephone installation and/or rental
Meals-on-wheels
Laundry service
Luncheon clubs
Home help
Day care
Residential care
School uniform grant
Free school meals
Holidays

Although not specific to people with disabilities, Unemployment Benefit, Widows' Pensions and payments from the Family Fund were also sometimes involved

f. unsuitable provision of an aid or appliance (mainly local authority housing, Home Help Service, appliances supplied by Social Services Departments and vehicles supplied through the Department of Health and Social Security):
62 problems

g. non-take-up through ignorance of the existence of a benefit or of the procedure for claiming it (DHSS centrally administered benefits, Supplementary Benefits, local authority provisions, prescription waivers, wheelchairs and DHSS vehicles):
37 problems

h. non-take-up through prohibitive cost to the client (mostly Home Help Service):
6 problems

i. non-take-up through refusal to apply for, or continue with, a benefit (mostly Supplementary Benefits):
11 problems

j. multiple issuing agencies for benefits covering the same need (Family Fund, Supplementary Benefits, and local authority Social Services Department):
4 problems

k. benefit only obtained on review or appeal following an initial refusal (mainly Attendance Allowance and Supplementary Benefits):
47 problems

l. client wrongly informed about a benefit (mostly Sickness/Invalidity Benefit and Supplementary Benefits):
27 problems

Social Security and National Health Service benefits contributed 268 of the problems, of which 71 concerned centrally administered benefits and the remainder, including 167 concerning Supplementary Benefits, were administered through local offices.

Which benefits caused the problems?

National Insurance benefits

Benefits administered through Department of Health and Social Security local offices presented relatively few problems in the study. Several reasons may be advanced for this; it is likely that, since there is no element of discretion in their administration, they are less problem-ridden than means-tested benefits. On the other hand, difficulties arising from these benefits may well tend to be referred to local National Insurance offices rather than to DIG and thus would not be proportionately represented in this sample.

Particularly notable, however, were several cases of incorrect information given to claimants by DHSS officers. One of these is discussed in some detail in Chapter 7 (page 209). Another particularly striking National Insurance problem concerned Mr C, a paraplegic who lacked two contributions to the National Insurance scheme due to two weeks' unpaid holiday, and was therefore deemed ineligible to claim Sickness Benefit. Mr C's employer was not allowed to pay these two contributions, even as a goodwill gesture, since, as stated under section 8(1) of the National Insurance Act 1965:

'.... no person shall be entitled to pay any contribution under this Act other than a contribution which he is liable to pay.'

Mr C himself was eligible to contribute only at the Class III rate, which would not, in any event, entitle him to Sickness Benefit. The outcome was that yet another disabled person was forced on to means-tested Supplementary Benefit, the only suggestion by the local office being that he should claim Non-Contributory Invalidity Pension (NCIP) in due course. This NCIP would, however, be fully taken into account when assessing Mr C's Supplementary Benefit requirements and would thus in no way affect his weekly income. Moreover, NCIP does not carry with it the supplements and Exceptional Needs Payments built into the Supplementary Benefit system.

Industrial disablement benefits, war pensions, Retirement Pensions, Widows' Pensions and Family Income Supplement did not figure largely in any of the problem categories. The Non-Contributory Invalidity Pension was too new a benefit to be widely represented in the case histories.

Attendance Allowance

Among centrally administered DHSS benefits the Attendance Allowance presented the largest number of problems, almost all of which related either to refusal through ineligibility or to allowances obtained only on review or appeal. Many claimants who were refused the allowance were forced to apply for review – often several times – before the benefit was granted. Among the most insistent applicants were those for whom the present system offered no other form of payment, either as of right or means-tested, and who thus were left with the task of proving their need for attendance as the only way of obtaining *any* benefit. Something like two-thirds of rejected claimants, however, do not apply for a review. This is unfortunate in that a large proportion of applications are successful on review; the experience of DIG's correspondents tends to confirm this.

It would, however, be unfair to imply that the large proportion of Attendance Allowance reviews noted in the study accurately reflects the present situation. Many relate to the period when no separate lower-rate allowance existed and therefore nothing could be granted when a claim to the full allowance was not felt to be justified. In fact the great majority of the reviews recorded in DIG's files date from before 1974, which lends support to the view that the eligibility criteria have gradually become more clearly established in practical terms.

Private Car Allowance

The Private Car Allowance, introduced by the Secretary of State for Social Services in 1972 as an alternative to the three-wheeler for handicapped people, was represented by a number of claims rejected on grounds of ineligibility because the strict medical criteria – the same as those for the issue of three-wheelers – had not been met by applicants. The Mobility Allowance, which in part replaced this allowance in January 1976, was at the time of this study scarcely represented in the case files, but the anomalous overlap remaining between the two mobility benefits was beginning to become apparent. Several times, the unfortunate situation of present ineligibility and future preclusion from any benefit emerged from the correspondence, often expressed in bitter terms. One such case related to an elderly married couple, both of whom were disabled and over retiring age. Having been unsuccessful in obtaining the Private Car Allowance before the introduction of the new Mobility Allowance, they have had to resign themselves to their future ineligibility for any statutory mobility help regardless of whether their conditions deteriorate, and to spending the greater part of their remaining years within the confines of their own home. Had they been assisted under the old system, the help given would have continued beyond retirement age.

Another example concerned non-take-up of the Private Car Allowance because the claimant was not informed of its existence until very shortly before the introduction of the Mobility Allowance came into force. With insufficient time for a claim to be processed before the closing date in January 1976, and with no new claims being accepted thereafter, this allowance could not be awarded; but the claimant will have reached retirement age by the time his age group comes to be considered for Mobility Allowance, and will thus be debarred. Had the claim for the Private Car Allowance been made earlier and been successful, however, the benefit would have been payable beyond retirement age and for as long as the claimant satisfied the conditions of eligibility.

The present situation is one where certain disabled people over retirement age receive mobility help whilst others with similar disabilities and mobility needs do not, and this is precisely the kind of anomaly which leads to incomprehension and bitterness among those intended to benefit from the system.

DHSS vehicles (Invacars) Several users of the DHSS Invacar (now in process of being phased out) found reason to complain about the unsuitability of the vehicle. Generally speaking, the arguments against the use of the Invacar have been twofold: firstly, that it was considered by many to be at best unreliable and at worst a danger to the driver and to other road users and, secondly, that disabled people should not be forced to drive alone.

The basic design of the Invacar has long been a contentious issue and frequent complaints about its reliability emerged from the case histories. Correspondence revealed evidence of frequent breakdowns, so that some disabled drivers preferred not to use the vehicle after the experience of being left stranded. One correspondent complained that he had been forced to abandon his employment because of the consistent unreliability of his Invacar. This problem is especially pointed since one of the most telling arguments for the provision of invalid vehicles was the need for disabled people to get to their place of work.

A related problem, equally pointed, concerned an Invacar driver who had been provided with a vehicle in order to get to his place of employment, and who was then made redundant. To compound the emotional and financial problems of redundancy, the user found that his vehicle was taken from him, since he was deemed no longer to require it for employment purposes. However, on approaching the Disablement Resettlement Officer to seek other employment the bewildered client was informed that he could not be considered for a job *until he had transport*, just when transport was being denied him *because he had no employment*. The publicity given to a number of such cases has led to a ruling that in future Invacars should not be withdrawn from their users immediately employment ceases, thus avoiding this kind of situation. But by then the issue of Category 3 Invacars had already been discontinued, and only a dwindling minority were helped by this change.

The Mobility Allowance has permitted a greater flexibility in certain directions. For those who opt to take the Invacars, however (at the time of writing, this means only people who would be eligible for Mobility Allowance but whose age group has not yet been phased in), there still remain the fundamental problems of the unreliability of the vehicle and the need for it to be driven by the handicapped person alone. It seems difficult to justify, in any terms, the obligatory separation of a family setting out on holiday, because the disabled father is unable to travel on public transport with his wife and children and has to make the journey in isolation in his Invacar.

Supplementary Benefit

Almost half of the families in the 1,300 case histories derive all or part of their income from Supplementary Benefit, and the various elements of Supplementary Benefit constitute the largest group of identified problems (of the 420 problems identified in the study, 167 – almost 40 per cent – related to Supplementary Benefit).

Three problem types emerged from the study: the first quantifiable in terms of refusals of benefit and wrong information given to claimants by DHSS officers, the second also quantifiable, being instances of unmet need once a benefit has been granted, and the third, more difficult to quantify but no less real, being that of unsympathetic treatment of clients by DHSS officers.

Refusal of benefit

In twenty-nine cases elements of Supplementary Benefit were refused on grounds of ineligibility, leaving a degree of unmet need which was expressed in the questionnaire or correspondence. Of these refusals, the largest number concerned discretionary Exceptional Needs Payments, as many being for clothing as for all other items.

Significant also was the apparent reluctance of DHSS officers to exercise their power to give discretionary lump-sum payments to non-recipients of Supplementary Benefit whose income falls only slightly outside the qualifying limit. Moreover, it was clear that these people were, generally speaking, unaware of their right to claim such discretionary payments.

In the vast majority of cases of refusal, the claim devolved on to charitable organisations which, because of their own financial difficulties, were not always able to help.

Inadequate benefit

It was disturbing to find, however, that even where elements of Supplementary Benefit had been granted, there were seventy problems relating to inadequacy of benefit. Amongst these figured families who had had to watch a lifetime's savings dwindle away to a level sufficiently low to allow a claim to Supplementary Benefit to be made, only to discover that the allowance, once granted, did not even cover their basic needs. The bulk of these problems concerned the basic rate of benefit, although almost as many involved Exceptional Circumstances Allowances and Exceptional Needs Payments. Heating allowances were shown to be inadequate in twelve cases. Inadequate resources to cover their fuel costs were particularly noticeable amongst disabled elderly people, many of whom required to maintain a high room temperature day and night because of their particular ailments (such as arthritis), and several such handicapped individuals were recorded as having to forgo an adequate diet in order to afford the necessary fuel.

Allied to the problem of inadequacy of Supplementary Benefits appeared to be that of the sheer complexity of their calculation – clearly not a problem exclusive to Supplementary Benefit. Many claimants were unaware of how their weekly entitlement had been calculated, and often were uncertain as to what extra amount was being allowed for, say, heating, or whether any amount was being allowed at all. Few claimants appeared to have enough knowledge of the Supplementary Benefit system to be able to take the initiative and prove to their local DHSS office that their heating requirements were not being met, and this task was often done on their behalf by DIG.

Further confusion arose over the alternative of Rent and Rate Rebates to Supplementary Benefit. The difference often amounted to a quite substantial sum and yet involved a calculation which few claimants seemed capable of doing.

A notable instance of inadequacy of benefit involved an Exceptional Needs Payment of £8 granted for a coat and a pair of shoes, which at 1975 prices would hardly have bought one of the specified items. A subsequent 'voluntary deduction' was made out of the weekly rate and retained by the local office to cover clothing needs. The family had been labelled 'bad managers' by the local DHSS office, who had suggested to them that Attendance Allowance should be used to pay for necessary clothing. All this befell a family of nine, including a mentally handicapped and incontinent child, where both husband and wife were substantially disabled. Both the wife and the handicapped child qualified for Attendance Allowance and income was solely from this, Family Allowances and Supplementary Benefit.

Unsympathetic officials

Unsympathetic treatment by Supplementary Benefit Commission officers led to complaints of humiliation caused to claimants. Clearly, any system which may expect a family to strip beds and turn out wardrobes for a visiting officer's inspection in order to establish a claim to a bedding or clothing grant is bound to cause humiliation and resentment, but possibly more so to handicapped people, who tend to be more anxious than most to be independent of 'charity'.

Ignorance

Identifiable non-take-up problems relating to Supplementary Benefit were largely caused by ignorance of the existence of the different elements of the Supplementary Benefits system, particularly of Exceptional Needs Payments. Several cases came to light where the recipients of a lump-sum grant thought themselves debarred from receiving any further discretionary help. One family with a low income and clear eligibility to Supplementary Benefit had not even been aware of its existence until informed by DIG.

Refusal to claim

Less significant numerically, but no less important, are those eligible non-claimants who were aware of their right to obtain Supplementary Benefit yet refused to do so. There were more identified instances of non-take-up through refusal to apply in connection with Supplementary Benefits than with any other benefit or provision. It is important to note that there are people who are prepared to forgo means-tested Supplementary Benefits entirely rather than face all that these entail in terms of humiliation, stigma and inconvenience.

Local authority provisions

The Chronically Sick and Disabled Persons Act of 1970 was a milestone in terms of legislation concerning local authority provisions for the disabled. From the time when the Act came into force local authorities could no longer rely on their discretionary powers only, but had the *statutory obligation* not only to discover the numbers and needs of handicapped people in their area but also to supply whatever needs were found for services to the disabled to help them lead fuller and more comfortable lives. Notoriously, however, there are local authorities which, for various reasons, have not fully implemented this Act, especially where charged to satisfy needs 'in the light of local resources'.

Housing

Local authorities had been empowered to build units of housing especially designed for the disabled long before the CSDP Act, and the Act made the provision of such housing a statutory obligation. Of the cases in the study, however, the proportion of handicapped people living in specially built dwellings was minute. Local authority provisions of conventional housing were unsuitable in sixteen cases, for a majority of whom purpose-built accommodation apparently was not available in sufficient numbers, and adaptations to existing property had not proved to be feasible.

Of the remaining local authority provisions included in the study, the most notable problem areas were found to be Home Help Services (18 problems), telephones (25 problems) and home adaptations (17 problems). Collectively, local authority provisions to the disabled ranked second as a problem area to Supplementary Benefit.

Home Help Service

The Home Help Service was found to be a source of problems on two counts: firstly, on account of the expressed dissatisfaction of clients with home helps, mostly for their unreliability or for their failure to carry out designated tasks regularly or properly, and, secondly, on account of the assessment, on the basis of means, of the client's share of the cost of the provision.

The prohibitive size of their assessed contribution led four families to struggle on without home help provision, a situation which generally meant that the breadwinning member of the family had also to carry out the household chores. In one case Attendance Allowance was taken into account when assessing charges for a home help, although there is no evidence to show that this practice still continues.

Telephones

The CSDP Act provided for the supply of telephones for the housebound, with installation charges and rental paid by the local authority. But it was found that eligibility criteria were enforced with great rigidity, which led to frequent rejections.

There also appeared to be a 'grey area' of doubt between the terms 'housebound' and 'non-housebound', and it was difficult not to sympathise with those disabled people who, without being strictly housebound, would have great difficulty in reaching a public telephone, especially, as several pointed out, because these telephones were frequently vandalised.

In one Yorkshire city a telephone was refused to a disabled married couple, where both members were substantially disabled, over retiring age and living on Supplementary Pension, with no other resident in the household. A letter from their Social Services Department stated that the reason was that they

'have access to a telephone in a flat occupied by an elderly lady across the hallway from their own ... It is considered that this department has done all in its power to assist Mr and Mrs —'.

The background to this letter is illustrated by the following passages, extracted from three letters addressed to DIG by the couple concerned, dated 30.4.75, 21.9.75 and 11.11.75 respectively.

'My wife and myself are both disabled. We cannot get out only to the hospital by ambulance. If either of us wants the doctor we have to wait until a nurse calls or the home help comes, which is only one morning each week. We have no family so we cannot rely on them.'

'Regarding using the phone next door, the lady is very confused and would not like to be disturbed in the night or day. A few weeks ago we had to get the police for her as she had nearly blown us all up. She couldn't understand why we weren't paying her for using the phone.'

'When I needed the doctor at 2.25 am I had to shout for help for a lady who lives 32 steps high to get her to use her phone on our behalf. I cannot climb steps as I have already told you. If my wife starts to lose blood a doctor has to be called as soon as possible.'

In the questionnaire, the husband listed his ailments as asthma, chronic bronchitis, emphysema and duodenal ulcers, and his wife's as a heart condition, thyroid trouble, nerves, bad circulation, arthritis, etc., and stated that he himself had difficulty in walking further than five or six yards. The letter from the Social Services Department stated that:

'The Chronically Sick and Disabled Persons Act gives local authorities power to provide appropriate assistance, but as resources are limited, each application for services has to take into account the need of the applicants in relation to resources and the needs of others.'

It is clear that to create a system of statutory provisions for the disabled and yet disqualify cases of urgent need through insufficient resources is to make a mockery of the spirit in which the legislation was conceived and enacted.

Housing adaptations

The correspondence revealed, not surprisingly, that where house adaptations for the disabled are concerned, local authorities differ greatly in the extent to which they feel able to comply with clients' needs. A sizeable proportion of claims for help from the local authority concerned large-scale adaptations, such as the construction of ground-floor bathrooms, which are necessarily expensive to carry out. In six cases, it was considered that particular large-scale adaptations were of a type which could not feasibly be made. In others, the assessment of the family's contribution proved so high as to be beyond its means without financial support from charitable organisations. In one case in Warwickshire the local authority delayed inordinately its decision as to the feasibility of an adaptation, refusing to give a definite answer to the claimant and in fact suggesting an application to a voluntary agency even before it had itself definitely refused.

In an Inner London borough, a sufferer from Parkinson's disease, whose Invacar was frequently vandalised, was provided by the borough with a garage. Great efforts were required, however, including an appeal to the Parliamentary Under-Secretary of State, before the garage was provided with suitable access for the vehicle, although the necessary 'adaptation' involved no more than the removal of a three-foot section of 'dwarf' decorative wall. (This delay was added to the two years the householder had had to wait even to be supplied with the Invacar, during which time she had also had to appeal to a Supplementary Benefit Appeals Tribunal to prevent her heating allowance from being withdrawn.)

Aids and appliances

Essentially, the problems were those of delay in effecting provision – in one case a delay of nine months in providing a simple walking aid – and unsuitability of provisions once they were obtained. Often aids proved totally unsuitable and were left unused, or, because of a lack of correct information, the required aid was not supplied. One disabled person, living in Wales, requested a bath rail under the Chronically Sick and Disabled Persons Act; she was visited by a social worker and told that *rails* were not supplied by her Social Services Department, but that bath *seats* were available. After having accepted the bath seat, which was of little use, and having bought a bath rail privately out of a meagre income, the client was visited by a different social worker who assured her that bath rails were indeed provided by the department and that she had been ill-advised to buy one privately.

To compare the unit cost of a simple aid such as this with the total cost of its final installation in the client's home, including the time and transport costs of two social worker visits – not to mention the time which these social workers could have spent on other clients – again strongly supports the contention that the basic needs of handicapped people are financial, and that, given an adequate income, they would be far better able to provide themselves with the aids and appliances they require and leave local authorities with more resources to deal with problems of more pressing concern.

Disabled housewives

At the time of this study, disabled married women (other than a few who were National Insurance contributors in their own right) were excluded from every cash benefit in respect of their disability except one, the Attendance Allowance, and were excluded from the tabulation accordingly. There were 311 such women in the case files, but only 16 were 'contributors' receiving benefits in their own right. Of the remainder, 49 were retirement pensioners. Thirty-nine received Attendance Allowance. The other 201 women did not qualify for any benefit in their own right; 58 lived in families subsisting on Supplementary Benefit.

The problem has persisted up to the present because the disabled non-contributing married woman has always been considered to be 'not gainfully employed' and thus not entitled to any payment in respect of her disability to compensate for her lack of earning power or to ease the burden of looking after the home and caring for children.

At the time of writing, the Non-Contributory Invalidity Pension, based upon incapacity for paid employment, is broadly speaking payable to men and to women without husbands who do not qualify for National Insurance benefits. The government has now also established criteria whereby the disabled married woman may qualify for NCIP on the basis of her incapability both of paid employment *and* of performing normal household duties. Complications were considered to exist, however, in the establishment of criteria by which to determine incapacity to carry out household duties. This extension of NCIP was postponed once, as part of the cuts in government spending, and was eventually introduced in November 1977. This 'housewife's pension' is taken fully into account for Supplementary Benefit purposes, so that it offers no help to disabled married women in the poorest families.

It is expected that some 40,000 disabled married women will qualify for the 'housewife's NCIP'. However, the OPCS Survey estimated at nearly a quarter of a million the number of disabled 'housewives' (both male and female) who could not carry out normal household duties. It seems likely, therefore, that this benefit will go only a small part of the way towards solving the problem.

Until a comprehensive solution is found to the problem of the disabled housewife, there remains as much truth as in 1968 in the statement made in the Seebohm Report that 'special attention ought to be given to the financial needs of households which are suffering serious strain because of the disablement of one of their members but which cannot at present be entitled to Supplementary Benefit or other payments from the Ministry of Social Security'.

Conclusions

Almost from the beginning of the study it became clear that the most pressing problems facing the majority of cases resulted directly or indirectly from financial hardship. Many people found themselves, for various reasons, excluded from all the benefits introduced especially for the handicapped and thus swelled the numbers of those who had to be brought up to the official poverty level by means-tested Supplementary Benefits. The government's report *Social Security provision for chronically sick and disabled people* recognised that 'below pension age, the severest financial consequence of disablement is inability to earn'. However, it was evident from the study that disabled people over retirement age were not spared any of the financial hardship caused by disablement.

Even where the basic necessities of life were covered by benefits, the extra costs of disability clearly caused many problems and restrictions, including the extra cost of travel by taxi for those who are unable to use public transport, the lack of money for entertainment or even to mix with other people, the need to forgo holidays, and the many other costs detailed in Mavis Hyman's study (*The extra costs of disability*). The restrictions described in scores of moving letters in DIG's files are evidence to back the claim that disabled people will not be able to lead as normal and full a life as possible until the extra costs of disabled living are recognised. Evident, too, were the restrictions felt by many of the disabled people in the case histories which arose from inadequate housing, a large proportion being housed by local authorities who were not able to satisfy their special housing needs.

The Seebohm Report recognised in 1968 that 'without the basic essentials of adequate housing and adequate incomes there is no possibility of providing an effective family service for the physically handicapped'. There can be little doubt that the absence of these two elements enormously increases the dependence of disabled people on the local authority provisions of the Chronically Sick and Disabled Persons Act 1970. But despite this dependence, it cannot be claimed that the provisions of the 1970 Act can meet those needs which are not covered by the Social Security system. To make any such claim would be to ignore both the general inadequacy of the provisions and their non-availability to handicapped people in many areas, factors which were greatly in evidence in the DIG files. Clearly such provisions cannot be effectively administered until local authorities are provided with the necessary financial resources to implement fully their statutory obligations under the Chronically Sick and Disabled Persons Act.

Appendix Two

The *Sunday People* form

This form, prepared by the staff of the *Sunday People*, is issued by the Mirror Group Readers' Service for use with applications for the Attendance Allowance (see page 58).

Attach to official claim form

Extra relevant information

Can you get in and out of bed by yourself?

If you spill anything can you wipe it up?

Can you bathe yourself (do you need help getting in and out of the bath)?

Do you need help with your clothing or in any other way, when using the lavatory?

Can you dress and undress yourself?

Do you need help in getting in and out of bed?

Do you need help to climb stairs?

Do you use a commode and need help to do so?

Can you turn in bed without help?

Do you wet the bed?

If you go to the lavatory during the night do you need help?

Can you hear well enough to know if someone is at the door? Can you hear the radio?

Do you need others to bring in your shopping and other necessities?

Are you able to make youself understood, especially with the faculty of speech? Can you do this easily, or with difficulty?

Are you slow in fitting your actions to your thoughts (clumsy and accident prone?)

Are you unstable on your feet, fall about a great deal if left unattended?

Do you find it hard to make simple decisions?

How much of the day do you spend in bed?

Do you find it difficult to concentrate?

If you slip down in bed can you raise yourself?

Do you suffer from nightmares?

Do you need supervision when dealing with hot liquids in order to avoid accidents?

237

Are you continent all the time?

Can you control your bowels?

Do you sleep badly? (1) Does your breathing trouble you during the night? (2) Are you excessively nervous during the night?

Can you walk a short distance unaided?

Can you make yourself a cup of tea in safety?

Do you need a wheelchair in order to get about?

Can you answer the door in reasonable time if someone calls?

Can you get to the phone if it rings especially if you are upstairs?

If you are sitting down can you get up without help?

Can you see enough to (1) read (2) make a cup of tea safely (3) cross the road?

Do you need help to write letters and read books?

Do you need help to feed yourself?

Do you need supervision when standing or sitting near (1) fires and stoves (2) on landings near stairways (3) in the bath?

Do you need help to wash and dress your hair?

Bibliography

General

1. *Social Security statistics*. Department of Health and Social Security, 1974.

2. *Inter-departmental Committee on Social Insurance and Allied Services* (Beveridge Report). Cmd 6404, 1942.

3. *Supplementary Benefits handbook*.

4. Acts of Parliament mentioned in Chapter 1, in particular: National Assistance Act 1948; Supplementary Benefit Act 1966; Chronically Sick and Disabled Persons Act 1970; National Insurance (Old Persons', Widows' Pensions and Attendance Allowance) Act 1970; Housing Finance Act 1972; Social Security Acts 1973 and 1975.

5. 'Poverty as relative deprivation'. P Townsend, in D Wedderburn, *Poverty, inequality and class structure*. Cambridge University Press, 1974.

6. *Local authority and allied personal social services* (Seebohm Report). HMSO, Cmd 3703.

7. *Better social services*. Bedford Square Press of National Council of Social Services, 1973.

8. *No feet to drag*. Alf Morris MP and Arthur Butler, 1972.

9. *Mobility of physically disabled people* (Sharp Report). 1974.

10. *Report of working party on Mobility Allowance*. Central Council for the Disabled, June 1976.

11. *Commitment to welfare*. RN Titmuss, 1973.

12. *Development of the Welfare Rights Service in Manchester*. City of Manchester Social Services Department, 1976.

13. *Social Security provision for chronically sick and disabled people*: a report to Parliament by the Secretary of State, 31 July 1974.

14. *Supplementary Benefits Commission annual report 1975*. HMSO, Cmnd 6615, 1976.

15. *Preliminary report of study of allocation of hours to home help clients*. JS May. Unpublished report by Strategic Planning Division, Warwickshire Social Services Department. 13 April 1976.

16. *Report on a review of the service: meals-on-wheels service*. DS Ashford and TW Knapp. Management Services Unit, Social Services Department, Dorset CC. Internal Report no. 90/03/05, May 1976.

Clearing House for Local Authority Social Services Research, University of Birmingham
1973

17. No. 9: Havering CSDP Survey, September 1972.

18. No. 10: *General practitioners and social workers*. Avril Theophilus. Wiltshire.

19. No. 11: *Report on a pilot survey to examine the public's awareness of and attitude towards the Social Services Department*. Hillingdon, July 1973.

20. No. 12: *Seaside holidays for handicapped persons: an appraisal of the service*. JE Tibbett. Staffordshire.

1974

21. No. 1: *Client opinions*. Hillingdon.

22. No. 7: *Meals-on-wheels service in Bedfordshire*. March 1974.

1975

23. No. 2: *Meals service for the elderly*. J Oldfield. Warwickshire.

24. No. 5: *Sick and homeless in Grassmarket*. Louanne McCrory.

25. No. 7: *O/T services in Hillingdon*. January 1975.

26. No. 8: *Survey on aging*. East Sussex.

1976

27. No. 1: *Alarms for elderly and disabled in Portsmouth*. Hampshire Social Services Dept.

28. No. 2: *Determining an appropriate charging structure for the Home Help Service in Birmingham*. Abbas Baba.

29. No. 4: *Comparatively speaking*. Andrew Leigh. Wandsworth.

30. No. 5: *A study of mental handicap in Derbyshire*. RG Colman. *The supply of aids and adaptations*. CJ Melotte. Kirklees.

Family Fund research project, Department of Social Administration, University of York

31. *Variations in provision by local authority Social Services Departments for families with handicapped children*. March 1976.

32. *The handicapped child and the family*. Dennis Hitch, March 1976.

33. *Relationship between the Family Fund and statutory agencies with responsibilities for handicapped children*. FF/22, January 1975.

34. *A study of the mobility needs of handicapped children including a review of Family Fund policy on mobility and an appraisal of the Mobility Allowance*. FF/39, October 1975.

35. *Some practical consequences of caring for handicapped children at home*. FF/57, April 1976.

36. *Incontinence*. FF/58, June 1976.

37. 'For your client's benefit'. Jonathan Bradshaw. *Social Work Today*, vol. 7 no. 5, 27 May 1976.

38. *Care with dignity: an analysis of costs of care for the disabled*. Economist Intelligence Unit Report. Action Research Monograph, January 1974.

39. 'The implementation of the Chronically Sick and Disabled Persons Act'. Stanley Orwell and Joanna Murray. *Social Policy Research*, February 1973.

40. 'Cash benefits for disabled people'. EB McGinnis. *Social Work Service* no. 10. DHSS, July 1976.

41. *Local authority holidays for the elderly and physically handicapped.* Susan Stone. HMSO, 1973.

42. *Holidays: the social need.* Social Tourism Study Group. English Tourist Board, 1976.

43. *Interim report from Working Party on Holidays.* London Borough of Wandsworth Social Services Department, December 1975.

44. *Poverty*, no. 25, Spring 1973. Child Poverty Action Group.

45. *The supply of aids and adaptations.* CJ Melotte. Occasional Paper No. 3, Kirklees Social Services Directorate, May 1975.

46. *Nearly a million disabled people in poverty.* A Memorandum to the Chancellor of the Exchequer and the Secretary of State for Social Services from the Disability Alliance. March 1976.

47. *Occupational therapists: joint review by Area Health Authorities and local authorities.* DHSS Circular HSC (IS) 102, December 1974.

48. *The remedial professions and linked therapies.* DHSS Circular HSC (IS) 101, December 1974.

49. *Home Help Service – performance review.* Report of the Chief Officers' Management Team. Leicestershire CC, June 1976.

50. Report to Area Health Authority on Spinal Injuries Centre at Stoke Mandeville Hospital. Buckinghamshire AHA, October 1975.

51. Holyhead Information and Advice Project – Holyhead Library, Final Report. P Power and G Stacy, Gwynedd CC, October 1975.

52. *Citizens' Advice Bureau Mobile Van: Research Project.* Progress report no. 1. Gwynedd Social Services Department, July 1976.

53. 'Dear David Donnison', 'David Donnison replies'. *Social Work Today.*

54. *Client perception and awareness of Birmingham Social Services Department.*

55. *Crossroads care attendant scheme.* March 1976.

56. *The extra costs of disabled living.* Mavis Hyman. National Fund for Research into Crippling Diseases, April 1977.

57. *Planning to help the handicapped in Birmingham.* Birmingham Social Services Department, February 1976.

58. *Transport: a review of services to clients.* London Borough of Hillingdon, June 1975.

59. *Identifying the chronically sick and disabled in Reading.* AW Whitbread, RIPA, August 1973.

60. *Services for the mentally handicapped in Greenwich.* Programme Planning Section, London Borough of Greenwich, February 1975.

61. *The meals service in Bedfordshire.* Bedfordshire Social Services Department, October 1975.

62. *Two-parent families in receipt of Family Income Supplement, 1972.* DHSS. HMSO, 1975.

63. *The administration of the Rent Rebate and Rent Allowance schemes.* Charles Legg and Marion Brion. DoE and Welsh Office, September 1976.

64. *Housing for disabled people in Greater London.* Susan Tester. Greater London Association for the Disabled, December 1975.

65. *Towards a housing policy for disabled people.* Report of the Working Party on Housing of the Central Council for the Disabled, 1976. (Interim Report, published December 1974.)

66. *The annual report of the Council on Tribunals for 1973–74.* HMSO, April 1975.

67. *Research study on Supplementary Benefit Appeal Tribunals – review of main findings.* Kathleen Bell, DHSS. HMSO, 1975.

68. *Homelessness.* Joint Circular of DoE, DHSS and Welsh Office, February 1974.

69. *Notes for a review of provision of housing for the physically handicapped in Kensington and Chelsea.* Nick Miller. Kensington and Chelsea Social Services Department, April 1976.

70. *Adaptations to housing for people who are physically handicapped.* Joint Consultation Paper by DoE, DHSS and Welsh Office. February 1976.

71. *Compensation, maintenance and rehabilitation: the conflict in British policies for the disabled 1914–1946.* Dr HM Bolderson. LSE thesis.

72. *Annual Reports* of Department of Health and Social Security.

73. *The incomes of the blind.* J Reid. Disability Alliance, 1975.

74. *An ABC of services and information for disabled people.* B Macmorland. Disablement Income Group Charitable Trust, 1976.

75. *Disabled housewives on Merseyside.* Ian Earnshaw. Disablement Income Group Charitable Trust, 1973.

Administrative costs

1. *Annual abstract of statistics for 1975.* HMSO, 1976.

2. *Supplementary Benefits Commission annual report 1975.* HMSO, Cmnd 6615.

3. *Social Security statistics 1974.* DHSS. HMSO, 1975.

4. *Care with dignity: an analysis of costs of care for the disabled.* Economist Intelligence Unit Report. Action Research Monograph, January 1974.

5. *An analysis of social services costs in Hillingdon.* Hillingdon Social Services Department, June 1976.

6. *The extra costs of disabled living.* Mavis Hyman. National Fund for Research into Crippling Diseases, April 1977.

7. *The administration of the Rent Rebate and Rent Allowance schemes.* Charles Legg and Marion Brion. DoE and Welsh Office, September 1976.

8. *Home Help Service – performance review.* Leicester County Council Social Services Department, July 1976.

9. *Determining an appropriate charging structure for the Home Help Service in Birmingham (June–October 1975).* Abbas Baba. CHLASSR – No. 2, April 1976.

10. *Holidays 1976, resident escorts pay and conditions.* London Borough of Wandsworth Social Services Department, 4 December 1975.

11. *Draft estimates of 1975/76 and 1976/77 Social Services budget.* Buckinghamshire Social Services Committee, 1976.

12. Report to the Area Health Authority on Spinal Injuries Centre at Stoke Mandeville Hospital. Buckinghamshire AHA, October 1975.

13. 'The implementation of the Chronically Sick and Disabled Persons Act.' Stanley Orwell and Joanna Murray. *Social Policy Research*, February 1973.

14. *Local authority holidays for the elderly and physically handicapped.* Susan Stone. HMSO, 1973.

15. *Holidays: the social need.* Social Tourism Study Group. English Tourist Board, 1976.

16. *Planning to help the handicapped in Birmingham.* Birmingham Social Services Department, February 1976.

17. *Transport: A review of services to clients.* London Borough of Hillingdon, June 1975.

18. *Preliminary report of study of allocation of hours to home help clients.* JS May. Unpublished report by Strategic Planning Division, Warwickshire Social Services Department, April 1976.

19. *Report on a review of the service: meals-on-wheels service.* DS Ashford and TW Knapp. Management Services Unit, Social Services Department, Dorset CC Internal Report no. 90/03/05, May 1976.

20. *Identifying the chronically sick and disabled in Reading.* AW Whitbread. RIPA, August 1973.

21. *Personal social services statistics 1974–75.* CIPFA, April 1976.

22. *Social services statistics (estimates) 1975/76.* CIPFA, January 1976.

23. *Care of the elderly – an exercise in cost benefit analysis.* R Wager. IMTA, March 1972.

24. *Investigation into the effects of different caring environments on the social competence of mentally handicapped adults – progress report no. 2.* DM and DS Race. ORU, University of Reading, April 1976.

25. *Decisions and resources – social work services.* HMSO, 1976.

26. *Abstract of accounts for the year ended 31st March 1972.* London Borough of Hillingdon.

27. *An evaluation of future social services expenditure on behalf of the City of Leicester.* ESP, PA International Management Consultants Ltd, February 1972.

28. *Revenue budget 1976/77.* Social Services Committee, London Borough of Hillingdon.

29. *Organisation of the Home Help Service in Hillingdon.* London Borough of Hillingdon, March 1975.

30. *Work patterns of social workers.* London Borough of Hillingdon, February 1973.

31. *A computer-based welfare benefits information system: the Inverclyde Project.* M Adler and D du Feu. IBM, December 1975.

Non-take-up and publicity

1. *Take-up of means-tested benefits.* Ruth Lister. CPAG Poverty pamphlet no. 18, November 1974.

2. *'Take-up: the same old story'.* Ruth Lister. CPAG *Poverty*, no. 34, Summer 1976.

3. *Rate Rebates: a study of the effectiveness of means tests.* Molly Meacher, CPAG Poverty pamphlet no. 1, 1972.

4. *Handicapped and impaired in Great Britian.* Amelia I. Harris *et al.*, Office of Population Censuses and Surveys. HMSO, 1971.

5. *Work and housing of impaired persons in Great Britain.* Judith Buckle, Office of Population Censuses and Surveys. HMSO 1971 Pt. II.

6. *Income and entitlement to Supplementary Benefit of impaired people in Great Britain.* Amelia I. Harris *et al.*, Office of Population Censuses and Surveys. HMSO Pt. III.

7. *'The implementation of the Chronically Sick and Disabled Persons Act'.* *Social Policy Research*, February 1973.

8. *Report on the survey of chronically sick and disabled people resident in Newcastle upon Tyne.* City and County of Newcastle upon Tyne, 1972 (2 volumes).

9. 'Genericism and the handicapped register'. John Haggett. *Health and Social Service Journal*, 11 October 1975.

10. *The financial problems of families with handicapped children and an evaluation of the Attendance Allowance.* Family Fund Research Project, University of York, 19 November 1974.

11. *Social Security statistics 1974.* DHSS. HMSO, 1975.

12. *Claimant to be doubted?* Ruth Rooney and Rachel Woolf. Grassmarket Project Team and Citizens' Rights Office (Edinburgh), May 1975.

13. *Take-up of the Attendance Allowance.* Family Fund Research Project. University of York, February, 1976.

14. *Towards a housing policy for disabled people.* Report of the Working Party on Housing of the Central Council for the Disabled, 1976.

15. 'Providing more for less'. P Taylor-Gooby. *Municipal and Public Services Journal*, 28 November 1975, pages 1513–1514.

16. *The take-up of Rent Rebates and Allowances in Birmingham.* D Page and B Weinberger. Centre for Urban and Regional Studies (CURS) Research Memorandum, April 1975.

17. *The Batley welfare benefits project.* J Bradshaw, P Taylor-Gooby and R Lees. Papers in Community Studies, University of York, no. 5, 1976.

18. *The Haringey Rent Allowance project – second interim report.* Theresa Lewis, Department of the Environment, May 1975.

19. *Take-up of the Family Fund.* Family Fund Research Project Report, March 1976.

20. *The Home Help Service in England and Wales.* Audrey Hunt and Judith Fox. HMSO, 1970.

21. *The multi-purpose claim form scheme; interim report on an evaluation of the scheme in Salop.* June 1976.

22. *Financial provision for handicapped people in the United Kingdom.* Paper presented by B McGinnis at the Conference on Financial Provisions for the Handicapped organised by Action Research for the Crippled Child at York, UK, in September 1976.

Combined assessment schemes and the improvement of application forms

1. 'Providing more for less'. P Taylor-Gooby. *Municipal and Public Services Journal*, 28 November 1975, pages 1513–1514.

2. 'Knowing the form'. L Christmas. *Guardian*, 30 June 1976.

3. 'More welfare for less cost'. P Taylor-Gooby, *Poverty*, no. 34, Summer 1976.

4. *The multi-purpose claim form scheme: interim report on an evaluation of the scheme in Salop.* June 1976.

5. 'Forms: for official use only'. P Morris. *Community Care*, 5 January 1975.

6. 'Unravelling red tape'. G Weightman. *New Society*, 13 November 1975.

7. 'Just fill in this form – a review for designers'. P Wright and P Barnard. *Applied Ergonomics* 1975, 6.4, pages 213–220.

8. 'A Form of Trial'. M Brion and C Legg, *Housing Monthly*, August 1975.

9. 'Forms of complaint'. P Weight, *New Behaviour*, 7 August 1975.

10. *Breaking through the assessment charges web*. Report of Working Party on Assessment Charges. London Borough of Hammersmith, August 1973.

11. *Centralised index and assessment scales*. Public Accounts Review Committee, London Borough of Hammersmith, 16 December 1975.

12. *A computer-based welfare benefits information system: the Inverclyde Project*. M Adler and D du Feu. IBM, December 1975.

13. *Welfare benefits project – final report*. M Adler and D du Feu. *Bulletin of Clearing House for Local Authority Social Services Research* (1974), vol. 2, pages 1–51.

14. *Interim report on cash benefits for the disabled*. Tony Emmett. Lambeth Directorate of Social Services.

15. *Means-tested benefits – a discussion paper*. National Consumer Council, 1976.